Self-Regulated Learning

Critical Pedagogical Perspectives

Greg S. Goodman, *General Editor*

Vol. 15

The Educational Psychology series is part of the Peter Lang Education list.
Every volume is peer reviewed and meets
the highest quality standards for content and production.

PETER LANG
New York • Washington, D.C./Baltimore • Bern
Frankfurt • Berlin • Brussels • Vienna • Oxford

ADVANCE PRAISE FOR Self-Regulated Learning

"In this lively and informative book, Stephen Vassallo issues a clarion call to educators, policymakers, parents, and socially concerned citizens to look below the seemingly progressive, happy-faced surface of one of the most influential forms of purported advance in contemporary western education—classroom initiatives and programs that claim to promote students' self-regulated learning (SRL) so that they will be able to flourish in twenty-first-century schools and societies. Vassallo explains just how non-neutral, individualistic, and seductively supportive of political and economic disparities such programs can be. His critical application of historical, philosophical, and sociopolitical analysis to the self-regulation movement in our schools reveals a neoliberal agenda intent on doing good, but which is just as likely to further current states of political alienation, social injustice, and economic inequality. This is an important and timely book as many schools and teachers become increasingly enveloped by what Vassallo regards as a neoliberal mantra operating under the auspices of psychological expertise, technological wherewithal, and a rhetoric of twenty-first-century learning skills."

*Jack Martin, Burnaby Mountain Professor of Psychology,
Simon Fraser University; Co-Author of* The Education of Selves

"An engaging, informed and insistent critique whose scholarly analysis reveals how the key educational discourse of self-regulated learning, via its concepts and assumptions, bolsters an individualism that naturalises and pathologises social inequalities and endorses conformity. It is a key departure for the new critical educational psychology. The book offers a nuanced and rigorous analysis that proposes neither wholesale rejection nor endorsement of SRL but rather calls for critical reflection and political reformulation as a resource for effective individual and social action."

*Erica Burman, Co-Founder of the Manchester Feminist Theory Network and Co-Director
of the Discourse Unit and the Women's Studies Research Centre,
Department of Psychology, Manchester Metropolitan University*

"In utilizing a critical psychological analysis of key topics in education, including a critique of the limits of standard educational psychology, Stephen Vassallo offers a unique perspective that is both interesting and compelling. Using 'self-regulated learning' as a focal point for his analysis, Vassallo persuasively argues against traditional interpretations of what counts as academic success. He prods the reader to engage more thoroughly with what the contextual meaning of learning entails for situated individuals. This view opposes neoliberal orthodoxy and repositions socially situated, individually engaged learners as agents for intelligent change. Teachers, administrators, school psychologists, and policymakers would benefit from wrestling with the substantive issues Vassallo offers."

*Deron Boyles, Professor of Philosophy of Education, Georgia State University;
President of the John Dewey Society; Past-President of the American Educational Studies Association*

"In this book, Stephen Vassallo has presented a groundbreaking vision of a more critical educational psychology. He engages subtly with the politically-informed philosophical work of Foucault, Bourdieu and Freire to rework the study of self-regulated learning with clear, engaging, and thought-provoking arguments. This book also has direct relevance for classroom practice, giving teachers much-needed support for taking student agency or empowerment beyond the neoliberal assumptions of traditional methods in educational psychology that focus on the learning and achievement of the individual student. By reflecting critically on the 'self' of self-regulated learning, Vassallo gives the reader innovative possibilities for changing education to better acknowledge the cultural, historical, and socio-economic conditions of schools and classrooms, thus giving students and teachers new impetus for working together to transform education to meet the complex challenges hidden in our normative practices. This intriguing and scholarly book should be required reading for senior undergraduate and postgraduate educational psychology, as well as critical psychology, students."

Lise Bird Claiborne, Associate Professor in Critical Educational Psychology, University of Waikato, New Zealand; Co-Author (with Wendy Drewery) of Human Development: Family, Place, Culture

STEPHEN VASSALLO

Self-Regulated Learning

AN APPLICATION OF CRITICAL EDUCATIONAL PSYCHOLOGY

PETER LANG
New York • Washington, D.C./Baltimore • Bern
Frankfurt • Berlin • Brussels • Vienna • Oxford

Library of Congress Cataloging-in-Publication Data
Vassallo, Stephen.
Self-regulated learning: an application of critical
educational psychology / Stephen Vassallo.
pages cm — (Educational psychology: critical
pedagogical perspectives; vol. 15)
Includes bibliographical references.
1. Learning. 2. Self-culture. 3. Critical pedagogy. I. Title.
LB1060.V375   370.15'23—dc23   2013000602
ISBN 978-1-4331-1534-9 (hardcover)
ISBN 978-1-4331-1533-2 (paperback)
ISBN 978-1-4539-1063-4 (e-book)
ISSN 1943-8109

Bibliographic information published by **Die Deutsche Nationalbibliothek**.
Die Deutsche Nationalbibliothek lists this publication in the "Deutsche
Nationalbibliografie"; detailed bibliographic data is available
on the Internet at http://dnb.d-nb.de/.

© 2013 Peter Lang Publishing, Inc., New York
29 Broadway, 18th floor, New York, NY 10006
www.peterlang.com

All rights reserved.
Reprint or reproduction, even partially, in all forms such as microfilm,
xerography, microfiche, microcard, and offset strictly prohibited.

To the memory of sister Debbie
and to my two children, Anthony and Lily.

Acknowledgments

There have been so many people who have been instrumental for writing this book. I want to thank Greg Goodman for including my work in this important book series. Greg has supported my book in both direct and indirect ways. Indirectly, Greg's work in educational psychology serves as a pathway for my writing and has been inspiring and motivating. Directly, Greg provided feedback on the book prospectus, reading drafts of chapters, talking me through issues, and ensuring that I stayed on track. I want to thank Jeff Sugarman, who introduced me to the term *critical educational psychology*. Jeff selflessly gave his time to read several iterations of these chapters. His support and encouragement was instrumental for writing this book. I have had several important conversations with other critical psychologists that supported this work. Among them are Jack Martin, Tim Corcoran, and Tom Billington. This work would not have been possible without the support of Lynn Fendler. Lynn introduced me to a range of critical theories and patiently worked with me to understand them. In addition, Lynn gave me thoughtful comments on my chapter on neoliberalism. I want to thank Punya Mishra for always being supportive of my work. I want to thank Melissa Smythe who read several iterations of my chapter on socioeconomic class.

I have several colleagues at American University who have supported me while writing this book. I want to give special thanks to my dean, Sarah Irvine Belson, who worked with me to ensure I had time to write. Marilyn Goldhammer read the entire manuscript, and gave me suggestions that dramatically improved the book. I want to extend gratitude to Stacey Snelling. Stacey read parts of the book and provided thoughtful feedback. I have had many important discussions with Elizabeth Worden and Vivian Vasquez that occurred just at the right time to keep me focused and motivated. I have several other colleagues who always showed support for my work: Charlie Tesconi, Fred Jacobs, Adrea Lawrence, Stacie Tate, Bob Karch, Alida Anderson, and Alex Hodges. I am grateful to all who are part of the American University community for their support.

American University has amazing students who have supported this book project. Hannah Sher dedicated her time and effort to help me improve and finish the book. She helped me work through difficult chapters, read chapters several times, conducted important research, and provided brilliant editorial suggestions. The few weeks preceding submission, Hannah committed countless hours to helping me polish the manuscript. I want to extend a special thanks to Rachel Trello, who during her summer at the beach read every chapter of the book. She was meticulous with her editorial comments and raised several alternative points that enabled me to reflect on strength of my arguments. I am grateful to Ryan Barker, who read several iterations of my conclusion and provided thoughtful and insightful feedback. I want to thank Crystal Wright for reading several drafts of these chapters; she always pushed me to clarify my arguments. There are countless other students who engaged in conversations in and outside of class that helped me articulate my ideas. I am fortunate to be at American University and surrounded by bright, hardworking, and dedicated students.

The love of my family was especially instrumental for completing this book. After a long day of writing, leaving my eyes dry, head hurting, stomach empty, and a bit cranky, coming home to my children, Anthony and Lil, was rejuvenating, making it possible to do it all again the next day. I want to extend a special thanks to my wife, Frances Rosario. Writing this book required countless hours and a monopoly on focus and cognitive resources. Frances remained patient and supportive throughout this process. Of course, I would like to thank my mom, Margaret Marano, who supports me in countless ways. Her pride and interest in my work and my accomplishments nurture my dedication to scholarship. I would also like to thank my dad, stepfather, stepmother, and aunt Sara. My siblings, Vickie, Charlie, Billy, Eddie, Natalia, and Debbie, have always remained supportive of my work and engaged in numerous conversations (debates, really) with me regarding some of the topics discussed in this book. A special thanks is owed to my sister Debbie. Knowing how proud she would have been of this book, I was able to keep going at times when my energy was waning; she was a key source of strength. I have several other family members and friends, too many to name, who deserve recognition; thank you.

Table of Contents

Introduction: Empowerment, Academic Success, and
Critical Conversations 1
    Contextualizing the Analysis: Positionality and Reflexivity 3
    The Importance of Thinking Critically 13
    Critical Analyses: Tensions and Contexts 15

1   Critical Educational Psychology 19
    Introduction 19
    Educational Psychology 19
    Concerns with Educational Psychology 22
    Critical Educational Psychology 29
    Conclusion 35

2   Background on Self-Regulated Learning 37
    Introduction 37
    Historical Background 38
    Conceptual Distinctions 41
    Pedagogy: Content, Formats, and Environments 47
    Critical Concerns 52
    Conclusion 57

3   A Consideration of Agency in Self-Regulated Learning 59
    Introduction 59
    Agency and Determinism: Causality and Control 60
    Psychology and Agency 63
    Conclusion 82

4   Efficiency, Productivity, and Adaptability:
Neoliberal Subjectivity 85
    Introduction 85
    Neoliberalism and Schooling 86
    The Neoliberal Self 88
    Self-Regulated Learning and Neoliberalism: Conceptual Alignments ... 90

    Critical Reflections: Management of Self in a Neoliberal Context 99
    Conclusion 111

5 **Social Class in Self-Regulated Learning** **113**
    Introduction 113
    Socioeconomic Class 114
    Guardian Involvement, Self-Regulated Learning Development,
    and Class 117
    Characteristics of Self-Regulated Learning 125
    Conclusion 136

6 **Adaptation, Prescription, and Dependency: Critical Pedagogical Reflections on the Ethics of Teaching Self-Regulated Learning** **139**
    Introduction 139
    Critical Pedagogy: An Introduction 140
    Self-Regulated Learning from a Freirean Perspective 145
    Conclusion 158

Conclusion: Reject, Embrace, or Reflect **159**

References **169**

Introduction
Empowerment, Academic Success, and Critical Conversations

Educational practitioners, policymakers, and researchers continue to be interested in understanding the sources of student achievement. In these conversations, academic success and failure is attributed to a variety of factors such as socioeconomic class, family upbringing, a capitalist economic system, culture, hard work, motivation, intelligence, genetic predispositions, and effort, to name a few. This list reflects a range of sources that are traditionally considered both within and outside of individuals' control—though there is debate about which of these factors are actually under personal control and to what extent. Notwithstanding, contemporary educational psychologists remain focused on students' capacity to exercise control over their own learning. This focus is evident in the burgeoning interest in self-regulated learning (SRL), which is a self-steering process in which individuals target their cognitions, feelings, and actions, as well as features of the environment, in order to achieve their learning goals (Boekaerts & Cascallar, 2006; Hadwin, Järvelä, & Miller, 2011; Schunk & Zimmerman, 1997).

Educational psychologists construe SRL as the strategic harnessing, directing, and adapting of personal resources that enable individuals to overcome limitations resulting from their own cognitive mechanisms, instructional environments, and sociocultural conditions. Instead of being explicitly directed by others, self-regulating learners independently assess, set goals to master, and employ strategies to complete academic tasks. These learners do not passively receive the environment. That is, they do not rely on feedback or external instructions to formulate a course of action. Rather, they attempt to control and transform their environment, thoughts, and behaviors by planning a course of action that is geared toward the achievement of a learning goal. A major appeal of SRL is that academic performance is treated as dynamic and controllable, whereby individuals can strategically steer their learning and attain academic success.

There is a seductive quality to SRL. It is likely difficult to find educators who do not want their students to regulate their learning, as it may be assumed that the opposite of self-regulated is externally directed, dependent, passive, and undisciplined. Part of the seduction comes from the promises of home, empowerment, independence, and opportunity. Researchers contend that SRL supports the self-driven attainment of learning goals in contexts that are characterized by increasing diversity, worsening economic conditions, expansion and access to technology, competition for attention, and vast knowledge sources. SRL is implicated in navigating these conditions, as well as leveling the playing field. Researchers reason that SRL is both a part of and a means to continuously develop the necessary skill set to participate, function, and compete in 21st-century environments (Chong, 2006; Järvelä, 2011; Zimmerman, 2002).

As a result of the value associated with SRL, there is a myriad of books and articles exclusively dedicated to understanding the nuances and contours of SRL. Much of this literature is oriented toward improving the teaching and learning of SRL in a variety of formal and informal contexts. Educational psychologists tend to agree that SRL should be explicit in curricula, policy, and pedagogy. In addition, they tend to agree that teachers, guardians, and community members should work with students to support their SRL. Although there are a number of conceptual, methodological, and pedagogical debates in the literature, researchers are unified by the ideas that SRL is (1) valuable for students; (2) a desirable pedagogical goal; (3) a universal human characteristic; (4) empowering; (5) necessary for preparation in 21st-century environments; and (6) a neutral, value-free, and natural form of human engagement.

This book is a departure in that a critical educational psychology (CEP) perspective is applied to the analysis of SRL in order to problematize conventional assumptions and invite critical conversations. CEP is a commitment to draw from inter- and intradisciplinary perspectives and methodologies to examine ethical, political, practical, and ideological contexts related to educational psychology phenomena. In other words, it involves drawing from perspectives within and outside of psychology in order to consider the critical contours of concepts and practices within educational psychology. The foundational assumption in this book is that SRL is not neutral, value-free, ahistorical, or disconnected from power. Rather, SRL is tangled in the politics of control, conformity, disempowerment, governance, marginalization, and oppression.

The methods, perspectives, and commitments within psychology are not always adequate to explore these possibilities. Therefore, in this book, I draw from poststructural theory, sociocultural theory, sociology, psychology, and critical pedagogy to explore nuances of SRL that are not typically featured in educational psychology discourse.

A major concern is that researchers and practitioners are committed to student empowerment via SRL without adequately considering ethical nuances, as well as diverse meanings and possibilities. Therefore, the purpose of this book is to further the conversation on SRL by conducting a critical analysis. I think of the term "critical" in neither positive nor negative terms, and I strive to avoid endorsing, rejecting, valuing, and devaluing SRL. Rather, I think of critical as being attuned to historical, philosophical, cultural, and ethical complexities. In this regard, this critical analysis is intended to disrupt taken-for-granted assumptions in everyday discourse of SRL. This type of work is essential because, as critical psychologists argue, psychological discourse can be implicated in the production and maintenance of a number of unintended, negative consequences by decontextualizing its origins and ignoring its underpinnings (Fox, Prilleltensky, & Austin, 2009a). The analysis can generate a broad range of possibilities for thinking and acting in relation to SRL. If critical conversations are not part of the discourse, then SRL will continue to be viewed as strictly empowering, agentic, and valuable, concealing possible ways that it produces and maintains inequality.

Contextualizing the Analysis: Positionality and Reflexivity

My interest in critically analyzing SRL emerged as I was struggling in my pursuit of a doctoral degree in educational psychology. Early in my studies, my advisor suggested that my difficulty in the program resulted from my inability to self-regulate my learning. Although at that point I had limited exposure to the concept of SRL, I was unable to articulate dissatisfaction with his assessment. For the next few years I worked diligently to understand the notion of SRL as it was depicted in the educational psychological and broad psychological literatures. Concomitantly, I was exposed to a broad range of philosophical, sociological, methodological, and ethical landscapes that enabled me to detect and deliberate over concerns with SRL, in general, and my advisor's claim, in particular. Consequently, I constructed a personal narrative that reflects my discomfort with the attribution of my struggles in graduate school to a lack of SRL.

I begin with a brief narrative to contextualize my concern with SRL because efforts to produce knowledge are social and historical practices that involve human affairs (e.g., Bullock & Limbert, 2009; Holzman, 1997; Latour & Woolgar, 1986). Therefore, it is important to explore reflexivity and positionality in any act that is designed to produce and disseminate knowledge. Bullock and Limbert, two critical psychologists, define reflexivity as "the continual consideration of the ways in which the researcher's own social identity and values affect the data gathered and the picture of the social world produced" (p. 224). This post hoc narrative reflects recognition of the importance of identity and positionality in shaping ways individuals construct, interpret, and engage with the world. Although I link my personal experiences with my commitment to engage critically with SRL, my concerns extend far beyond the story I tell.

I identify as a white, Italian, working-class[1] male, who was born and raised in Brooklyn, New York. From 10 year-old till the time I left the state at the age of 25, I lived in a row home directly across the street from government-subsidized housing, often referred to as the "projects." Although the neighborhood changed over time, the composition when I lived there can best be described as economically disadvantaged and working class. In terms of racial composition, mostly African American and Latino families lived in the projects. In the row homes, residents were primarily white with a mixture of national backgrounds. The schools that I attended were nestled in this configuration of housing projects and single-family row homes, as well as just feet from a plant that processed human excrement. Like the neighborhood, the schools in this area had a mixture of diversity. The schools can be described as large and urban, with my high school having a graduating class of more than 700, and a student enrollment of approximately 3,400.

Throughout my K–12 schooling, I would not describe myself as interested, engaged, or successful. Along with all my other siblings, I attended a private Catholic school from first to fourth grade. To this day, I do not understand how that was possible. At that time, my mother lived alone and had five kids; my father was a city bus driver. It makes sense that for financial reasons I entered public schools in the fifth grade and stayed in the system until the completion of high school. In my junior high school (what some know as middle school), there were 12 general education classes. Using a well-defined tracking system, I was placed into the eighth best class. Institutionally, I was not recognized as a "good" student. Throughout this level of schooling, I never did homework on my own; instead, I copied other students' work. Overall, I had little interest in and motivation for institutional lessons. High school was not much different. Throughout my four years, I only partially read one book, seldom studied, and frequently failed to complete in-class assignments and homework. I seldom cut school but never showed interest in being there. In high school, I did not participate in extracurricular activities. Despite being disconnected, uninterested, and unmotivated, I consistently received B's throughout both junior high school and high school.

While at the secondary level, I accumulated few credentials that supported my marketability as a college candidate. Aside from abstaining from extracurricular activities, I scored under 1,000 on the Scholastic Aptitude Test. I took one advanced placement class, in which I performed poorly. The one area in which I did well was foreign language. I took the regents examination for Spanish language learning. I scored high on this exam, secured college credit, and was exempt from taking foreign language in college, an exemption that I found favorable at the time because it meant fewer requirements for graduation. Although my academic history was relatively unimpressive and my strength and drive as a student were questionable, at the end of my senior year I applied to Brooklyn College, a local institution that is part of the City University of New York consortium of colleges. As a result of family income level, I received full government support for tuition.

My decision to attend college was not informed by intrinsic or instrumental purposes. That is, I did not see the value of college as a pursuit for knowledge or as a means to an occupation. My decision to attend was informed by my desire to avoid occupational decisions and commitments while giving myself something to do. College, in particular, and schooling, in general, was not promoted in my family as an essential and naturalized element to life trajectories, nor was it viewed as a necessary and indisputable good. Of course schooling was valued in our home and my mother worked hard to prepare her children with the knowledge and skills to transition from home to school. Notwithstanding, schooling was not positioned as a naturalized element of a life course.

Despite the fact that schooling was valued in our home, the members of my family did not have a history of strong academic performance. As a child, my mother remained mostly in the home, my biological father was a city bus driver, and my stepfather, with whom I lived most of my life, worked as an electrician. None of these guardians had experience with tertiary education, nor were they "high" performers at the secondary level. Out of my five siblings, two dropped out of traditional high school; one eventually returned to get her diploma from an alternative secondary schooling program. My three siblings who graduated went to college but all dropped out. Despite the fact that I was the second youngest of a family of six, I was the first to receive a bachelor's degree. Two of my brothers returned to college later in their lives and received their degrees, one in journalism and the other in business. Neither of them work in those or related fields; instead they work in blue-collar jobs. Like me, my family members experienced challenges with navigating the demands of schooling.

My struggles with schooling at the tertiary level amplified. During my first two years, I missed classes, fell asleep during lectures, failed to turn in assignments, and seldom read for class. Midway through one semester, I stopped going to all my classes for no particular reason other than lack of interest. After two years, my grade point average (GPA) was 1.67, and, as a result, I was put on academic probation. During my third year at Brooklyn College, my academic performance began to shift, which was facilitated greatly by admittance into a well-resourced honors program that was designed to prepare top-performing undergraduates for graduate school. With a 2.0 GPA, a committee of peers and one faculty member, despite the fact that they admit and graduate students with a 3.5 GPA or higher, believed that I had the potential to be successful in this program. This belief was generated, propped up, and defended by a friend of mine who was in the program and who also happened to sit on the admissions committee. I met this friend in one of my classes and he suggested that I apply to the program. He was well respected in the program and his opinion carried significant weight. The next three years in this program were difficult but I managed to graduate with honors. After six years, I graduated with my bachelor's degree in psychology with a 3.5 GPA.

What role, if any, did SRL play in both my struggles and shift in performance? Could one conclude that my academic achievement was attributable to improvements in SRL? While at Brooklyn College I did not know of the concept of SRL. It is not common for individuals to describe their engagement and performance using this term. Perhaps it is more common to use related concepts such as disciplined, caring, motivated, strategic, and hard working. Regardless of the language, I do not attribute my academic outcomes to the exertion of personal, planned, and strategic control over learning. In fact, I attribute my improved performance to a number of factors beyond my control. I was lucky to have met somebody who sat on the honors program's admissions committee and then benefit from his influence. Once in the honors program, my college education was drastically different from previous years. The program was conducive to developing a strong sense of community with faculty and peers, which was made possible by small class sizes, a student cohort, and sustained faculty investment. Many of the honors courses validated diverse cultural knowledge and experiences, and afforded me the opportunity to affirm my sense of personhood and pursue topics of interest. The honors faculty were patient and supportive while I worked to resolve course incompletes and F's. I was in a well-resourced program in which I was given extra support, attention, and resources.

Although the educational climate was dramatically different, my academic struggles did not entirely fade. I had difficulty writing papers, forming arguments, understanding advanced texts, and researching. Notwithstanding these struggles, I received all A's in my honors courses, and A's and B's in all other courses. Again, an important question is what role, if any, did SRL play in this performance? Did I experience success in the program because of improvements in SRL? Were some of my persistent struggles a result of my inability to self-regulate my learning well?

It is challenging to capture my experiences of control when in the honors program. Arguably, it is difficult to capture self-regulatory control at any given moment. Therefore, I am reluctant to unequivocally conclude that my success was a result of SRL. However, I do not believe that I was self-regulating my learning, or at least doing it well. Contemporary researchers tend to agree that all individuals are capable of and attempt to regulate their learning. Only, some individuals are better at it than others. Although I persisted in the face of challenge, studied, and worked hard, I did not see myself as strategic, intentional, and reflective. Did I have to experience myself as in strategic control in order to have been exercising such control?

The above questions are important because academic performance is often attributed to purposeful and intentional engagement. From this line of thinking, it makes sense to associate academic success with SRL. If students are successful in school, then the reasoning follows it must have been because of their strategic and intentional engagement. The corollary to this reasoning is that if students are unsuccessful then they could improve by becoming strategic, reflective learners. Success and failure are explainable in terms of SRL. Of course, researchers recognize that not all success and failure in schooling are explainable in this way; however, many identify SRL as a significant factor. Identifying SRL as a significant factor positions individuals as personally responsible for their outcomes and endorses the view that all individuals have an equal opportunity to be successful (Vassallo, 2011). Ostensibly, all individuals need to do is make the right choices and take advantage of those opportunities.

Coming from a working-class background and being a first-generation college graduate, it makes sense that one would conclude that I was shifting my socioeconomic position through my intentional, goal-directed, and strategic engagement in which I was able to take advantage of every available opportunity. One problematic assumption underpinning this conclusion is that I had the same opportunity as everybody else in my class position, including my siblings. As a struggling student I gained access to an elite honors program because of who I knew. I did not have the same credentials, knowledge, or dispositions as students who typically applied and were admitted. Opportunity is not always "equal." Although SRL can be tied to opening up some opportunities, it is doubtful that I could have gained access to this program at the time I did by being intentional and strategic. Perhaps, one could argue that if I were intentional and strategic throughout schooling I could have acquired the credentials to gain access to the honors program. However, as is clear from the narrative, having the knowledge, skills, and dispositions to strategically navigate the demands of schooling were not part of my home discourse, nor were they something I developed in school.

Another problematic assumption with associating my academic success with SRL is that I took advantage of the opportunity presented to me and persisted because of choices, hard work, and strategic behavior. However, it is clear that luck (i.e., meeting a student committee member), a shifting educational environment, and special treatment contributed to improved performance. The notion of SRL, and related concepts, invites educators and researchers to overstate the degree to which personal control is responsible for performance, while ignoring other explanatory factors. These assumptions can lead teachers, researchers, and policymakers to (1) view individuals as deficient and the sole sources of their predicaments; (2) ignore disparities in opportunity; and (3) focus on changing individuals to address educational problems. Arguably, chance, relationships, and a particular educational environment led to a significant shift in my performance and academic trajectory, not an intervention to make me a strategic learner.

However, let us assume for a moment that my improved grades at the undergraduate level were a direct result of my self-regulation. There is a question about whether or not self-regulating my learning was empowering. My experience in college reflects Fine and Burn's (2003) description of a tension that working-class youth experience in school. They state:

> For . . . working-class youth and young adults . . . "opportunities to succeed" may tear at the fabric of biography, identity, loyalty, and belonging. Often tithed, materially and/or psychologically, exiting one's class status (having a "great chance"), or betrayal

of one's "home class," and terror of one's "new environment," may double as cruel seduction. Every "terrific opportunity" may be filled with the potential for abandonment and shame. Every "offer" may be tainted with the weighty sense of those left behind. (p. 850)

This tension captures my experiences and the "choices" that I confronted. The more I was successful in school, the more I became fractured and conflicted, and the greater the psychological chasm between my home and me.

This tension makes sense. Critical theorists tend to agree that schools are middle-class enterprises, as they reward, value, validate, and teach knowledge, skills, and dispositions that align with middle-class culture (e.g., Brice-Heath, 1983; Brantlinger, 2003; Fine & Burns, 2003). So, if SRL supports academic success, and academic success produces chasms between me and my community, then regulating my learning to be successful in school carries with it a sense of loss. Arguably, all learning comes with loss as it involves acquiring new, as well as letting go of, ideas, dispositions, beliefs, and identity. However, this loss means something different for working-class children than for middle-class children. In addition, success in schools for working-class individuals is implicated in the maintenance of a cultural hierarchy in which middle-class dispositions, beliefs, practices, and ways of knowing become validated as the culture of power.

One could argue that the problem here is not SRL but rather the contentious educational contexts in which SRL is employed. Although this argument seems reasonable, analyses of SRL cannot be divorced from educational contexts and goals. Schooling is political, ideological, and cultural. If individuals are expected to regulate themselves within schools, then they are ultimately entangled in these contexts. If SRL supports academic success, educational psychologists must be attuned to the politics of that success.

The concern here extends beyond the contexts in which SRL is employed and the sense of loss that is evoked. SRL itself is tied to identity, ways of being, and knowing. SRL was not just a learning gimmick that I could have exercised without having a certain identity, along with particular thought processes, desires, and behaviors. Setting goals, deliberating over a repertoire of strategies, self-evaluating, and strategic planning were activities that I seldom observed in my home, especially in relation to academic tasks. My mother was always somebody who acted quickly to solve the countless problems she experienced raising six children. Forethought, planning, and personal evaluations did not precede action, or at least they were not modeled or cultivated in our home. My academic engagement resembled this orientation; I just tackled academic tasks. I did not have the requisite disposition and skills to plan, reflect, evaluate, and monitor my learning.

Arguably, all engagement indicates SRL, as goals, intentions, evaluations, and problem-solving processes are used in all activities of our lives. Thus, Martin and McLellan's (2008) query is relevant to consider. They wonder what distinguishes SRL from quotidian experiences and actions. If all actions are strategic and goal directed, then what makes some self-regulated activities better than others? One possibility has to do with the degree to which SRL enables individuals to adapt to academic situations and perform well in schools. In fact, a defining feature of SRL is adaptation to school demands, often with the connotation of academic success. If SRL supports adaptation to and success within school and schools reproduce inequality, then SRL can be implicated in reproducing inequality.

Up to this point, my concerns with SRL can be summed up in the following questions: (1) Does academic success always indicate SRL? (2) Does SRL enable individuals to experience success in environments that are discriminatory? (3) Does regulating learning involve being a particular kind of person, one that can potentially conflict with an existing sense of self and home culture? (4) Can we always know when one is exercising strategic control over learning? and (5) What makes some self-regulatory actions better than others? Although these questions have critical importance, a major concern is about the framing of the conversation for my academic performance. Using the concept of SRL to explain my academic performance limits the conversation, which is structured around a binary of personal and external control. Critical theorists tend to eschew binary thinking. Although I validate this way of thinking by reflecting on the sources of control for my academic performance, the conversation must move beyond these limits.

To continue with the narrative, until the honors program I had never considered attending graduate school. After graduating from Brooklyn College I spent one year working for the New York City Housing Authority's social services division, with the intention to apply for graduate programs in psychology. I applied to eight PhD programs in psychology, despite the fact that I had little idea what a dissertation was, how to conduct research, or the purposes of PhD programs. I wanted to attend graduate school because of expectations from peers and faculty from the honors program and my desire to continue learning, while avoiding the confinement of working in a 9–5 job. Although I was surprised at the time, I understand why all my applications were rejected. A peer, who I met in the honors program, had been attending Michigan State University in the teacher education program. She suggested that I apply to their educational psychology doctoral program. Although I had never heard of the field, I wanted to continue my schooling and, therefore, applied to the program. My friend, who herself was highly regarded in the program, passed along my materials to a prestigious and influential faculty member, as the deadline for submitting applications had passed. My materials were reviewed and I was granted a face-to-face interview, which resulted in my admittance to the program.

After seven years, at the end of the 4–7 expected range for completion, I received my PhD. Not unlike previous levels of schooling, I experienced a number of challenges. Without familiarity of educational psychology and a research direction, I meandered through the doctoral program. My struggles with understanding challenging texts, writing well, and making persuasive arguments continued. My advisor seemed to know unequivocally that my challenges were a result of poor SRL, an attribution that was likely supported by the association between success and SRL. I experienced challenges in the doctoral program for several reasons, one of which ostensibly might be a result of ineffective SRL. Also, being in the program required me to have certain kinds of knowledge, goals, interactive patterns, and thinking processes—ones that were unfamiliar to me despite the fact that I was in a program that was designed to prepare me to navigate this kind of environment. At both the graduate and undergraduate levels, I had to become something significantly different from what I was. Being successful was not just about setting goals, employing strategies, and monitoring both the self and academic progress but also about being somebody different—one that became foreign to my home community.

It was not until writing this book that I felt as though I was effectively regulating my learning. During this nearly two-year-long process, I developed an outline for the book and plan that included a timeline and benchmarks. Throughout, I reflected on the conditions that best supported my productivity and efficiency for achieving my goals, which were strategically adjusted when needed. I formed and adapted goals, employed a variety of strategies to achieve those goals, and observed which strategies worked well. Particular attention was paid to the kinds of environments that were most conducive to writing so I could try to protect and re-create them. I recognized when I needed breaks and explored rejuvenating leisure activities. When self-deprecating beliefs emerged, I mitigated them through reason in order to sustain motivation. I maintained a tight focus by limiting reading and writing to only those sources that were deemed relevant for writing the book. There was a great deal of time dedicated to this project.

Although these efforts enabled me to achieve my goal of completing the book, these self-regulatory activities did not feel empowering. Regulating my book writing meant living with a new set of rules and values—some that I found beneficial and others that I found problematic. I felt constrained and obligated, bound by the requirement to be efficient and productive. In part, these regulatory efforts were organized around my effort to pursue preformulated, institutionally sanctioned norms for performance. As requirements for productivity and efficiency are increasing in higher education for faculty members, I find SRL to be effective for meeting these demands. Balancing teaching, service, and other scholarly activities, my time had to be strategic and instrumental. I ensured that when at my peak in terms of cognitive energy, I needed to be focused on the book. Thus, I had to study and learn about myself so I could use that information to be productive. I considered myself self-regulating when writing the book and such activities were instrumental for completing the book.

These regulatory efforts, however, were accompanied by problematic realizations. In recognizing myself as self-regulating effectively, I found myself increasingly accepting of institutionally sanctioned knowledge, dispositions, and expectations for productivity. My motivation, goals, and aspirations were aligned with institutional norms and expectations. Arguably, in previous contexts, there was not such a neat alignment, possibly explaining academic challenges. Relationships with friends and family were rendered superficial. During this time, new relationships were difficult to forge because of time constraints. Or new relationships were formed that could support my effort to write the book. Learning to academically self-regulate, or at least understanding myself as counting as a self-regulating learner, did not mean a simple shift in behavior. It was reconditioning orientations to academic tasks, looking inward for sources of empowerment, remaining narrowly focused on a particular task, relating to people in certain ways, and changing what I desired and aspired to do—all in the interest of achieving a normative standard of performance and productivity. It seems to me that although I struggled academically, schooling contributed to conditioning me to become a self-regulating learner. Although these strategic activities have enabled me to achieve my writing goals, I had to develop a certain set of values, rules, and norms for engagement that aligned with institutional goals.

To conclude that I was struggling in graduate school, or even at any preceding level of education, because I was not self-regulated ignores the politics of the curriculum knowledge toward which I was supposed to regulate myself, what it means to self-regulate for somebody who is unfamiliar with this form of engagement, ways in which SRL is entangled in culture, personal and familial history, and how SRL engenders subordination to institutional demands. The construction of this narrative is not intended to serve as a basis for rejecting SRL. Instead, it is offered in order to raise critical questions—ones that need to be adequately explored if researchers, teachers, and policymakers commit to shaping pedagogy to teach students to regulate their learning.

The Importance of Thinking Critically

SRL is almost exclusively considered a valuable and empowering form of engagement—one that good teachers will foster, invite, and reward. In addition, SRL is associated with the alleviation of social problems, democratic participation, lifelong learning, and human agency. Proponents believe that SRL expands freedom of action by enabling individuals to select, influence, and construct their own circumstances. Therefore, SRL is associated with the state of empowerment or is described as something students need to be empowered to do. Researchers reason that regulating learning can mitigate the potential challenges related to diverse student populations, nonlinearity of knowledge sources, large class sizes, economic inequalities, increased access to technology, and the abundance and structure of knowledge sources. With the value associated with SRL, it is not surprising that research on SRL continues to show steady increases in each subsequent decade starting from its emergence as a formal object of study in the early 1980s (Martin, 2004a; Post, Boyer, & Brett, 2006). Concerned that SRL is not explicitly widespread in curricula, policies, and pedagogy (Hilden & Pressley, 2007; Winne, 2005; Zimmerman, 2000), educational psychologists are committed to developing conceptualizations and pedagogical models that can be applied to classrooms.

If not already doing so or committed to doing so, it is likely that teachers will be confronted with the expectation to teach students to regulate their learning. Educational psychology is a foundational course for preservice teachers and contributes to production of criteria for what counts as highly qualified teachers. It is difficult to find an educational psychology text that does not include a chapter or section on SRL. Even contemporary educational rhetoric and reform signal a push toward SRL. For example, President Barack Obama's

(2009b) speech to children in schools reflected discourse that overlaps with SRL. He stated, "They [referring to certain named students] faced challenges in their lives just like you [addressing students all across the country] do. But they refused to give up. They chose to take responsibility for their education and set goals for themselves." Although responsibility is not interchangeable with SRL, it is closely related, especially when accompanied with ideas such as hard work and goal setting. Messages of personal responsibility and individual accountability are prominent in current federal education policy and rhetoric.

In addition, there is an expanding discourse on 21st-century competencies (21CC) which aligns with SRL. There are several organizations that have produced overlapping frameworks that describe competencies that individuals need to navigate and succeed in the 21st century (Organisation for Economic Co-operation and Development [OECD] Competencies; Partnership for 21st-Century Skills, Assessment and Teaching of 21st-Century Skills; Council on 21st-Century Learning). According to an OECD (2005) report, a competency is "more than just knowledge and skills. It involves the ability to meet complex demands by drawing on and mobilizing psychosocial resources (including skills and attitudes) in a particular context" (p. 4). Examples of these competencies include self-direction, adaptability, flexibility, critical literacy, ability to execute, and interpersonal management. As Wolters (2011) appropriately shows, these competencies are aligned with SRL. Given that several states have already adopted this framework in their curricula, and several more states are likely to follow suit, teachers are likely to confront expectations to teach students to regulate their learning even if not explicitly organized around the concept of SRL.

The increase in SRL research, the growing popularity of 21CC, and national education discourse make it likely that teachers will be confronted with the expectation to explicitly craft their pedagogy in ways that foster SRL. Therefore, a critical conversation about SRL is timely and necessary. Although researchers and theorists integrate multiple perspectives in research on SRL (e.g., Perry, 2002), as well as recognize the need for examining the sociopolitical context related to this construct (e.g., Boekaerts & Corno, 2005), the perspectives and methods for studying SRL have focused almost exclusively on the conceptual, methodological, and pedagogical complexities—all with the intention of making teaching and learning SRL widespread and effective. Although these foci have value and are important for advancing research, it is essential that researchers, practitioners, and policymakers critically consider diverse interpretations of SRL in order to encourage nuanced conversations and ethically informed practice.

In general, it is important for educational psychologists to integrate critical perspectives that push the boundaries of our discourse. As Gallagher (2003) argues, the field of educational psychology is often considered to be a neutral, objective, scientifically validated body of knowledge. SRL, for example, is considered a natural human disposition that can be studied and formally developed using carefully crafted scientific tools. However, my position in this book, and the position of critical psychologists in general, is that psychological discourse is historical, ideological, philosophical, political, and cultural. Like other educational psychology concepts, such as memory, metacognition, critical thinking, and self, SRL is embedded in and endorses philosophical, ideological, cultural, and political contexts. Further, educational psychological ideas can be implicated in both disempowerment (e.g., Kincheloe, 1999b) and empowerment (e.g., Cleary & Zimmerman, 2004). Therefore, it is important that policymakers, researchers, and practitioners understand these possibilities that surround the application of educational psychology phenomena..

A critical analysis of SRL is important for exploring taken-for-granted and ignored assumptions and providing the tools to reflect on the range of possible dangers surrounding this concept. If I believe that my academic outcomes result strictly from my self-regulatory effectiveness, I might ignore educational inequalities and erroneously engage in self-blame or self-adulation for my predicaments. If I believe that regulating my learning was a natural human disposition, I might pathologize myself for not embodying and manifesting SRL better. The notion of SRL can shape how people understand and relate to themselves, as well as how they live. If the contexts of SRL are understood, then it is possible to engage in reflections about whether or not to endorse this way of engaging. That is why Bird (1999) contends that critical analyses are important for developing innovative educational practice. A CEP perspective is intended not to supplant certain forms of inquiry within educational psychology. Rather, it is intended to invite reflections on ignored tensions, complexities, naturalization of phenomena, and effects of educational psychological discourse on students and teachers.

Critical Analyses: Tensions and Contexts

The purpose of this book is to use a variety of tools to illuminate ignored tensions and complexities with the discourse of SRL. As research on SRL is applied to all levels of education and subject domains, the analyses in this book are broadly applicable. With that said, the arguments and reasoning in some of the chapters are heavily informed by research related to students and teachers from kindergarten to the 12th grade. Each chapter is dedicated to a particular focus or theoretical perspective. Some perspectives are both conceptually incompatible and compatible. My aim is not to produce a theoretically coherent critique. Rather, it is to draw from as many perspectives as possible to illuminate different tensions and critical concerns. Therefore, many of the chapters can stand as independent analyses. However, there are common threads that unite the chapters. Although not always explicit, each chapter invites critical reflections on individual human agency, which is the particular focus of chapter 3. In relation to this thread, issues related to empowerment and disempowerment run throughout the book. All chapters illustrate ways that SRL is not neutral, value-free, or independent of power.

The first two chapters are overviews. In chapter 1, I elaborate on CEP and discuss its importance. The parent field of psychology has made strides in integrating critical perspectives, yet educational psychology is lagging behind. Few explicitly discuss the possibilities for what a CEP perspective can look like. This chapter is a starting point for the production of such possibilities. CEP is a commitment to examine widely held ideas, concepts, beliefs, and methods in educational psychology through intra- and interdisciplinary lenses in order to consider ways that our field is implicated in dynamic and subtle workings of power. Organized around this commitment, three themes for critical analyses are discussed: polyvocalism, emancipation, and sociohistoricism. This conceptualization of CEP is a key starting point for a dialogue on how we can push for, frame, and organize critical work within educational psychology. This chapter also reveals my critical commitments, in general, and my approach to this book, specifically.

In chapter 2, a thorough background on SRL is provided. SRL has been part of the educational psychology literature for more than three decades. During this time, the conceptualization of, methods for studying, and models for teaching SRL have evolved. Although the value of and commitment to teach SRL remain unquestioned, the discourse is not monolithic. The tensions and evolution of the literature are discussed. I conclude the chapter by highlighting critical questions and concerns that receive little to no attention in conversations about SRL. These include (1) ways in which teaching SRL endorses a narrow self that is individualistic and a priori; (2) SRL is tied to supporting efficient and effective obedience to institutional mandates; and (3) the ends of SRL are tied to contentious educational environments.

Each of the following chapters can stand as independent, yet related, analyses. In chapter 3, I focus on the notion of agency in SRL. Agency is defined as one's ability to make choices that shape life conditions and outcomes (Martin, 2004b). SRL researchers implicitly presume some conception of agency or, at least, a position in response to "the question of agency" (e.g., whether agency is affirmed or denied in self-regulation). It is surprising and curious that agency is rarely mentioned in the educational psychological literature on academic self-regulation, let alone given extensive or adequate treatment. Literature from a variety of fields, such as sociology, psychology, and philosophy are used in order to illuminate the commitments related to the assumptions and implications of agency in SRL. I argue that much of the discourse on SRL is underpinned by a narrow, philosophical conception of agency.

Chapter 4 is about how SRL involves harnessing subjectivity so that individuals can operate in neoliberal environments. Neoliberalism is well known as an economic logic that is undergirded by the belief that the best way to ensure prosperity and equal opportunity is to transform all economic and social arrangements to operate like the free market. Therefore, objectives are to transform institutions to maximize choice, deregulate activity, and support competition. Neoliberal environments work if individuals adopt neoliberal selfhood, a self that is a competitor in the marketplace and is driven by self-interest as pursued and rationalized through an economic logic of productivity and efficiency. The discourse of SRL is entangled in neoliberal logic and neoliberal conceptions of selfhood. From the association with neoliberalism, SRL is not independence from power but a way to tie students' propensities and aspirations to a specific set of institutional, economic, and political aims.

In chapter 5, I turn to research on socioeconomic class by comparing research related to middle- and working-class individuals, to consider the norms that are endorsed both in research on SRL development and representations of effective SRL. For the former, guardians are implicated in the development of children's academic self-regulation. That is, there are certain forms of interactions, dispositions, and knowledge that are associated with SRL development. Analysis of socioeconomic class and guardian involvement reveals a similarity between what middle-class guardians know and do, and those conditions that are identified as important for SRL. For the latter, representations of effective SRL align with middle-class children and the features of selfhood that guardians try to cultivate. That which counts as effective academic self-regulation in contemporary educational environments reflects the knowledge, skills, and dispositions of middle-class children. I do not suggest that working-class children are incapable of SRL and that guardians do not and cannot cultivate it. Rather, that norms and expectations related to SRL that are featured in the literature are associated with class norms.

In chapter 6, I draw from the critical pedagogical philosophy of Paulo Freire. In particular, I consider his ideas related to adaptation, prescription, and dependence to show how SRL is entangled in obedience, subordination, and oppression. Drawing from Freire, teaching students to self-regulate their learning: (1) targets individual psychological changes that render individuals adaptable to existing pedagogical arrangements; (2) is guided by a logic to prescribe a certain kind of self and form of engagement; and (3) produces problematic relationships of dependence. From a critical pedagogical perspective, adaptation, prescription, and dependence are tools of oppression. Therefore, the association among SRL, empowerment, and agency are put under serious scrutiny. Although I use Freire's work to suggest that teaching SRL is incompatible with the ideals of critical pedagogy, the point is that his book is intended as a key point from which to launch new commitments and practices related to the study of and engagement with SRL, ones that are attuned to power, politics, ideology, culture, and identity. Although I illuminate a number of key critical nuances, more work is needed to continue pursuing the dialogue on SRL.

Note

1. According to my occupational status, level of education, income, and assets, my identification as working class is contested by many criteria for class categorization. Identification is entangled in a two key questions: who has the authority to categorize and what criteria reflect categories? Although most categorization schemes locate me as middle-class, I do not identify myself that way. There are a couple of issues with my identification. First, I recognize that my self-identification as working class is possible because of the middle-class privilege. Second, I am not recognized as working class by those across the class spectrum, especially those who fit criteria for working class. Notwithstanding, my history and family are working class. Although class groups are not politically homogenous, my politics are more aligned with a stereotypical working-class platform than a middle-class one. In addition, I reject the metaphor that I have "made it out" of my family's class. Working class status is not something that I find unfavorable and in need of escape. So I reject a label that has me moving out of something.

Chapter 1
Critical Educational Psychology

Introduction

Critical educational psychology (CEP) is a commitment to examine widely accepted ideas, concepts, beliefs, and methods in educational psychology through intra- and interdisciplinary perspectives in order to consider ways that the discourse of our field is implicated in the workings of power. This means explicitly considering ways educational psychology is entangled in issues of freedom, control, governance, oppression, discrimination, marginalization, empowerment, and disempowerment. These issues are seldom explored because of an assumptive context that educational psychology discourse is neutral, value-free, and consistent with supporting individual empowerment. To support efforts to engage critically with the discourse of our field, I offer three possible themes for inquiry: polyvocalism, emancipation, and sociohistoricism. This conceptualization of CEP is one way to construct critical possibilities, and it should serve merely as a starting point for a dialogue on how we can push for, frame, and organize critical work within educational psychology.

Educational Psychology

Educational psychology is a subfield of the parent field of psychology and is heavily influenced by general psychology and its subfields, which include, but are not limited to, developmental psychology, social psychology, and cognitive psychology. Bird (1999) captures this characteristic, defining educational psychology as any area of education that is informed by psychological theories or techniques. Educational psychology is also informed by perspectives outside the conventional boundaries of psychology, such as evolution, philosophy, and biology, just to name a few. Drawing from a rich landscape of perspectives both within and outside of psychology, educational psychologists study what people think, do, and know in relation to particular environments where education and training are intended to take place (Berliner, 1993).

The field of educational psychology is a relatively modern construction, emerging over the last two centuries. However, researchers argue that what typically falls within the purview of the field has been around for centuries (Berliner, 1993; Grinder, 1989; Woolfolk-Hoy, 2000). Berliner suggests that since the time of the Passover ritual, individuals have been concerned with individual differences, assessment, human development, the nature of subject matter, problem solving, and transfer of learning—all foundational areas of educational psychology. In addition, Plato and Aristotle are viewed as theorizing about the nature of knowledge in ways that resemble some contemporary constructivist ideas (Berliner, 1993; Grinder, 1989). John Comenius (1592–1670) was the first to suggest that children learn differently across ages—a foundational idea to Jean Piaget's theory of cognitive development (Grinder, 1989). Further, John Locke (1632–1704) is associated with empiricism, which is the broad idea that all learning is attributed to external sources. Although few contemporary educational psychologists are strict empiricists, the attention to the social world in learning and development informs much contemporary educational psychology discourse (Pintrich, 2000).

Although with deep historical roots, figures over the last two centuries have been instrumental in molding the field. Some of these figures include Johann Friedrich Herbart, John Dewey, William James, G. Stanley Hall, and Edward L. Thorndike. During the 19th and 20th centuries, the general field of psychology was transitioning away from its philosophical foundations to an increasing reliance on science (Billig, 2008). Concomitantly, a debate about whether or not education can be studied scientifically was occurring (Berliner, 1993). The formation of psychology as a science and the acceptance that education can be studied scientifically was significant for the formation and relevance of educational psychology (Berliner, 1993). Like the trend in general psychology (Billig, 2008), educational psychologists departed from their philosophical roots and aligned with the logic and practices of the natural sciences in order to gain legitimacy as an authority in education policy and practice.

E. L. Thorndike, who Berliner contends is generally recognized as the father of educational psychology, suggested that only scientifically empirical work should guide education. Berliner describes Thorndike's faith in experimental psychological science and statistics as unshakable. Thorndike believed that people were as easy to study as toads and stones and that teaching and learning are mechanical, predictable, and subject to laws similar to the natural world.

Like many other educational psychologists in the early part of the 20th century, Thorndike conducted his studies in laboratory settings and relied on experimental methods. Although the knowledge and practices from this time continue to inform contemporary discourse, the laboratory research that was designed to construct universal and generalizable principles of learning were criticized for being disconnected from the messiness and complexity of classroom settings (Berliner, 1993; Woolfolk-Hoy, 2000). In addition, some of the educational psychologists who endorsed laboratory experimentation for studying teaching and learning expressed disdain for the perspectives and experiences of teachers and students, commitments that further alienated these researchers from the relevance of classroom life (Berliner, 1993).

Not all educational psychologists agreed with studying learning in laboratories (Berliner, 1993; Woolfolk-Hoy, 2000). Notwithstanding, it was not until the 1950s after the launch of Sputnik that psychological research was focused on the classroom (Woolfolk-Hoy, 2000). Today, a significant portion of educational psychology research is conducted in classrooms. In fact, Berliner contends that a defining feature of our field is the application of psychological tools, knowledge, and concepts to the study of individuals in educational contexts. The assumption is that there are specific things about teachers, students, curricula, and schooling environments that require its own field of study within psychology. With the shift to classrooms, Berliner contends that educational psychologists became interested in and validated the experiences of teachers and students. However, the commitment to science for constructing generalizable principles related to teaching, learning, and development persisted.

The shifts from the laboratory to the classroom and from disdain to interest in experiences of students and teachers have contributed to certain trends in our field (Berliner, 1993). These trends include recognizing the value of both large-scale quantitative measures as well as small-scale qualitative measures. Another trend is what Berliner refers to as "psychologizing school subjects" (p. 65), which is an approach to the study of learning that is concerned with the thinking of the learner, the structure of the discipline to be learned, and the form of explanations available to the teacher. The assumption is that studying teaching and learning involves a consideration of the interaction between different variables. Another trend relates to assessments. Berliner associates standardized assessments with the logic and commitments of Thorndike and argues that contemporary educational psychologists are likely to endorse multidimensional qualitative and quantitative assessments of educational phenomena. Other trends include viewing intelligence as incremental and diverse, moving away from isolating the self from the world, and recognizing, at least to some degree, the sociopolitical context of our work. As in any field, the knowledge, tools, assumptions, and commitments within educational psychology have evolved and will continue to do so.

Despite the fact that theorists were skeptical about the relevance of educational psychology for teaching (Woolfolk-Hoy, 2000), the discourse of our field pervades educational conversations, policies, and pedagogy. Today most teacher preparation programs have an educational psychology component, even if it is referred to by another name. Psychology is intertwined in everyday educational discourse. Behavior management, identity, learning styles, self-esteem, parenting styles, self-regulation, pedagogy, human development, and morality, to name a few, are all areas of inquiry for educational psychologists. The National Board for Professional Teaching Standards, the organization responsible for defining the criteria for national certification, evaluates teachers' understanding and application of different theories of learning and development. Specifically, teachers must demonstrate an understanding and sensitivity to theories informed by Jean Piaget and Lev Vygotsky, the two titans of cognitive developmental theory. In addition, teachers must show that they can structure their lesson plans based on the information-processing theory of memory. There are countless examples in which educational psychology informs institutional policies and practice, as well as everyday discourse related to teaching and learning.

Concerns with Educational Psychology

Notwithstanding the evolution and qualities of the field, educational psychologists are committed to certain assumptions, philosophies, methodologies, and conceptualizations. These include normalizing human thoughts and behaviors, treating their tools and knowledge as neutral and value-free, reducing academic success to isolated variables, endorsing narrow ideals of selfhood, relying on science as the gold standard of inquiry, and ignoring historical contexts. Packer and Tappan (2001) contend that the diversity of perspectives within our field has enabled educational psychologists to overcome some of these limitations. They reason that the inclusion of diverse perspectives encourages people to examine their own values, positions, and assumptions. However, there are certain assumptions that seldom get challenged, and there is an absence of the kinds of perspectives that can adequately support critical engagement, especially in the area of self-regulated learning (SRL).

Individualism and Selfhood

Bird (1999) asserts that educational psychologists are committed to ideological individualism, which means the individual is both the problem and solution to social, economic, and educational problems. In general, psychologists are accused of this commitment (Tolman, 2009). A central concern with this ideology is that individuals are viewed as the site of reformation, while environmental situations, such as interpersonal evaluations, asymmetrical social relationships, institutional arrangements, and diagnostic tools, are ignored. To illustrate, some sociological researchers observe that working-class children tend to perform more poorly in schools than their middle-class counterparts (e.g., Gorlewski, 2011; Willis, 1977). To address this disparity, an intervention based on ideological individualism may involve targeting and changing working-class children's thought processes, aspirations, self-perceptions, behaviors, and home environments. Ignored in this approach, however, is the way schools are a middle-class enterprise, in that they value, validate, and reward the habits, skills, dispositions, and knowledge of middle-class culture. Ideological individualism orients researchers and educators to construe disparities in education as an individual psychological problem rather than a systemic problem. Thus, ideological individualism can invite deficit-based thinking and conceal subtle ways that power operates in schools, as class-based identities can be marginalized and cultural hierarchies maintained.

Ideological individualism also endorses a narrow conception of self and personhood. Attributing success and failure to individual psychological phenomena divorces persons from their relational and constitutive ties. Educational psychologists tend to endorse a kind of selfhood that can be described as rational, interior, isolated, and separable from historical contexts. Martin (2007) argues that these features of selfhood underpin the two types of self that dominate educational psychology: scientific and expressive. The scientific self is committed to studying, knowing, and controlling thoughts and behaviors for the pursuit of personal enhancement. The expressive self is committed to understanding and expressing uniqueness, private emotions, and experiences in order to develop one's "full potential." The scientific and expressive selves endorse the idea that individuals are furnished with internal mechanisms for control and are responsible for their thoughts, behaviors, and outcomes.

The expressive and scientific selves are pervasive in educational psychology discourse, as evidenced by research related to SRL, self-esteem, metacognition, self-concept, motivation, and identity. There are concerns with these selves as they are rational, a priori, and narrowly oriented toward the self. Cushman (1990) argues that expressive and scientific selves lack a strong sense of historical and sociocultural origins, a condition that he contends invites acquisitiveness and consumption. He describes these selves as empty because meaning and identity is garnered from commodities. Gergen (2009) suggests that such selves threaten psychological well-being, inviting isolation, a search for self-esteem, and perpetual anxiety. Martin, Sugarman, and Thompson (2003) argue that these selves pose challenges for democratic participation. The problem is that pedagogical interventions that are designed to teach SRL, for example, encourage and endorse a narrow sense of self that invites troubling consequences.

Part of the issue is that many educational psychologists view expressive and scientific selves as a natural human feature. However, some sociocultural theorists do not take the self and its contents as a priori and suggest that institutional discourse contributes to the production of selfhood (e.g., Cushman, 1990; Gergen, 2009; Martin, Sugarman, & Thompson, 2003; Mead, 1934). That is, the self is a cultural artifact that develops from one's interactions with others. Taking up the aim to teach students to regulate their learning involves shifting educational environments, implementing direct pedagogical interventions, and shaping home environments in ways that inscribe and endorse a particular type of self that is argued to be narrowly oriented toward self-development and self-interest. Treating the self as an artifact invites dialogue about different ways of being, and how certain educational environments value, validate, and inscribe may actually narrow ontological possibilities.

There is evidence that some SRL researchers embrace a view of self that is constituted in relation to a particular time and place. This commitment is evident in the relatively recent concepts of co-regulation and socially shared regulation. The self that underpins these notions is socially embedded. However, in these conceptualizations, the social is treated as influencing a priori internal mechanisms. As Martin, Sugarman, and Thompson (2003) contend, treating the social as influential preserves individualistic views of selfhood and makes a neat separation between person and world—a distinction that many critical psychologists question. If the social is influential, then there must be a substance that already exists that is being influenced. Often, the existing substance is characterized as being independent of time, place, and cultural constitution.

Technical Rationality

Another concern with educational psychology is the strict reliance on the logic and methods of science (Gallagher, 2003; Martin & McLellan, 2008). The assumption is that valid and standard measurements and calculation of the variables that shape academic performance can shape "best" teaching practices that predictably produce certain outcomes. Gallagher (2003) describes this view of education as underpinned by technical rationality because teaching is reduced to technical steps. This rationality can be summed up in the following way: if X is known, then Y can be implemented to produce outcome Z. The "X" can be any number of things related to knowledge of students, including their socioeconomic class, race, gender, academic history, interests, desires, goals, and parents. Not all educational psychologists are concerned with these features of personhood. Another debate within the field relates to the degree to which characteristics of students are universal or constituted as a result of the interactions between culture, biology, history, and chance. Notwithstanding this ontological debate, educational psychologists across the board remain committed to the assumption that if they know their students and implement sound scientifically based pedagogical practices, then certain outcomes can be produced. The reliance on technical rationality makes sense given the status of science in contemporary educational discourse. Educational psychologists try to remain relevant within education and vie for jurisdiction over decisions regarding policy and practice.

Technical rationality is especially present in research on SRL. Researchers suggest that SRL research needs to be advanced by improving valid, reliable, and generalizable data so that pedagogical interventions can be effective (Boekaerts, Maes, & Karoly, 2005; Schunk, 2008). Boekaerts, Maes, and Karoly (2005) state:

> The greatest challenge for the coming decade is . . . to consolidate the conceptual, methodological, assessment-based, and interventive insights gathered across many disciplines . . . to achieve a greater sense of systemisation, generalisability, and . . . external validity. Moreover, the integration of the science and practice of self-regulation would take a giant step forward were we to seek greater clarification of our meanings and standardisation of our measurement and treatment procedures. (p. 307)

These authors argue that SRL research needs to be advanced by ensuring concepts, interventions, and measurements are standard, valid, and generalizable. The underlying assumption is that conceptual agreement and standardized measures can support the production of generalizable principles for how to teach students to academically self-regulate.

Specifically in the area of SRL, Martin and McLellan (2008) argue that the expansion of measurement, the consolidation of conceptualizations, and purported improvements in interventions are important objectives, but they do not adequately support developments in research on SRL. Martin and McLellan recognize the importance and value of empirical work for conceptual development. However, SRL is tied to a number of philosophically and ethically contested concepts. Therefore, Martin and McLellan argue that it is a mistake to believe that the improvement of the conceptualization and methods of SRL can occur strictly through empirical work. They state that "empirical investigation will not cure the conceptual ills of psychological research in the area of self-regulation. Indeed, the mistaken belief that it will only adds to the considerable confusion already evident in the scholarly literature" (p. 441). Like other widely accepted ideas and concepts in educational psychology, SRL must be examined using historical, cultural, and philosophical analyses.

Both the logic of technical rationality and its ethics need to be critically considered. In terms of the former, it is essential to consider what it means to "know" students and how that knowledge is entangled in issues of power. What categories are used to construct students? What is viewed as comprising features of students? Can that constructed knowledge of students serve as the basis for effective educational interventions? The degree to which we can know students and the efficacy of that knowledge to inform pedagogical interventions needs critical scrutiny. In terms of ethics, a critical exploration of the effects of student knowledge must be conducted. If knowledge of students is possible, supporting efforts to predict and control outcomes, there needs to be careful consideration of the kinds of outcomes that are produced and how student knowledge equips authorities with the tools to efficiently and effectively produce particular outcomes. Educational psychologists ignore these concerns and are guided by the assumption that rigorous scientific method will yield sound facts that can ultimately be used to support the academic process and student empowerment.

Educational psychologists who draw from sociocultural theory challenge some of the prevailing methodological and conceptual assumptions within their field (e.g., Perry, 2002). However, they also operate with and endorse a commitment to technical rationality. Sociocultural theorists have been instrumental in transforming how SRL is understood and studied. They pushed researchers and practitioners to use qualitative methods to understand how contexts interact with students to invite SRL. These contributions, however, were not a departure from technical rationality but were designed to make it more effective. Educational psychologists suggest that sociocultural theory is instrumental for enriching understandings of phenomena by illuminating the social and environmental components of SRL. The logic is that if all variables, such as individual dispositions, environmental structures, interpersonal interactions, pedagogical structures, culture, and identity are known, then better interventions can be developed and implemented to effectively teach students to self-regulate their learning. The underlying assumption is that phenomena, such as SRL, are complex, but through improved science, all variables contributing to the development and enactment of SRL can be discerned and controlled.

Historical, Cultural, and Philosophical Contexts

The reliance on science for validation, legitimacy, and relevance invites the perception that educational psychology discourse is neutral, value-free, and ahistorical (Gallagher, 2003). A number of educational psychology concepts, such as the child, adolescence, memory, and self, to name a few, that are foundational to educational psychology are naturalized and normalized. There are few conversations about how our core disciplinary concepts and ideas emerged within a particular time and place. Some critical theorists have conducted historical analyses of foundational educational psychology concepts. Notable examples include Erica Burman's book *Deconstructing Developmental Psychology* (2008), Tina Besley's book *Counseling Youth: Foucault, Power, and the Ethics of Subjectivity* (2002), and Nancy Lesko's book *Act Your Age!: A Cultural Construction of Adolescence* (2001). These authors denaturalize and historicize concepts such as the child, adolescence, and development.

For example, Lesko (2001) conducted a historical analysis of the notion of adolescence in order to trace our contemporary understanding to a historically specific context. Lesko does not analyze when the notion first emerged in history. Rather, she focuses on the late 1800s, which is when adolescence took on a different form. Lesko focuses on the influential work of G. Stanley Hall, one of the grandfathers of educational psychology, who was working in a time when the United States was attempting to construct a certain social order, increase virility, and expand. In the late 1800s, Lesko contends the sciences of anthropology and psychology were used to study children to achieve these broad goals and mitigate emerging social anxieties. Lesko argues that psychologists in the 1800s viewed adolescence as the key "stage" for socializing individuals to achieve these national goals. In this context, adolescence became reified through increased visibility via psychological measurements and evaluations. Adolescence was something to be controlled with emerging administrative practices, which were viewed as necessary to produce a particular social order with particular types of people.

One of the issues that Lesko (2001) raises is that a white, male, Western perspective informed the way adolescence was understood and the vision of society. The visibility, measurability, and controllability of adolescence were accompanied by the discourse of normalization. That is, there was a normal way to be an adolescent, experience adolescence, and emerge from adolescence. Of course, such norms were, and continue to be, tied to cultural, historical, and political contexts. If researchers and educators ignore these contexts, there is a danger of treating being and identity as beyond social change and critique. In addition, there is a danger of concealing ways in which power operates to form truths about who we are.

In addition to being historically situated, the discourse of educational psychology is entangled in culture norms, values, and politics (Gallagher, 2003; Kincheloe, 1999b; Martin, 2004a). For example, Pino-Pasternak, Whitebread, and Tolmie (2010) conducted a meta-analysis of the research on guardian involvement and SRL. They observed that most research studies were conducted with affluent white families who had plenty of schooling experience. Their claim is consistent with what others have observed about the discourse of educational psychology, namely that it tends to reflect and represent white, middle-class people (Gallagher, 2003; Kincheloe, 1999a). Aligned with this assessment, I argue in this book that the discourse of SRL endorses middle-class guardian practices and representations of middle-class children. The dangers of narrowly reflecting populations can lead to the exclusion of diverse ways of thinking, beliefs, habits, and practices, while normalizing and validating others.

Noting concerns with educational psychology is not intended as a call to abandon the tools, methods, and conceptualizations of the field. Instead, the suggestion is to broaden our understanding by including diverse representations of concepts and methods and situating them within particular historical, political, and cultural contexts. Bruner (1996) argues that including alternative meanings supports the understanding of concepts rather than renders them ambiguous and irrelevant. Although educational psychology certainly makes room for alternative meanings, as the field is comprised of diverse perspectives, there are certain commitments and assumptions that have not adequately supported critical engagement. To adequately support a critical agenda, there must be (1) recognition that educational psychology is bound to a specific set of beliefs and assumptions that are culturally, historically, and philosophically bound; (2) critical interrogation of these assumptions; (3) conversations about power and opportunity; and (4) explorations of potential consequences related to the discourse of educational psychology.

Critical Educational Psychology

Pushing for the integration of critical inquiry into a subfield of psychology is nothing new. There is compelling work in areas such as development psychology (e.g., Burman, 2008; Holzman, 1997; Bradley, 2005), counseling psychology (e.g., Corcoran, 2007), community psychology (e.g., Nelson & Prilleltensky, 2005), and social psychology (e.g., Parker & Shotter, 1990). In addition, there is a broad perspective called critical psychology. Many critical psychologists share a commitment to discern and mitigate inequality by examining ways social, historical, and cultural arrangements produce different opportunities and advantages. Critical psychologists tend to believe that mainstream psychological practices and knowledge can contribute to differences in opportunity and pursuits for humanity (Burman, 2008; Durrheim, Hook, & Riggs, 2009; Kincheloe, 1999b; Teo, 2009). Therefore, a primary concern of critical psychologists is to develop the tools needed to recognize and address inequality.

Critical psychologists recognize that their scholarship, commitments, and tools do not guarantee the production of truth or the awareness that can "free" individuals from the constraints of psychology and other structural arrangements. Notwithstanding, there is still a commitment to critically engage with prevailing assumptions and commitments of the discipline. Such critical psychological inquiry is intended to support the production of a range of possibilities for thinking, behaving, and interacting.

Although the parent field of psychology, and some of its subfields, has made strides in integrating critical perspectives, educational psychology is lagging behind (Bird, 1999; Martin, 2007). In 1999, Bird charged that, "the field of educational psychology is in many ways one of the furthest from the critical project in psychology" (p. 22). Nearly a decade later, Martin (2007) makes a similar claim as it relates to the burgeoning body of studies in educational psychology with the *self-* prefix. He states:

> It is surprising that relatively little attention has been paid to conceptualizing the kinds of self that are assumed in this body of scholarly work or to interpretations of the sociocultural and institutional contexts within which these conceptions have developed and flourished. The relative absence of such conceptual and interpretive work seems espe-

cially striking given the considerable attention that has been devoted to critical consideration and interpretation of psychologists' self-related studies in other areas of psychology. (p. 79)

As another example, educational psychology is not featured in either the first or second editions of the book *Critical Psychology: An Introduction* (Fox, Prilleltensky, & Austin, 2009b). In general, there tends to be an absence of critical educational psychology scholarship, both from within and outside the conventional boundaries of the field. This absence is a concern because critical psychologists implicate the discourse of psychology in a number of unintended, negative consequences. Therefore, the infusion of psychology in everyday educational discourse warrants sustained and explicit critical attention. Yet few educational psychologists advocate this focus (cf. Kincheloe, 2005; Goodman, 2008).

There is evidence that critical perspectives have marginally entered educational psychology conversations (Bird, 1999; Corcoran, 2007; Gallagher, 2003; Kincheloe, 1999a; Martin, 2006; Sugarman, 2011; Vassallo, 2011). Goodman (2008) and Kincheloe (1999b, 2007) have made significant strides in developing a critical perspective within educational psychology. Kincheloe has worked on a perspective called postformal educational psychology, which is defined by a commitment to illuminate ways that the dominant discourse within educational psychology marginalizes, renders invisible, and silences diverse ways of knowing. Postformal educational psychology introduced Paulo Freire's work in conversations about the limitations of cognitive theory (Kincheloe & Steinberg, 1993; Kincheloe, 1999b). Although this perspective is still focused on cognitive critiques (e.g., Malott, 2011), it has been used in other areas of study (see Kincheloe & Horn, 2008) and is sometimes referred to as critical constructivism (Goodman, 2008; Kincheloe, 2005). This perspective is pioneering and is an essential part of a CEP landscape. My concern is that adopting this label can narrow the critical scope because of the epistemological and ontological connotations related to the notion of constructivism. In addition, this perspective tends to be aligned with an emancipatory agenda informed by the neo-Marxist perspective of Paulo Freire. The conceptualization of CEP offered here encapsulates this perspective but is not reducible to or definable by it, as CEP does not necessarily align strictly with any political, economic, psychological, and philosophical rationality.

The conceptualization of CEP offered here is one possibility for organizing a critical focus. CEP is a commitment to examine widely held ideas, concepts, beliefs, and methods in educational psychology through intra- and interdisciplinary lenses in order to consider ways that our field is implicated in dynamic and subtle workings of power. Not unlike critical psychologists, critical educational psychologists are concerned with the ways psychological discourse can contribute to inequality, though specifically aimed at educational contexts. I present three themes of critical work: polyvocalism, emancipation, and sociohistoricism. Polyvocalism involves pushing the boundaries of foundational and taken-for-granted concepts by integrating a variety of voices and representations in the dominant discourse. The second theme, which is aligned with the first, involves an explicit commitment to emancipatory change by way of reforming structures and conditions of oppression and discrimination. The third critical theme relates to sociohistorical perspectives. Those writing in this tradition are concerned with understanding the conditions that make ideas, practices, and concepts possible given certain historical circumstances. Although critical inquiry can vary, there are underlying commonalities, which include (1) commitments to diverse perspectives; (2) critiques of dominant discourse; (3) skepticism toward universalism, neutrality, and radical individualism; (4) concerns about inequality; and (5) ambivalence toward the scientific method.

The three themes discussed here are not necessarily mutually exclusive and can all be integrated into critical scholarship. This conceptualization in no way represents a rigid representation of what CEP is or can be. Rather, the definition and framework laid out here reflects a particular organization that should be negotiated, interrogated, contested, and continuously developed. I want to present a starting point for a dialogue on how we can push for, frame, and organize critical work within educational psychology. The themes are not listed in any particular order. That is, critical scholarship does not follow a linear developmental trajectory in which sociohistorical perspectives are the endpoint. Each theme contributes to the critical landscape and invites reflection on the complexity of educational psychology discourse.

Critical as Polyvocal

Scholarship that integrates multiple voices and representations to broaden the understanding of the dominant ideas, concepts, and assumptions within educational psychology is polyvocal. There are two strands in this theme. The first relates to the use of different perspectives in order to highlight different meanings and representations of the dominant discourse. Gergen (2009) nicely illustrates this commitment by drawing from the feminist scholarship of Carol

Gilligan, the social behaviorism of George H. Mead, the sociology of Erving Goffman, and the cultural psychology of Jerome Bruner, Jaan Valsiner, and Lev Vygotsky, to name a few, to push his readers to rethink what it means to be in the world. Gergen challenges the idea that individuals have isolated consciousness, psychological cores, and minds separable from people and places. In his book, he argues for a substantially different view of selfhood from the one that underpins and pervades educational psychology. Work like this provides new possibilities for understanding, endorsing, and valuing certain kinds of selfhood. Opening up ontological possibilities was possible by integrating diverse perspectives, especially those that challenge core disciplinary assumptions.

Polyvocality can also take the form of cultural research. This commitment involves disrupting the dominant discourse by examining different qualities of thinking, knowing, and being. This strand can involve cultural examinations attuned to the differences related to a number of educational psychology concepts. For example, researchers have conducted studies to examine the different ways individuals from different countries regulate their learning (Hamamura, Meijer, Heine, Kamaya, & Hori, 2009; Higgins & Spiegel, 2004; Uskul, Sherman, & Fitzgibbon, 2009). In one study, Hamamura and colleagues compared North Americans with East Asians, who were respectively described as approach-oriented (motivated to win or excel) and avoidance-oriented (motivated to avoid a loss). These culturally specific orientations were shown to shape one's regulatory processes and task engagement. A commitment to polyvocalism involves understanding these differences so they can be recognized, validated, and valued in educational contexts.

This strand also includes comparisons across groups within a particular context. Focusing on socioeconomic class, Kincheloe (1999a) argues that the forms of intelligence that are tested, valued, and validated in schools reflect the intelligence of middle-class culture. He argues that working-class culture values different kinds of intelligence that are not included in schools. Luttrell (1989) makes a similar argument related to class and gender. She contends that working-class mothers have specific ways of feeling and being that are distinct from their middle-class counterparts. These feelings, which Luttrell calls "emotional capital," of working-class mothers clash with what is institutionally recognized and validated (p. 33). In this book, I explore class-based differences in the self that can influence the qualities and quantities of SRL. The assumptions underpinning this strand of research are (1) that individuals across different identity groups will manifest educational psychological phenomena in fundamentally different ways; and (2) the dominant ideas in educational psychology are representative of a particular population, excluding and rendering invisible diverse ways of knowing, doing, and being.

Polyvocality can be viewed as a way to democratize educational psychology by accounting for multiple perspectives to inform research and practice. Packer and Tappan (2001) reason that these types of research studies encourage reflections on positionality and value judgments. Committing to polyvocalism does not necessarily mean giving each voice and representation equal weight in pedagogical and research decisions. More so, it has to do with recognizing diversity, situating it within cultural context, and generating awareness of the implications buying into certain ideas over others. Polyvocalism can be important to support teachers' ability to differentiate instruction, be culturally responsive, and reflect on interactions between pedagogy and students' cognitive structures.

Critical as Emancipatory

Commitments to polyvocality can illuminate ways that educational psychology constructs are representative of a particular group. These insights can lead to modifications of instructional environments that are inclusive and inviting. Additionally, these insights can provide teachers with knowledge of their students, so they can monitor them and intervene when necessary in culturally responsive ways. For example, it has been argued that African Americans distrust school personnel, see performing well in school as white and see schooling as a white institution (Ogbu, 2003). With this understanding of a group's mind-set, teachers can directly target their pedagogical interventions at changing or harnessing that mentality in ways that foster adaptation to an existing classroom order. They might implement pedagogical changes that include hanging pictures of influential African Americans, hiring African American teachers, or incorporating a month of African American recognition. These efforts may democratize the educational context but do little to challenge broad structures of inequality.

A commitment to polyvocalism alone does not support an emancipatory agenda. That is why Fox, Prilleltensky, and Austin (2009a) state that critical work in psychology is not just aimed at minor institutional reform. Instead, often informed by Marxist and neo-Marxist notions of power, this theme of critical work is directed at understanding and reforming broad social structures that are responsible for oppression and unjust social orders. Emancipation can include changes in individual psychology as long as they are concurrent with changes in worlds. As McLaren (2007) warns, changing individuals without changing oppressive structures are symptomatic of subordination and oppression. Freire's (1987, 2000) educational philosophy is a good example of an emancipatory theme. Like other critical theories (e.g., Giroux, 2009; McLaren, 2007), Freire starts with the assumption that schools are rife with inequalities. A danger, as Freire warns, is that working to change students' perceptions, motivation, and beliefs without addressing that inequality is dehumanizing. Emancipation occurs not by adapting to unequal school structures but by transforming them. The goal of an emancipatory inquiry is unmask, make explicit, and change structural inequalities.

Critical as Sociohistorical

Another theme of CEP involves not just commitments to diverse perspectives and emancipation but also to illuminate the historical and cultural constitution of ideas within educational psychology. While this work can involve emancipation and polyvocalism, it is not defined by these themes. Rather, sociohistoricism can be defined by what Billig (2008) calls "historical reflexivity." He states that historical reflexivity "requires at its minimum that psychologists trace the origins of their psychological ideas, linking them to broader historical and ideological contexts" (p. 20). Similar to polyvocalism, sociohistoricism has multiple interrelated strands.

In one strand, theorists and researchers examine ways social, cultural, and historical events contribute to the constitution of psychological phenomena, which are treated as emergent and in no sense prior to their sociocultural surroundings. Kirschner and Martin (2010) describe this approach as relational and historical. Martin, Sugarman, and Thompson's (2003) work on self and agency is an excellent example of this line of thinking. For years, people have reflected on the sources of control over their lives and circumstances. Some take extreme positions and attribute causes of what people think and do to individual decisions or structural circumstances. Working against such determinism, Martin and colleagues reason that humans are agents in that they interact with the world in ways that enable them to be influenced by and influence meanings and categorizations, which are specific to a particular historical and cultural moment. The aim of this scholarship is to explore the links between historical and cultural context to the formation of particular kinds of people. This line of inquiry is focused on the constitution of psychological phenomena.

Another strand of sociohistorical analysis involves tracing the origins of psychological ideas and linking them to broad historical and ideological contexts. This strand is different because the historical and relational emergence of psychological phenomena is not the focus. Rather, the aim of this work is to disrupt naturalized ideas that are taken for granted by illuminating ways in which historical, cultural, and political contexts shape possibilities for how to think about people. As noted earlier, Burman (2008) and Besley (2002) conducted historical analyses of the notions of child and adolescence. While their research does not ontologically invalidate these concepts, they situate their emergence through carefully crafted historical analyses. Rose (1999) provides another example of this type of analysis. He explores the ways that the concepts, rules, authorities, procedures, and techniques, of what he calls the "psy" disciplines, produce ways of speaking truths about people. The position is that given particular historical, political, social, cultural, and ideological conditions, certain truths can be formed and techniques can be developed that make it possible to think about people in certain ways. Those operating with this commitment focus on illuminating historical, philosophical, social, and cultural conditions that make it possible and impossible to form certain truths.

Conclusion

Although the parent field of psychology has made strides in integrating critical perspectives, educational psychology is lagging behind. In order to support the integration of critical perspectives, I present a conceptualization of CEP, which I define as drawing from multiple perspectives to explore ways in which disciplinary tools, models, concepts, and methods are entangled in power. I offer three themes for what this critical work can look like. The CEP landscape presented here is a key point for how we can push the critical dialogue in educational psychology. The purpose of integrating critical perspectives within our field is not to suggest a wholesale rejection of the discourse of educational psychology. Rather, the purpose is to open up the possibility for rejecting, embracing, and resisting it. Any critical work should at minimum invite these possibilities.

This CEP perspective serves as a lens through which I engage with SRL. Typically SRL is treated as neutral, value-free, and divorced from issues of power. However, I draw from research on socioeconomic class, neoliberalism, agency, and critical pedagogy to illuminate ways that SRL is entangled in compliance, subordination, culture, philosophy, and ideology. Aside from the pedagogical challenges with teaching students to self-regulate, there are ethical issues that must enter into conversations. Typically, researchers focus on improving the teaching and learning of SRL, without adequately considering the potential, the assumptions about people that are endorsed, and the underpinnings of this effort.

Chapter 2
Background on Self-Regulated Learning

> If you give a man a fish, you feed him for a day; If you teach a man to fish, you feed him for a lifetime. (Zimmerman, Bonner, & Kovach, 1996, p. vii)

Introduction

This old adage is cited in a manual designed for teachers to instruct students on how to regulate their learning. It reflects conventional meanings and assumptions that pervade the discourse on self-regulated learning (SRL). That is, teaching students the knowledge, skills, and dispositions for self-regulation supports independent, self-sufficient engagement that has long-term benefits. SRL is a self-steering process whereby students understand, and change if necessary, their own thoughts, emotions, and behaviors, as well as features of the environment, in order to achieve their goals. Supporting students' SRL is associated with possibility and empowerment because academic achievement is not viewed as static and uncontrollable. Rather, achievement is construed as dynamic and within personal control whereby individuals can overcome limitations in cognitive processing, instructional constraints, and social and cultural barriers.

Researchers implicitly and explicitly associate SRL with individual human agency because it is purported to expand freedom of action by enabling individuals to select, influence, and construct their own circumstances. SRL is almost exclusively associated with academic success (e.g., Greene, Bolick, & Robertson, 2010; Kitsantis & Zimmerman, 2006; Lodewyk, Winne, & Jamieson-Noel, 2009), the alleviation of social problems (e.g., Zimmerman, 1998, 2000), democratic participation (e.g., Yowell & Smylie, 1999), and lifelong learning (e.g., Lapan, Kardash, & Turner, 2002). From these associations, SRL is treated as a form of empowerment and something students need to be empowered to do.

Educational psychologists contend that all individuals can benefit from SRL training. However, SRL is often touted as especially beneficial for individuals and groups who are considered "at risk" (e.g., Butler, 2003; Harris, Graham, & Mason, 2003; Howse, Lange, Farran, & Boyles, 2003; Vick & Packard, 2008; Weed, Keogh, Borkowski, et al., 2010; Zimmerman, 1998). For example, referring to Benjamin Franklin, George Washington Carver, and Indonesian immigrants, Zimmerman (1998) states that these individuals went beyond their "humble origins" and "limited access to high-quality education" by educating and disciplining themselves, and by recognizing that "learning is a proactive activity requiring self-initiated motivational and behavioral processes as well as metacognitive ones" (p. 1). Others agree that SRL can support academic success for individuals from economically disadvantaged backgrounds. In addition, SRL is believed to be beneficial for individuals with special learning needs and those with histories of academic difficulties.

Few educational psychologists contest the value and importance of SRL. Despite this agreement, the discourse is not monolithic. There are a number of conceptual (what is SRL?), pedagogical (how can SRL be taught?), and methodological (how can SRL be measured?) debates within the literature. Much of the controversy results from diverse epistemological and ontological commitments and perspectives from which educational psychologists draw. Although diverse perspectives inform the discourse, there is an absence of perspectives that invite critical reflections on the philosophical, historical, political, and cultural contexts of SRL. In this chapter, I explore points of tension and key developments that are generally part of the conversation and end by highlighting critical questions that receive little to no attention.

Historical Background

SRL has been part of educational psychology discourse for more than three decades, first introduced in the late 1970s and formalized as an area of study in the early-to-mid-1980s. However, Martin and McLellan (2008) note that related concepts have been around for centuries. They suggest that theses concerning the broad idea of self-regulation have been available since at least the time of John Locke (1632–1704). Martin and McLellan add that almost all major Enlightenment, Romantic, and 20th-century philosophers had a good deal to say about matters of self-command, self-discipline, and self-control.

Going back further, some researchers connect Plato's philosophizing to contemporary ideas about self-regulation (Myrseth & Fishbach, 2009; Shanker, 2010). For example, Myrseth and Fishbach (2009) suggest that the notion of "akrasia," which is defined as the state of acting against one's judgment, relates specifically to an issue of self-control. Myrseth and Fishbach ask, "How does one pursue a goal offering larger long-run benefits when it conflicts with a temptation offering greater immediate rewards?" (p. 247). This question pertains directly to the exercise of self-control in the form of delay of gratification, an important process identified in SRL (Bembenutty & Karabenick, 2004; Mischel, Shoda, & Rodriguez, 1989).

Although theories of self-control have deep historical and philosophical roots, the Enlightenment marks a significant moment for this area of research. Porter (2001) notes that this period was characterized by the emergence of the scientific study of people, in which philosophers and scientists were interested in discovering (or perhaps constructing) laws that governed thoughts, behaviors, and the production of social environments. This commitment informs much of the psychological research that occurred within the 20th-century. In the early 1900s when behaviorism was the dominant paradigm, researchers were focused on how science could be used to understand stimulus and response bonds so that environments could be structured to predictably and reliably produce certain behaviors. However, in the latter part of the 20th- century, psychologists shifted away from the external influence over behavior to focus on using science to understand how thoughts, beliefs, and attitudes shape behaviors (Martin & McLellan, 2008). Today, educational psychologists operate with the assumption that through scientific study certain behaviors, thought processes, and psychological states could be known and intentionally shaped. More significant, such knowledge is believed to be necessary for supporting individuals' control over themselves and their worlds.

Over the last half of the 20th- century, the source of control over thoughts and behaviors were no longer located solely in external sources. Individuals were conceptualized as being furnished with inherent capabilities to exert control over themselves and their environments. Martin and McLellan (2008) identify a number of strands of psychological research that support this assumption: a cybernetic perspective (Wiener, 1948), the test-operate-test-exit model of feedback control (Miller, Galanter, & Pribram, 1960), and the information-processing model of memory (Atkinson & Shiffrin, 1968). These lines of research have one thing in common: individuals are conceptualized as interacting with environments and capable of exerting control over both themselves and their worlds by mediating environmental influences. These lines of scholarship serve as a foundation for the emergence of SRL.

When first studied, researchers were primarily focused on the cognitive mechanisms and processes individuals used when regulating their learning. They sought to characterize what self-regulated learners did, thought, and believed. This early research was conducted with academically successful students—as determined by teacher reports, grades, and standardized test performance—using interviews with students, observations of students, and self-report scales (e.g., see Zimmerman & Martinez-Pons, 1986). Of course there is a problem with the assumption that successful students are self-regulated. A variety of factors contribute to academic success, which cannot always be attributed to intentional and strategic direction of one's learning. Contemporary researchers have not fully challenged and explored this assumption. It is essential for moving forward that the association between academic success and self-regulation be treated cautiously, skeptically, and critically.

Early inquiries approached SRL from perspectives attributed to Jean Piaget and Albert Bandura (Post, Boyer, & Brett, 2006). From a Piagetian influence, some researchers believed that SRL was not possible until individuals reached formal operations and were capable of abstract thought, which includes thinking about one's thinking, or in other words, metacognition. Few researchers endorse this view today. In fact, Piaget is seldom explicitly referenced in contemporary SRL research. However, Albert Bandura, who is the major figure of social cognitive theory, is pervasively present and informs a great deal of the literature (Martin, 2004b; Post, Boyer, & Brett, 2006). Since this early influence by two major figures in educational psychology, SRL has been studied from a variety of perspectives.

SRL research burgeoned in the 1990s and continues to show steady increases (Martin, 2004a; Post, Boyer, & Brett, 2006). Post, Boyer, and Brett (2006) describe the 1990s as driven by what they call "expansionist fervor" (p. 10). A number of articles and handbooks have been published that elucidate a variety of componential features, which include, but are not limited to, behavioral regulation, personality, emotions, well-being, goal structures, and community. During the expansionist period, a variety of perspectives and methods have been used to study SRL, especially those with a social emphasis (e.g., McCaslin & Burross, 2011; Perry, 2002; Järvelä & Järvenoja, 2011; Volet, Vaurus, & Salonen, 2009). McCaslin and colleagues (2006) characterize the history of SRL research in terms of waves. They argue that the first wave emphasized a number of individual processes for academic self-regulation. The second wave is characterized by the replacement of the "idiosyncratic constructions of the individual learner with a perspective of the social-embeddedness of a cultural participant" (McCaslin et al, 2006, p. 237). In this second wave, emphases are on the social world, identity, and meaning. Some of the perspectives that inform this inquiry include, but are not limited to, ecological (Yowell & Smylie, 1999), Vygotskian (McCaslin & Hickey, 2001), and Deweyian (Prawat, 1998).

Conceptual Distinctions

Although diverse perspectives inform the field, Martin (2004b) contends that SRL research is organized into two camps: constructivist and sociocultural. The foundational assumption of constructivist theories is that individuals construct their own meanings, goals, and strategies from the information available in the external environment as well as information in their own minds. Often in conflict, sociocultural theories are underpinned by the idea that SRL is situated within historical and social contexts, is always in relation to environmental demands, and is separable from culture. The sociocultural and constructivist division informs a number of methodological, conceptual, and pedagogical debates.

Sociocultural theorists treat SRL as an event, as opposed to a disposition (e.g., Perry, 2002). An event interpretation means that SRL is the enactment of strategic learning that results from individuals operating with others in a particular context. This view is underpinned by the assumption that all individuals are capable of SRL given the right contextual conditions, which include opportunities for choice, control, mastery, peer collaboration, and self-evaluations (Perry, VandeKamp, Mercer, & Nordby, 2002). Researchers are interested in exploring ways that task conditions, pedagogical structures, interaction patterns, and curricula invite SRL. There is empirical support for this position as researchers repeatedly show that with varying degrees of support, all children from a range of ages and abilities can regulate their learning effectively (e.g., Perels, Merget-Kullmann, Wende, Schmitz, & Buchbinder, 2009; Perry & Drummond, 2002; Vidal-Abarca, Mañá, & Gil, 2010).

Those who endorse a dispositional interpretation, which aligns with the constructivist camp, acknowledge that SRL is tied to contexts. However, they see academic self-regulation as an individual cognitive skill that can be trained or promoted through the aggregation of experiences, which can be transferred to new situations. The dispositional treatment of SRL is concerned with understanding and shaping cognitive and motivational mechanisms that enable individuals to exercise control (e.g., Zimmerman, 2002). Proponents of a disposition perspective believe that individuals can draw on their experiences in order to proactively implement self-regulatory strategies and thought processes across contexts and domains. From a disposition perspective, SRL has social origins as it develops over many hours of practice and training. Those who endorse this view agree that contexts can trigger or quell a disposition to self-regulate; however, the source, qualities, and quantities of SRL are internal.

These conceptual differences are associated with methodological and pedagogical commitments. Those who are committed to an event perspective are likely to use observations, interviews, running records, and discourse analysis to measure SRL. They will pay attention to the interactions between individuals and tasks. Those who are committed to a dispositional perspective are likely to focus on the individual as the unit of analysis. Researchers may interview and observe individuals and administer self-report scales, surveys, and questionnaires. From a dispositional perspective, pedagogy involves directly training students or providing self-regulating models. From an event perspective, SRL pedagogy involves facilitation and dialogue. The former involves structuring contexts that are conducive to SRL. The assumption is that if tasks and environments are structured in certain ways, then students will not need direct guidance from the teacher to self-regulate. The latter involves engaging in consistent communication in order to adjust interactions and contexts in ways that support regulatory learning. These pedagogical differences are elaborated in upcoming sections.

Although the differences between constructivism and sociocultural theory have shaped the conversation, there is a contemporary framework that is gaining traction for distinguishing theories of regulated learning. Three concepts are included in this framework: SRL, co-regulated learning, and socially shared regulated learning (Hadwin, Järvelä, & Miller, 2011). Hadwin, Järvelä, and Miller (2011) use the term "regulatory learning theory" as an umbrella under which to capture these concepts (p. 66). Given a strong emphasis on the social world for academic regulation, they use this term to avoid the connotations of isolation and individualism related to the "self" prefix. This framework is not entirely distinct from Martin's (2004b) way of organizing the literature into constructivist and sociocultural camps. The concept of SRL aligns with constructivist logic in which dispositional and other internal regulatory mechanisms are emphasized. The concepts of co-regulated learning and socially shared regulated learning align with a sociocultural perspective in which context, interactions, and culture are emphasized.

Regulatory Learning Theory

Self-Regulated Learning

The term "SRL" is associated with the constructivist camp, which emphasizes regulatory processes as constructing meanings, goals, and strategies from individuals' minds, as well as information available in the external environment. From this perspective, it is believed that an action is not self-regulated until there is intentional action corresponding with established goals (Bandura, 1997; Zimmerman, 2000). That is, strategic action directed at learning can be constituted as self-regulated in as much as students use personal processes, such as self-observation, goal setting, planning, and reflection, to guide behavior and mediate environmental contingencies in pursuit of learning goals. Those who endorse this view recognize the social influence on SRL; however, they construe individuals as having a priori internal mechanisms that enable them to mediate environmental messages and exercise strategic control over themselves and their worlds. Hadwin and Oshige (2011) suggest that the notion of SRL is construed as a developing process that is merely assisted by task modeling and feedback. Although SRL is believed to have social origins, thoughts and actions are believed to be irreducible to the social context in which SRL is enacted.

Co-Regulated Learning

The notion of "self" in SRL can be interpreted as individualistic, isolated, and divorced from social and cultural influence. Concerned about these connotations, some researchers adopt the notion of co-regulated learning, which is grounded in a Vygotskian view of learning and development (e.g., Hadwin & Oshige, 2011; McCaslin, 2009). Hadwin and Oshige (2011) define co-regulated learning as "transitional processes in a learner's acquisition of SRL, during which members of a community share a common problem-solving plane, and SRL is gradually appropriated in response to and directed toward social and cultural contexts" (p. 258). This concept emphasizes sharing the regulatory burden with capable others, with the eventual transition to individual self-regulatory thoughts and practices. Co-regulation involves the relationship among cultural (a force that transforms personal biology and social relationships into cultural beliefs and expectations), social (situations, opportunities, and relationships), and personal sources of influence (potential and readiness) (McCaslin, 2009). The appropriation of self-regulatory practices occurs through activity, engagement, and mutual relationships where individuals bring certain skills to learning tasks. The notion of co-regulation emphasizes the intersubjective development and enactment of academic self-regulation.

Socially Shared Regulated Learning

Another type of academic regulation is referred to as socially shared regulated learning, which emphasizes collective activity that is directed at shared goals. Essentially, this is a collective form of regulation through which goals and standards are co-constructed and end products are shared. From this perspective, personal goals guide regulatory efforts. However, personal goals are inseparable from social goals and are pursued through interactions with others. Ultimately, the desired end product of this process is socially shared cognition. From this perspective, everybody is not believed to think and act in the same way. Rather, goals, thought processes, identity, and behaviors are understood relationally and complementary to a shared goal. Research in this area focuses on individual roles and individual regulatory processes—but within social contexts—and considers individual roles and processes as part of a socially constructed process.

Conceptual Compatibility: Integration and Interaction

Some educational psychologists raise concern that the expansion of research on regulatory learning has led to the emergence of definitions and conceptualizations that are unclear and disconnected (Boekaerts & Corno, 2005; Schunk, 2008). As a response, researchers work to consolidate and show compatibility across various accounts of regulatory learning (Boekaerts & Corno, 2005; Volet, Vaurus, & Salonen, 2009). Researchers suggest that in the aggregate the different takes on SRL contribute to a broad picture of regulated learning. As Packer and Goicoechea (2000) suggest, sociocultural theories are helpful for considering how context shapes thoughts and behaviors, while constructive theories are helpful for considering what individuals take away from situations and how they contribute to environmental dynamics. Researchers argue that it is essential to adopt an approach to SRL that allows researchers and teachers to focus simultaneously on the students' self-regulation of the learning and motivation process, as well as on the environmental triggers and conditions that affect these processes (Butler, 2002; Järvelä & Järvenoja, 2011; McCaslin & Burross, 2011; Volet, Vaurus, & Salonen, 2009). The assumption is that students come with experiences, propensities, and histories that contribute to shaping a dynamic classroom structure, which iteratively interacts with personal factors in ways that shape possibilities for SRL. In other words, individuals have dispositions that shape an event, which iteratively works to shape dispositions. This view of SRL can be called interactionist (Järvelä & Järvenoja, 2011).

In addition to constructing compatibility across accounts, all theories of SRL share common features (Boekaerts & Corno, 2005; Martin & McLellan, 2008; McCaslin & Burross, 2011; Zeidner, Boekaerts, & Pintrich, 2000). For example, Boekaerts and Corno (2005) explain, "All theorists assume that students who self-regulate their learning are engaged actively and constructively in a process of meaning generation and that they *adapt* [emphasis added] their thoughts, feelings, and actions as needed to affect their learning and motivation" (p. 201). With the emphasis on adaptation, researchers suggest that effective and productive self-regulated learners do not adopt a habit or a routine set of skills or strategies; rather, they respond to new learning challenges in productive ways by strategically altering tasks, perceptions, goals, plans, identities, and strategies. SRL as an adaptive process is an element in all accounts.

In addition, Hadwin, Järvelä, and Miller (2011) identify four major tenets that underpin all regulatory learning theories: (1) regulated learning is intentional and goal directed; (2) regulated learning is metacognitive; (3) learners regulate behavior, cognition, and affect; and (4) regulated learning is social. Others note similar points of overlap across accounts of regulatory learning theory (e.g., Boekaerts & Corno, 2005; Greene & Azevedo, 2007; Martin & McLellan, 2008). Researchers generally agree that regulated learning involves cognitive, behavioral, and affective regulation in the processes of goal setting, performance monitoring, and task- and self-evaluation. Researchers also agree that SRL is a natural human process that all individuals attempt to and are capable of using, but do so in various ways, frequencies, toward different ends, and in relation to different contexts (Bandura, 2001; Boekaerts & Corno, 2005; Higgins & Spiegel, 2004; Paris, Byrnes, & Paris, 2001; Winne, 2005; Zimmerman, 2000).

From these assumptions, researchers are less likely to describe individuals as self-regulated or not self-regulated, as if it were a stable disposition, an essential quality of only certain individuals, or entirely independent of contextual configurations. Rather, it is common to describe differences in SRL in terms of quantities and qualities rather than deficits (Zimmerman, 2000). To capture differences, researchers use a number of binary classifications: novice and expert (Zimmerman, 1998), functional and dysfunctional (Zimmerman, 2000), effective and ineffective (Zimmerman, 2000), strong and weak (Schmeichel &

Baumeister, 2004), adaptive and maladaptive (Boekaerts & Corno, 2005), and high and less (Abar & Loken, 2010). Contexts are also classified (high or low) in terms of their likelihood to support SRL (Perry, Nordby, & VandeKamp, 2003).

Other common features across accounts of regulated learning theory relate to mechanisms and processes. Greene and Azevedo (2007) contend that researchers overwhelmingly correlate a mastery goal orientation with effective SRL. A mastery orientation involves the pursuit of a learning goal for the sake of gaining competence. This orientation is in contradistinction to performance goals, such as pursuing a goal for a grade or social perception. The assumption is that those who pursue mastery are likely to persist in the face of challenge, sustain motivation, set challenging goals, seek support, and self-motivate. Those who effectively self-regulate their learning set goals that are conducive to academic goals, and they continuously reflect on and adjust goals accordingly. Although researchers may disagree about the sources that influence the pursuit of mastery, this goal orientation is nonetheless an important feature of SRL.

The importance of and requirement for self-evaluation, self-awareness, and self-knowledge are featured in all theories of SRL. Having self-awareness means knowing one's own level of understanding, in addition to knowing strengths, weaknesses, ways of thinking, and beliefs—all fundamental to metacognition—that support efforts to adjust oneself or the environment to improve learning. Self-awareness is also about understanding one's thoughts and actions in relation to learning outcomes. That is, proponents of SRL reason that effective self-regulating learners understand that what they do and think contributes to their learning outcomes. They understand how perceptions, attitudes, and beliefs contribute to particular behaviors and outcomes. Self-awareness also involves understanding environmental contingencies. Individuals contribute to producing environmental circumstances, which have a reciprocal influence on thoughts and behaviors. Awareness of environmental contingencies can provide individuals with the knowledge to shape responses or change environments to produce the effects they want. Understanding environmental contingencies involves the scientific investigation of self, which includes constant vigilance, intense observations, recording of data, and the analysis of personal information.

The use of learning strategies is also a key feature of SRL. The use of strategies requires that learners have a repertoire of strategies from which to choose, and also the self-knowledge and skills for task evaluation to decide on the appropriate strategy. Educational psychologists call this conditional knowledge.

The assumption is that not all learning strategies are appropriate for all tasks and that individuals must evaluate the conditions, whether personal or external, that make one strategy more or less effective for a specific task. Strategy use will depend on individual learners: what has worked for them in the past, what can work for them now, what they are capable of doing, what goals they want to achieve, and what the task requires. Although the decision for which strategies to use for what task depends on self-assessments and task evaluations, researchers agree that specific qualities and quantities of learning strategies are indicative of effective SRL.

For example, help-seeking is an important strategy for SRL. With the importance on the social world for SRL, interacting with others to achieve a goal is essential. Not all forms of help-seeking are considered effective for self-regulatory efforts. Self-regulatory help-seeking involves confining questions to just those hints and explanations needed to independently finish performing a task (Puustinen, Lyyra, Metsäpelto, & Pulkkinen, 2008). Such help-seeking requires the monitoring of performance, the awareness of difficulties that cannot be overcome, and the wherewithal and self-determination to remedy that difficulty by requesting assistance from knowledgeable others (Newman, 2002). Self-regulatory help-seeking does not count as such when questions are asked needlessly (e.g., when individuals are capable of solving problems themselves) and when the help-seeking is designed to limit cognitive engagement.

Despite debates and controversies, theories of SRL share a number of common features and assumptions. The major differences across these theories relate to how SRL develops and what should be done to facilitate it. Some differences also relate to processes and mechanisms. Notwithstanding, many features and tenets of regulated learning are shared. In this analysis, the term "SRL" is used broadly with the commonalities in mind and not to signify a particular brand of regulatory learning theory. Accordingly, many points of critical reflection can be generalized to the broad regulatory learning literature.

Pedagogy: Content, Formats, and Environments

Although researchers argue that all students try to regulate their learning in some way, some students have goals, thought processes, beliefs, and learning strategies that compete with effective SRL. In addition, some environments are implicated in curtailing self-regulatory efforts. Therefore, much of the contemporary expansion of SRL research is attributable to the development of SRL pedagogy. In this literature, researchers work to understand how to best teach students to academically self-regulate. The idea of teaching SRL can be interpreted broadly to include any implicit or explicit pedagogical intervention or structure that can be tied to efforts to cultivate or invite students' SRL. Thus, teaching SRL can mean structuring environments or it can mean direct strategy instruction, for example. In the literature, pedagogical conversations circulate around issues of what actually needs to be taught (e.g., learning strategies and thought processes), how to deliver instruction (e.g., direct instruction or facilitation), and what environments are most conducive for SRL (e.g., opportunities for choice, student-centered, or teacher-centered).

Pedagogical Content: What Students Need to Learn

Researchers emphasize different targets for SRL pedagogy. Some of these include, but are not limited to, self-awareness, awareness of environmental contingencies, thought processes, and learning strategies. There are a number of tools that support such self-investigation: journals (e.g., Du Bois & Staley, 1997), graphs (e.g., Kitsantis & Zimmerman, 2006), logs (e.g., Zimmerman, Bonner, & Kovach, 1996), and computer technology (e.g., Azevedo, Johnson, Chauncey, & Graesser, 2011; Wang, Peng, Cheng, Zhou, & Liu, 2011). In addition to learning techniques for self-investigation, researchers argue that individuals need to acquire a repertoire of learning strategies and the conditional knowledge for when to use them. Strategy instruction is an essential component in most SRL pedagogical models. Strategies can include, but are not limited to, help-seeking, self-observations, self-questioning, taking organized notes, and documenting and evaluating learning behaviors.

Although educational psychologist may treat the setting of goals as a natural human disposition—a commitment that requires critical scrutiny—when it comes to academic learning, there are specific kinds of goals and goal structures that are needed for academic self-regulation. For example, academic learning involves setting a distal goal with a number of proximal goals. Individuals must learn to set goals, execute a plan to achieve those goals, monitor progress toward goals, and mitigate the effects of competing goals. They must also learn how to strategize their engagement in order to achieve their learning goals. Students must learn to maintain attention over their goals by setting, monitoring, and adapting them.

Pedagogical Formats

Few researchers disagree about what students need to learn in order to effectively self-regulate their learning. However, they disagree on the form of pedagogy that is required. In general, researchers suggest that SRL requires an explicit commitment (Bednall & Kehoe, 2011; Cleary, Platten, & Nelson, 2008; Martinez-Pons, 2002; Stoeger & Zeigler, 2011; Winne, 2005). Stoeger and Ziegler (2011) argue that it is well accepted that students can and need to become proficient self-regulated learners (i.e., planning, strategizing, evaluating situations, focusing, and adapting) through explicit pedagogical efforts, which can be in the form of cognitive training or environmental structuring. Pedagogy that is designed to teach SRL can be thought about in terms of distinct, yet not mutually exclusive, formats: modeling, direct instruction, facilitation, and dialogue.

Modeling

Modeling is the key pedagogical strategy undergirding the social cognitive perspective of SRL. This pedagogical commitment is about showing and demonstrating self-regulatory thoughts and behaviors. In schools, teachers and students can share their self-regulatory thought processes and behaviors as they engage in learning tasks, and can serve as models by illustrating and being vicariously reinforced for their engagement. Modeling can be used to support strategy development, improvements in self-efficacy, and foster effective self-regulatory thought processes. There is a significant body of literature that explores factors that contribute to effective modeling. The assumption is that if principles of effective modeling are used, then students will emulate observed behaviors and thoughts, which can be appropriated and adapted to meet new contextual demands.

Direct Instruction

Researchers argue that SRL requires direct instruction, which means explicitly and with guidance teaching students ways to think and behave. Although direct instruction is not typically used as a sole pedagogical format in SRL models, Winne (2005) argues that it is a necessary element. For example, Graham, Harris, and Troia (1998) propose a six-stage instructional model that begins with teacher-directed discussions on self-regulatory procedures, task evaluations, and appropriate plans for actions. Transactional strategies instruction begins with teachers describing and explaining how to use SRL strategies (Pressley, El-

Dinary, Wharton-McDonald, & Brown, 1998). Housand and Reis (2008) correlate teachers' explicit metacognitive strategy instruction with effective SRL. Although researchers disagree about the amount of direct instruction needed for SRL development, many agree that SRL instruction requires intentional, explicit, and structured interactions aimed at teaching SRL.

Facilitation

Aligned with a sociocultural perspective, some researchers suggest that teaching SRL involves shaping instructional contexts in ways that invite SRL (e.g., Perry et al., 2002), a pedagogical format referred to here as facilitation. Specifically, providing students with opportunities for choice, control, influence over assessments, and peer collaboration is shown to invite student SRL. Miller, Heafner, and Massey (2009) argue that it is difficult for students to learn to regulate if the contextual conditions are not conducive to that form of engagement. Shanker (2010) contends that group- or student-centered activities, in which students have the space to express their emotions and choose their activities, are likely to invite SRL by tempering counterproductive emotions, sustaining alertness, producing calmness, and engendering deep engagement. Teaching SRL in this format is about shaping environments in ways that support the enactment of SRL and interjecting only strategically to support students' self-regulatory efforts.

Dialogue

Some sociocultural researchers emphasize the importance of dialogue for learning to academically self-regulate. This format is more interactive than the previous ones. Although all formats involve dialogue to some extent, this format is characterized by an evolving relationship in which students and teachers develop a mutual understanding about expectations and possibilities for self-regulatory behaviors. The assumption is that not all environments can have the same effects on students and not all students can engage in SRL in the same way. Therefore, consistent communication can contribute to a mutual and evolving understanding of SRL. From these interactions, individuals can learn to engage and control their own self-regulated learning by observing others, requesting help, being prompted, or experimenting with self-regulation in conjunction with supportive others.

Many SRL pedagogical models make use of multiple formats, although some researchers place stronger emphasis on certain ones over others. The emphasis is important because pedagogical formats align with particular assumptions of SRL. For example, the modeling and direct instruction align with a dispositional perspective by suggesting that SRL is trainable. It is not uncommon for the notion of training to accompany research-related SRL pedagogy (e.g., Stoeger & Ziegler, 2011). Viewed as trainable, teaching SRL is considered gradual, concerted, and dispositional. In this regard, teaching SRL involves (1) continuity across time and place; (2) complementary and similar pedagogical structures across a variety of spheres; and (3) opportunities to practice.

Researchers who align with a sociocultural view of SRL are likely to favor facilitation, as they tend to see SRL as an event. From this perspective, SRL is less about development and training and more about enactment and facilitation. Such a commitment leaves room for different regulatory possibilities, both in the form of SRL instruction and manifestation of student SRL. This approach also works against an overly individualistic approach to SRL by implicating pedagogical conditions in the form and content of SRL. Those who favor facilitation are committed to SRL pedagogy that is centered on understanding structural conditions and their relationship to student dispositions for the enactment of SRL. Butler (2002) does raise concern, however, that an overemphasis on contextual conditions for inviting SRL challenges a fundamental assumption and appeal of SRL, namely that individuals can overcome certain limitations by harnessing their personal resources to control learning outcomes.

Instructional Environments

Focused on the interaction between contexts and personal dispositions for SRL suggests that there are limitations with generalizing pedagogical conditions. However, there are specific conditions that tend to be associated with inviting and developing student SRL. For example, researchers tend to agree that opportunities for choice and control are features of classrooms that invite and support the development of SRL (e.g., Cleary & Zimmerman, 2004; Housand & Reis, 2008; Paris & Paris, 2001; Perry et al., 2002; Zimmerman, 1998). In addition to choice, Perry and colleagues (2002) argue that collaboration, nonthreatening evaluations, self-evaluations, and opportunities for mastery are key features of classroom environments that invite and support the development of SRL. Housand and Reis (2008) studied self-regulating learners within a gifted education program. They contend that classrooms characterized by choices, complex tasks, volitional control (e.g., time and independence for task engagement), metacognitive prompting (e.g., weekly reflections), explicit strategy instruction (in the form of modeling and direct instruction), student participation in assessment, and materials that allowed students to reflect and track their progress (e.g., reading logs) invited SRL. Paris and Paris (2001) suggest that adopting project-based learning encourages mastery, collaboration, and self-evaluations. They define this form of learning as student-designed inquiries of real problems in real contexts.

Educators must exercise caution, however, if relying on generalized assumptions about what kinds of environments are best for SRL. For example, opportunities for choice, personal control, and peer interactions are associated with a student-centered approach, which is associated with supporting SRL (e.g., Zimmerman, 2002). However, McCaslin and Burross (2011) suggest that direct instruction was more supportive for students in their research study than was an approach in which the teacher assumed a facilitative role. This research study reminds us to carefully consider universal claims about the potential and possibilities related to particular pedagogical conditions for supporting the development and enactment of SRL. For these reasons, as contemporary researchers suggest, attention must be paid to the interactions between individuals and educational context (e.g., Hadwin & Järvelä, 2011; Järvelä & Järvenoja, 2011; McCaslin & Burross, 2011).

Critical Concerns

Contemporary educational psychologists remain committed to exploring conceptual methodological and pedagogical challenges with SRL in order to support its integration in practice and policy. In regard to this effort, there has been considerable progress, as evidenced by the consolidation of concepts and pedagogical models. Although conventional debates are not fully resolved, contemporary conversations tend to be focused on pedagogical concerns. This focus makes sense given the presumptive context that SRL is valuable for all students, can level the playing field, and is a source of empowerment. There is relatively little scholarship related to the ethical, cultural, and philosophical complexities related to SRL itself and the implications of teaching it (cf. Martin & McLellan, 2008).

To some extent researchers recognize the need to move beyond conventional conversations and debates. In 2005, Boekaerts and Corno suggested that researchers needed to "examine the socio-political dimensions of the construct [SRL]; that is to say, they should study its semiotics and what it means to establish a goal for all students to become self-regulated learners" (p. 226). In addition, researchers also suggest that the significance of culture for SRL needs to be considered (e.g., Volet, Vaurus, & Salonen, 2009). Despite these calls, conversations about SRL have not been broadly inclusive of the sociopolitical and cultural dimensions. Further, I am skeptical that if fully realized, these lines of inquiry can adequately support critical conversations, unless researchers begin with the premises that SRL is not neutral, value-free, divorced from issues of power, and unequivocally empowering. Starting with these premises, I explore the kinds of personhood that underpin SRL, the values within the discourse, and complexities surrounding empowerment.

Self and Personhood

The notion of self, which is an essential, yet implicit and assumed, element in SRL theorizing, is a political, historical, and cultural artifact. Ignoring the historical and cultural constitution of self gives validity to the idea that SRL is a natural human proclivity or disposition. Martin and Sugarman (2001) argue that the self is a particular kind of understanding that is situated within a historical context. Influenced by George Herbert Mead, Martin and Sugarman theorize the self as a social artifact, something that emerges as a result of activity and relationships. From this view, the sociocultural world does not determine the self but provides the background from which individuals extract and continuously form ideas and theories about themselves. If the self forms and is continuously formed in relation to our world, attention needs to be paid to the kinds of self and personhood environments that are designed to support SRL invite and inscribe.

As Sugarman (2011) contends, education is fundamentally about the making of persons. Within any educational configuration, certain kinds of persons are valued, validated, and inscribed. Thus, teaching SRL can be implicated in shaping particular kinds of persons. Conducting a critical analysis of the selves within educational psychology, Martin (2007) contends that the self of SRL is underpinned by what he refers to as scientific and expressive selves. The scientific self is componential, executive, rational, knowable, controllable, internal, and ahistorical. The scientific self sees itself as distinct from the world, knowable, and, therefore, capable of control over itself. It is a self that is believed to be naturally furnished with the internal cognitive mechanisms that enable one to reflect on, monitor, and control thoughts and behaviors. The scientific self is fragmented as individuals are construed as having compartmentalized psychological features and executive functions that enable them to monitor and control themselves. The expressive self is committed to discerning, expressing, and developing a sense of identity. It is a self that is strongly aligned with classical liberal political philosophy about expressing opinions, freely exploring tastes, forming a "healthy" sense of self, having choices, and pursuing personal interests.

In contrast to the expressive and scientific selves, Martin (2007) discusses a type of selfhood that he calls communal, which he argues appears little in educational psychology literature. The communal self exists in dialectic between the self and social. It is a self that is understood to take form and emerge in a historical time and place. Thus, the communal self is relational and recognizes its historical constitution by reflecting on ways that certain contexts make identity possible. Martin (2007) discusses these forms of selfhood to make the point that selfhood is not a priori, predetermined, fixed, universal, or natural. Rather, the self can take different forms as a result of interactions between biology, history, and culture. However, teaching SRL involves endorsing expressive and scientific selves, which are implicated in creating a sense of personal isolation, emptiness, consumption, voids in communal involvement, and challenges for democratic participation (Cushman, 1990; Gergen, 2009; Martin, 2004a). There is real concern for the kind of self that underpins and is endorsed in SRL, especially as attention to SRL increases. Critical focus must remain on the kinds of selves endorsed in SRL, the effects of these selves, and how such selves are historically, philosophically, and culturally embedded.

Individual and Social Betterment

The conception of self is entangled in other critical concerns, one of them being the distinction between individual and social betterment. It is common for SRL researchers and theorists to express the need for individuals to improve control over emotions, thoughts, and behaviors for the purpose of improving academic performance. In this regard, the discourse of SRL focuses on individual betterment, without adequate contributions to civic virtue. As Martin (2004a) argues, "Knowing how to study effectively, or to motivate oneself are important and useful, but hardly equate with hallmarks of personhood such as civic virtue and responsible living" (p. 22). The critical concern here is focused on the degree to which SRL endorses self-interested goals and social goals. Martin raises concern that a self with a profound interiority, a predisposition for self-mastery, and detached from historical and cultural terrain produces patterns of consumption that serve individual needs.

One might argue that self-interested pursuits benefit society. For example, researchers contend that SRL could be used to support socially desirable behaviors, academic achievements, and a number of other so-called social problems, such as smoking, teen pregnancy, and crime. Improved academic performance could be connected to national interests to compete globally and create a superior workforce for the American economy. On a microlevel, individuals who self-regulate their learning can serve as models for others and, therefore, be a valuable resource for social improvement. Considering these examples, it might seem reasonable to associate SRL with social betterment because of individual betterment. Notwithstanding, there are a number of critical questions: (1) Who decides what is betterment (both for the individual and social)? (2) Does individual betterment have to align with an institutional objective? (3) What political logic underpins this association? (4) Who actually benefits from people operating with the ethic that individual pursuits are for the social good? Fox, Prilleltensky, and Austin (2009a) argue that individualism disproportionately hurts individuals from groups with little political, economic, and cultural capital. In this regard, an ethic of self-interest can be implicated in the reproduction of inequality.

Empowerment and Agency

SRL is typically associated with empowerment and agency. Agency is defined as one's ability to make choices that shape life's conditions and outcomes (Martin, 2004b). Yowell and Smylie (1999) define empowerment as "students' capacities to understand behavior-outcome relationships within given contexts and their belief that they have the capability to enact the behaviors necessary for such desired outcomes" (p. 478). Cleary and Zimmerman (2004) state that "empowerment can be thought of as a process by which individuals gain control over their lives" (p. 542). SRL is treated as a process by which individuals exercise control over their learning outcomes. There is a humanistic quality associated with SRL that stems from a heightened sense of self-control and personal responsibility, which educational psychologists tie to democratic participation, lifelong learning, self-sufficiency, academic success, and upward mobility.

However, there is little consideration of ways that SRL is disempowering. As suggested above, inviting and requiring self-interest can actually disempower certain individuals and groups. Another way to think about disempowerment and SRL has to do with compliance and surveillance. Martin and McLellan (2008) suggest that one can interpret SRL as "the disguised manipulation of student self-surveillance in the service of the institutional mandates of schools" (p. 2). That is, those who regulate their learning can be viewed as using seemingly self-directed behavioral and thought processes to comply with institutional mandates. In fact, Post, Boyer, and Brett (2006) state that definitions of SRL from the 1990s included compliance as a feature. They state:

> Self-regulation "is the ability to comply with a request, to initiate and cease activities according to situational demands, to modulate the intensity, frequency, and duration of verbal and motor acts in social and education settings." In addition Kopp highlights the sophisticated cognitive system enabling a young child "to postpone acting upon a desired object or goal, and to generate socially approved behavior in the absence of external monitors." (p. 5)

In the above quotation, SRL is associated with compliance and the production of socially approved behaviors. Noncompliance to school expectations can serve as indices of failure at self-regulation. So, is SRL, or what at least counts as effective SRL, doing what one is supposed to do without being told to do it?

Educational psychologists encourage the institutionalization of SRL; that is, they want to make it widespread and explicit in curriculum and practice. It is difficult to imagine how this institutional focus can avoid imposing particular sequences for thoughts and behaviors. Thus, Martin and McLellan (2008) question the degree to which SRL actually reflects autonomy. They state:

> It is by no means always clear that the highly scripted and externally imposed sequences of strategic activity and instruction evident in many studies and interventions in the area of students' self-regulated learning leave adequate room for the fostering of true self-determination with respect to students' choice and enactment of their learning and study strategies. (p. 82)

Within schools, it might be difficult to avoid taking up the aim to teach SRL without scripting students' engagement, or without validating and rewarding behaviors that match preconceived ideas about what SRL looks like, while punishing or invalidating behaviors that are misaligned with SRL. Critical attention needs to be paid to how SRL is entangled in compliance to institutional mandates.

The Ends of Self-Regulated Learning

The critical conversation surrounding compliance must extend to the politics and power of schooling environments. That is, consideration of the contexts in which SRL is employed needs to be part of the conversation. This element is important because, as critical theorists argue, schooling environments are rife with inequalities and contradictions that are protected and resistant to change (Freire, 2000; McLaren, 2007). For example, schooling curricula are interpreted as representative of white, middle-class men—resulting in the silencing and marginalization of identities and diverse ways of knowing. Some view standardized tests as biased, supportive of a neoliberal agenda, and aligned with a factory model of teaching and learning (e.g., Gorlewski, 2011). In addition, researchers consistently observe that curricula are different across class backgrounds in ways that help to reproduce class hierarchy (e.g., Anyon, 1981; Journell, 2011). For example, middle-class children are exposed to both explicit and implicit curricula that prepare them to fill middle-class occupations. Whereas, working-class children may be exposed to curricula designed to get them to perform rote procedures and follow orders. Given these contexts, SRL may be mobilized to efficiently produce a particular social order.

Notwithstanding these contradictions and asymmetries in schooling environments, researchers are focused on improving SRL, which involves efficiently and effectively adapting to learning environments. In this regard, some researchers and practitioners implement pedagogical interventions to support students' regulatory efforts to learn state-mandated content and improve performance on standardized test scores (e.g., see Miller, Heafner, & Massey, 2009). Therefore, critical scholars may see the regulation of learning institutionally mandated curricula to be in conflict with empowerment, social justice, and freedom because it validates problematic learning environments. Critical inquiry must involve close examinations of the contentious educational contexts in which SRL is encouraged, valued, and employed.

Conclusion

Due to the value associated with SRL, researchers focus on better conceptualizations, measurements, and pedagogical interventions. Although there is significant debate surrounding SRL, there are several points of agreement and common features that unite researchers who operate in different academic camps. Certain assumptions and commitments about SRL continue to remain taken for granted, naturalized, and divorced from issues of power. Although some educational psychologists have begun to conduct critical analyses of SRL, considerable work needs to be done. The following chapters involve drawing from diverse perspectives, ones not typically integrated in research on SRL, in order to examine ethical, philosophical, cultural, and pedagogical complexities related to the discourse of SRL. That is, I conduct a critical educational psychology analysis of SRL.

Chapter 3
A Consideration of Agency in Self-Regulated Learning

Introduction

Hadwin, Järvelä, and Miller (2011) state, "Contemporary perspectives of learning recognize that learners actively control their own learning and outcomes. Agency refers to the capacity to intentionally plan for, control and reflect upon our actions; agency is what makes us human" (p. 66). Self-regulated learning (SRL) presumes and affirms the idea of agency and is positively associated with SRL. However, the question persists about how much control individuals can exercise over their lives, in general, and learning, in particular. Notions such as determinism, fatalism, and structure suggest that we do not unequivocally exercise control over circumstances and outcomes. A central concern is that the discourse of SRL can invite overstatements about the degree of personal control that is responsible for academic outcomes. Assuming agency and overstating personal control can direct attention away from the role that schooling arrangements, pedagogical conditions, and curricula play in academic outcomes.

Although foundational to SRL, agency is often ignored. The lack of attention is of concern because agency is controversial, contentious, and understood in various ways. Theories of agency are underpinned by different assumptions about the nature of personhood, human thought, experience, action, and social systems. As a foundational element, researchers and theorists need to be explicit and clear about the assumptions of agency that are endorsed in SRL. Without such explorations, conversations on the roots, limitations, and critical concerns about SRL are difficult to forge (Martin, 2004a). The lack of attention to the complexities of agency may also invite contradictory educational practices. For example, if SRL is unequivocally viewed as a form of agency, then one may commit to teaching students to academically self-regulate and justify those pedagogical decisions based on student empowerment. However, teaching SRL may seem to empower students to exercise their agency, but it actually serves as an instrument to encourage complicity, compliance, and obedience. In this regard, associating SRL with agency and empowerment comes into serious question. In order to support ethically informed practice and reflection, it is important to be clear about the assumptions of agency in the discourse of SRL.

Agency and Determinism: Causality and Control

Questions and debates about agency have been around for centuries. Throughout much of this history, controversies were framed in terms of determinism and free will, which Bandura (2006) describes as terminology that is a "throwback to medieval theology" (p. 165). Although such terminology at times enters contemporary discourse, the notions of structure and agency commonly frame discussions related to causality and control over life circumstances. Agency and structure represent two extreme and opposing points on a spectrum. From an agency position, individuals are solely responsible for their life situations because of the choices they make. Some of the vocabulary that is associated with this position is intention, conscious will, voice, and individual responsibility. Different mechanisms are identified as sources of agency. For example, Searle (2007) views the capacity to reason and deliberate over anticipated actions and nonactions as essential for personal control. Some researchers identify goal setting and reflection as key sources of agency, as these psychological processes are believed to free one from external determination (Bandura, 1989; Zimmerman, 2000). Others see agency as constructing knowledge and mediating environmental messages (Bruner, 1990; Winne, 2005).

The notion of structure is on the other end of the spectrum. Structure can be understood as external and internal entities that are responsible for thinking, action, and outcomes. Some examples of structure include, but are not limited to, families, economic systems, schools, communities, biology, and language. The idea is that structures are comprised of parts that contribute to a system that is responsible for thought, action, and social configurations. Despite the fact that the notion of structure is a naturalized part of discourse, there is not always agreement about what constitutes a structure and whether or not structures exist (Archer, 2003; Giddens, 1984; King, 2009; Lizardo, 2010; Sawyer, 2002; Sewell, 1992). For example, Sawyer (2002) notes that many sociologists are committed to the idea that "social structures and group properties do not really exist, but are merely ways to summarize individual behavior in the aggregate" (p. 286). Aligned with this position, King (2009) writes, "Whenever individuals act, they instantiate the rules of structure. . . . Structure, as virtual rules, and systems, as institutions, are conveniently conflated in the acting individual, so that individuals reproduce the system" (p. 263). These sociologists challenge the idea that there is such a thing as a structure or that a structure is anything other than the coordination and aggregation of individual actions. In psychology, Ratner (2000) describes Jerome Bruner and Jaan Valsiner as committed to this idea as well. He summarizes their perspective by stating, "Society is composed of individuals. In Bruner's view, society is a forum for individuals to negotiate meanings in their face-to-face interactions. In Valsiner's view, society is the sum of personal meanings devised by individuals" (p. 416).

Assuming one believes in the existence of structures, questions remain about their genesis (i.e., how they form), mutability (i.e., how they change), and function (i.e., what roles they play). Some researchers argue that individuals can influence structures while others treat them deterministically. For example, Bowles and Gintis (1976) espouse an economically deterministic position. They argue that the laws of capitalism exist prior to and independent of individual action, and these laws predictably govern and shape behaviors and life outcomes. In another example, the brain is believed to have distinct parts and functions that when working together make certain thoughts and behaviors possible. That is, what we do, think, and become results from the structure and function of our brains, which are shaped through interactions with our environments. However, one can argue that individuals control, at least to some degree, their brains either by selecting different environments or changing thought patterns. Although debates persist about the genesis, mutability, and function of structures, the key idea is that there are configurations and relationships between systemic parts that are implicated in determining, or at least shaping in part, what individuals do and think.

The term "structure" itself is not as explicitly pervasive in psychological literature as it is in other disciplines such as anthropology, economics, and sociology. Psychologists tend to use notions such as social, cultural, environmental, and even psychological to refer to structural entities. Ratner (2000) disagrees that these concepts should be conflated with the notion of structure. Regardless of the conceptualization and terminology, agency is counterbalanced by concepts that are organized around the idea that there are forces beyond personal control that shape thoughts, behaviors, and outcomes.

The notions of structure and agency can evoke a number of seeming dualisms, such as individual and world, willful and determined, empowered and dominated. Contemporary researchers and theorists tend to avoid these dualisms; it is uncommon to take an extreme position on the question of agency, as many agree that explanations for thoughts, actions, and outcomes are shaped by a mixture of forces. Some contemporary theorists are committed to compatibilism, which is characterized by the assumption that structure and agency are not opposing but offer a nuanced understanding of causality and control (Martin, Sugarman, & Thompson, 2003). Notwithstanding, there is still considerable disagreement about how structure and agency are compatible. Questions persist about what can one control, how much control one can exercise, which structures matter, and what effect structures have on circumstances and outcomes. Other questions are:

1. Is agency an actual state or is it an experience?
2. Is agency intentional and conscious, or can it be automatic and unconscious?
3. Is it an individual or social phenomenon?
4. Does it develop or are individuals naturally agentic?
5. Can and should agency be taught?
6. What is the role of the historical and social context for agency?
7. What are the mechanisms and processes that make agency possible?
8. How much of what people do is determined by what they control and how much is determined by forces outside of one's control?
9. When is an action agentic and when is an action just an action?

Underpinned by assumptions about the nature of personhood, experience, social systems, and actions, responses to these questions will vary. Furthermore, answers to these questions will shape how teachers understand themselves, students, and teaching responsibilities. For example, if teachers overstate the degree to which intentional, purposeful, and rationally controlled processes shape student outcomes, they may assume that (1) those who perform well in school do so because of their choices; (2) all students have the same choices; (3) educational structures afford equality of opportunity; (4) educational structures are neutral; and (5) pedagogical interventions must involve teaching students to make good choices. As another example, if one believes that agency must be taught or at least individuals must be taught how to exercise their agency, teachers may encourage relationships of dependence wherein students may only realize their agentic power by learning institutional lessons.

Psychology and Agency

Within the discourse of psychology, Wegner and Pennebaker (1993) argue that the assumption that individuals can exercise control over themselves and their environments is a relatively new idea that emerged around the 1950s. Before then, when behaviorism was the dominant learning paradigm, intentions, purposefulness, and goals were designated as parapsychological phenomena. Skinner (1971), a prominent behaviorist, contended that the associations between stimuli and consequences governed action; thought was merely a by-product of these bonds, not the source of action. Although Wenger and Pennebaker argue that individual control is a recent phenomenon, Skinner argues that for centuries people have found it difficult to move away from attributing thoughts and actions to internal and controllable components. Despite the historical association and contested nature of personal control, educational psychologists tend to accept the idea that individuals actively control their learning by setting goals, directing attention, inhibiting impulses, employing psychological defenses, and employing cognitive strategies.

However, Sugarman and Sokol (2010) contend that psychologists continue to implicitly and explicitly wrestle with the question of agency. They state that scientific psychologists use "deterministic language of behavioral contingencies, statistical regularities, neurophysiological states and processes, computational functions and models, or evolutionary biology" (p. 1). They suggest that universalizing laws and mechanisms undermine conceptions of individual control. On the other hand, clinical psychologists are strongly committed to the idea that individuals have freedom of choice and can exercise personal control in solving problems, coping, making decisions, and shaping their thoughts. Aligned with a clinical commitment, Cleary and Zimmerman (2004) suggest that SRL communicates messages of hope and empowerment because students can rely on personal resources to achieve one's learning goals by overcoming psychological and environmental limitations.

A critical analysis of agency in SRL is not intended to communicate messages of despair and disempowerment, question the value of SRL for academic success, or take a position on whether or not SRL is unequivocally an expression of agency. Rather, the intention is to highlight particular assumptions of agency that are endorsed in SRL theorizing and to discuss limitations of those assumptions. The analysis begins with an exploration of agency in the social cognitive view, which informs a significant portion of SRL literature and is followed by considerations of agency in co-regulation and socially shared regulation. Although there are points of difference across the theories, certain assumptions about agency are shared. Concerns with these underlying assumptions are explored. The central goal of this analysis is to highlight the different ways that SRL both affirms and disaffirms agency.

SLR: A Social Cognitive Perspective

The social cognitive perspective is associated with Albert Bandura and advanced by two prolific SRL researchers, Barry Zimmerman and Dale Schunk. The social cognitive treatment of SRL has a strong contemporary presence (Post, Boyer, & Brett, 2006); aside from the myriad of research articles informed by this perspective, this view of SRL is present in widely used educational psychology textbooks (Ormrod, 2011; Santrock, 2008; Woolfolk-Hoy, 2007). From this perspective, an action is not self-regulated unless there is intentional action corresponding with established goals (Bandura, 2006; Zimmerman, 2000). The notions of proaction and reaction are used to capture this element.

> SRL is viewed as proactive processes that students use to acquire academic skill, such as setting goals, selecting and deploying strategies, and self-monitoring one's effectiveness, rather than as a reactive event that happens to students due to impersonal forces. (Zimmerman, 2000, p. 16)

According to Bandura (2006), the sources of proactive engagement are intentions (e.g., the goals individuals set), forethought (e.g., deliberation over possible futures), self-reactiveness (e.g., executing a plan of action), and self-reflection (e.g., the assessment of behaviors, thoughts, goals, and performance). Social cognitive researchers believe that in exercising agency one is self-regulating and in self-regulating one is exercising agency. That is, SRL and agency imply each other. Therefore, Martin (2004b) appropriately characterizes this view as a "theory of agency as self-regulation" (p. 135).

Individual Agency, Proxy Agency, and Reciprocal Causation

Although social cognitive theorists emphasize personal processes and resources in SRL, the social world plays a fundamental role. Notions such as proxy agency and reciprocal causation are intended to capture the social component of SRL. Bandura (2001) argues that individuals cannot make anything happen at any given time and likewise cannot shape their lives entirely from personal resources. In fact, he argues that few social cognitive–oriented researchers actually believe that individuals are "autonomous agents" who serve entirely as independent causal forces. Strategic learners must use social resources to achieve personal goals. Proxy agency, also called socially mediated agency, involves influencing others who have the resources, knowledge, and means to act on one's behalf in order to achieve personal objectives (Bandura, 2006). Proxy agency is tantamount to strategic help-seeking. Bandura (2006) also uses the notion of collective agency to describe groups' strategic efforts to pool their knowledge and resources to attain a collective goal. This form of agency is given little attention in the SRL literature.

Despite the inclusion of proxy and collective agency, the social cognitive view of SRL is heavily underpinned by the notion of individual agency, which involves the use of personal resources to influence oneself and the environment. Social cognitive researchers do not deny that the environment has influences; however, they argue that personal processes can be used to exercise control over environmental conditions. The idea is that the environment, behaviors, and psychological states and processes can reciprocally influence each other—a model of SRL referred to as reciprocal causation. In this model, environmental cues and consequences shape behaviors and psychology. But if individuals develop awareness of those contingencies, they could actively change, shape, and mitigate their effects. Bandura (2006) reasons that just as the environment can exert influence over individuals, the self can influence the environment.

To illustrate the process of reciprocal causation, consider a hypothetical student named Markus who is a college senior majoring in psychology. Markus just received his psychopharmacology midterm exam score, which was a 79 (environmental feedback). With the exception of his introductory psychology course, he had received A's in all of his psychology classes. Markus recognized (psychology) that his studying (behavior) was inadequate but he was not being reactive. That is, he did not wait to receive his score before evaluating his study strategies and setting goals. Like all other exams, he was proactive in his studies, as he set study goals (psychology), managed his time (behavior), and implemented study strategies (behavior) that worked for him in the past. Upon feedback (an environmental influence), Markus realized that he needed to reconsider his study strategies (behavior) for this particular course. As a result of past success, Markus believed (psychology) that he could improve, but he believed that his repertoire of learning strategies was limited. Therefore, Markus enrolled in a learning strategies workshop (changing the environment), which was focused on teaching skills for self-evaluation, analyzing tasks, monitoring performance, setting appropriate goals, and using effective strategies.

Ontology of Agentic Capabilities

From a social cognitive perspective, agentic capabilities emerge from the interactions between individuals and their worlds. Bandura (1989) calls this theory "emergent interactive agency" (p. 1175). From this theory, all individuals are believed to be capable of SRL, but some lack the necessary perception, behavioral skill, and self-knowledge to exercise that control (Bandura, 2006; Cleary & Zimmerman, 2004; Pintrich, 1995; Shanker, 2010; Svinicki, 2010; Wehmeyer, Palmer, Agran, Mithaug, & Martin, 2000). Zimmerman (2000) writes:

> Our regulatory skill or lack thereof is the source of our *perception of personal agency* [emphasis added] that lies at the core of our sense of self . . . it [SRL] entails not only behavioral skill in self-managing environmental contingencies, but also the knowledge and the sense of personal agency to enact this skill in relevant contexts. (pp. 13–14)

The use of the term "perception" reveals an underlying commitment of agency. Perception connotes an individual construction that may or may not be objectively verified or justified, a construction of something that is subjective. From this understanding, the main obstacle to exercising control over learning involves subjective misreading of possibilities and potentialities that lead individuals to believe they do not have control. It is assumed that all individuals can exercise control provided they have the right perceptions, which includes high and accurate self-efficacy. Individuals must believe that they can affect their academic performance through their own personal resources. Individuals must learn to associate their thoughts and behaviors with particular outcomes.

Pedagogy that is aligned with this theory is focused on the goal to shape students' perceptions, knowledge, self-evaluations, monitoring mechanisms, and skills so they can exercise their agency. Individuals must become scientists investigating themselves by (1) documenting thoughts and behaviors; (2) measuring personal changes and outcomes; (3) calculating environmental contingencies; (4) observing oneself; and (5) strategically manipulating personal and environmental variables. Individuals can use self-efficacy scales, learning strategy logs, journals, personal charts, and time management logs. The underlying assumption is that all students have agentic capability and can influence themselves and their environments provided they have comprehensive self-knowledge.

In the social cognitive, perspective agency and SRL imply each other. Individuals are conceptualized as those who are influenced by environmental and behavioral forces but can also influence those components as well. According to social cognitive theorists, all individuals are capable of agentic self-regulation; factors such as self-knowledge, perception, and environmental awareness support or curtail the exercise of self-regulatory control. The logic is that individuals can exercise control over their learning by monitoring, evaluating, and reflecting on beliefs, thought processes, behaviors, and environmental contingencies. This view of agency aligns with what Sugarman and Sokol (2010) refer to as an idealistic view of "agentive internalism," which is a term used to group theories of agency that construe individuals as being furnished with a priori agentic capabilities and internal mechanisms as the source of agentic activity (p. 2). There are several concerns with this view of agency.

Agentive Internalism: Proaction, Calculability, and Personal Control

Sugarman and Sokol (2010) argue that agentive internalist perspectives emphasize the significance of internal causation and control by theorizing the ways internal structures and processes furnish individuals with the capability to make intentional choices, originate action from within, and render action voluntary. Labeled as an "idealist" view, Sugarman and Sokol argue that internal causation is rooted in Kantian and Cartesian metaphysics whereby individuals are treated as possessing unique characteristics that serve as the sources of thought and action (p. 2). Kant's philosophy is associated with Enlightenment thinking, which includes the idea that through reason and scientific study humans can know and control themselves. Descartes is also associated with Enlightenment thought and is well known for theorizing the separation between mind and world. Informed by Kant and Descartes, agentive internalist views are underpinned by a conception of the individual "as possessed of some form of transcendent agent and/or a complex of internal structures and processes (e.g., executive processes, metacognition, self-regulation, self-control, self-concept, self-efficacy, and so on) by which agency is generated, expressed and experienced" (Sugarman & Sokol, 2010, p. 2). By identifying these philosophical roots, Sugarman and Sokol provide a starting point for identifying the philosophical underpinnings of a social cognitive view of SRL and agency.

The separation of mind from world makes it possible to conceptualize isolated individuals who are in control of both themselves and their worlds, especially when individuals are construed as being furnished with internal capacities that enable them to construct knowledge, mediate environmental information, and make autonomous choices. Separating the person from the world invites the possibility of neatly identifying a source of thoughts and actions. As evidenced by their use of the terms "proactive" and "self-generated," social cognitive theorists suggest that sources of thought and action can have a discernible and unequivocal starting point, one that is attributable to the individual. Expressing skepticism, Martin and McLellan (2008) ask:

> Is it really possible to make such distinctions [between internally and externally originated thought and action] on the basis of whether or not the goal-setting, strategic acting, monitoring, and evaluation said to attend the worldly activity of human persons is self-generated and self-determined versus occasioned and determined externally by circumstances and others? (p. 10)

The authors highlight an enduring complexity of agentive internalism. The difference between action that originates from internal sources and action that is socially determined is no simple matter. Martin and McLellan point to a debate over which philosophers have deliberated for years: (1) are individuals the authors of their thoughts and actions; (2) can individuals know when they authored their thoughts and actions; and (3) does authoring a thought or action necessarily signify agency?

Some psychologists question the degree to which thoughts and actions are actually under personal control. Individuals may believe they know when actions are theirs because they experience themselves as causing them. However, people can be mistaken about the authorship of their thoughts and actions. Individuals may encounter situations that profoundly mislead them about the origins of action; they can come to believe that they have performed actions they did not or that they were not the source of actions that were in fact their own. To explain this phenomenon, Wegner and Wheatley (1999) propose a theory of "apparent mental causation." As the title suggests, attributing cause to psychological processes and mechanisms are merely apparent because of the contiguity between thinking about an action and performing it. They argue when individuals think about an action in advance of its occurrence and when alternative sources of the action are not known, individuals mistakenly attribute cause to themselves.

Contrary to social cognitive theorists, Wegner and Wheatley (1999) are critical of the idea that conscious intention and forethought are responsible for the production of behaviors and are a source of agency. In general, they question the degree to which psychological sources are causal in general. Wegner and Wheatley argue that "personal agency is a perception that results from interpretation, it is a conscious experience that may only map rather weakly, or perhaps not at all, onto the actual causal relationship between the person's cognition and action" (p. 481). Wegner (2002) argues that people do not naturally assign authorship to themselves but must learn to do so. He writes, "We are not intrinsically informed of our own authorship and instead must build it up virtually out of perceptions of the thoughts and the actions we witness in consciousness" (p. 218). Social cognitive theorists agree that individuals must build an understanding of how thoughts and behaviors play a causal role. The key difference, however, is that social cognitive theorists suggest that learning how one's thought and actions are causal is merely recognizing what is already true. Whereas Wegner suggests that individuals construct an explanatory narrative about causality that is not necessarily actual.

Carver and Scheier (2000) argue that researchers who are interested in the question of agency have focused mainly on individuals' need to feel as though they are in control as opposed to actually being in control. The perception of control is believed to increase the probability of the occurrence of adaptive self-regulatory thoughts and behaviors. If students do not believe that they could achieve their learning goals through their own strategic efforts, then they may display less resilience, effort, and commitment to overcome learning challenges (Bandura, 2001). Therefore, it may seem adequate to focus on producing the perception of control. From a social cognitive perspective, such a focus makes sense because control is assumed and actual, and those who do not exercise it have faulty perceptions.

One problem with this view of agency is that it endorses the view of society as a meritocracy, which is the idea there are no direct oppressive structures limiting students' opportunities. The assumption is that all individuals have an equal opportunity to acquire the credentials to compete for prestigious social positions and economic capital. Those who perform well in school do so because of personal factors such as hard work, motivation, cognitive skills, and discipline. Unequal pedagogical arrangements, the distribution of resources, and sociocultural factors, such as race, gender, and ability are not sources of inequality; social inequalities remain at the level of the individual, not contradictions and asymmetries in institutional settings. Assuming and overstating personal control can direct attention away from the role that schooling arrangements, pedagogical conditions, and curricula play in student thoughts, behaviors, and outcomes.

Another reason that it is problematic to assume individuals have agentic control relates to ideological individualism. If individuals are assumed to have control and are responsible for their outcomes, then academic, economic, and social problems are addressable at the level of the individual. In classrooms, students can be blamed for whatever problems emerge or are constructed. The corollary is that pedagogical interventions will be directed at reforming students to address those problems. Zimmerman (2000) exemplifies this line of thinking when he constructs teen pregnancy as an academic, social, and economic problem, and self-regulation as the solution. There are several issues with this line of reasoning. Teen pregnancy is not inherently a problem, but it becomes one because of certain cultural values and structural conditions that make it a problem. So, addressing the so-called problem means getting all people in line with particular values and structures. In this regard, individuals may not be viewed as agentic unless they play by a specific set of rules and comply with institutional and cultural norms; hence, a paradox.

Let us come back to the example of Markus to explore this paradox. Although he employed strategic behaviors when studying for his exam (perhaps a result of internalized scripts), Markus relied on an external prompt to reevaluate his engagement. The compass for the effectiveness of his response is tied to institutional norms for academic success. There is no depiction of an authority figure orchestrating Markus' actions to reevaluate himself and implement personal changes. However, Markus had to learn a set of conventions, thought processes, and behaviors that generated value for grades, a disposition to meet academic demands, a commitment to self-knowledge, and strategies for self-guidance. Markus is equipped with a number of tools, dispositions, techniques, and aspirations that enable him to seemingly direct himself to pursue personal goals that have a clear alignment with institutional norms and expectations for academic success. A concern with SRL is that it resembles and enables compliance.

Some SRL researchers explicitly associate SRL with compliance (Chong, 2006; Post, Boyer, & Brett, 2006). Post, Boyer, and Brett (2006) state:

> Self-regulation "is the ability to comply with a request, to initiate and cease activities according to situational demands, to modulate the intensity, frequency, and duration of verbal and motor acts in social and education settings." In addition Kopp highlights the

sophisticated cognitive system enabling a young child "to postpone acting upon a desired object or goal, and to generate socially approved behavior in the absence of external monitors." (p. 5)

Like these researchers, Chong (2006) argues that conforming to social expectations and norms, staying focused on tasks regardless of competing interest, and delaying gratification are self-regulatory commitments that are essential for successful academic engagement. These researchers do not view such compliance as antithetical to agency. In fact, suppressing impulses, desires, interests, thoughts, and behaviors for socially and academically acceptable ones are viewed as the epitome of agency (Chong, 2006; Bembenutty, 2009; Shanker, 2010). The idea is that impulses, desires, and dispositions—sources of thought and action that are not willful—are not governing thought and action but are rather under willful control. An inability to comply with school demands may indicate a lack of agency. Therefore, resistance to schooling may be considered antithetical to agency.

This position is a problem as agency can be viewed as resistance to institutional norms and practices, especially those that are endorsed and valued in schools, which are not neutral and value-free. Compliance to school demands may mean different things to certain groups. As will be discussed further in the book, schools are often referred to as middle-class enterprises because the knowledge, skills, and dispositions associated with middle-class culture are rewarded, valued, and validated (Anyon, 1981; Bernstein, 1971; Giroux, 2001; Gorlewski, 2011; Lareau, 2003; McLaren, 2007; Willis, 1977). For example, Gorlewski (2011) argues that composition and literature in schooling endorse middle-class values of individualism, upward mobility, and glorification of authority. For working-class and economically disadvantaged students, mismatches between curricula and cultural conventions may require them to suppress their values, identities, and dispositions in favor of ones that appropriately reflect middle-class conventions. Compliance for working-class children can mean subordination to pedagogical arrangements that protect a cultural hierarchy.

Researchers observe that working-class students tend to resist schooling in various ways (e.g., Finn, 2009; Gorlewski, 2011; Ogbu, 1993). One way, as Gorlewski (2011) contends, "Working-class students exercise agency by constructing oppositional cultures through and in written discourse" (p. 200). Ogbu (1993) makes a similar observation in terms of race. Schools are not only viewed as propagating and protecting class conventions, but racial ones as well.

Like working-class youth, Ogbu argues that black students develop what he calls an "oppositional frame of reference" to schooling because of the propagation of values associated with white people. As a consequence, Ogbu contends that for some black students doing well in school is seen as "acting white." Given the problems with schooling environments, dropping out and minimizing effort can be the preservation of identity, values, dignity, and humanity. Suppressing resistance and complying with institutional demands can then be interpreted as subordination to educational contexts that privilege certain groups over others. Therefore, resistance and disengagement to schooling can reasonably be agentic and empowering.

There is another issue related to compliance. Social cognitive researchers make the distinction between reactivity and proactivity. This distinction is complicated because internal mechanisms can be furnished by external sources. Sociocultural researchers argue that so-called internal processes and mechanisms, such as goal setting, planning, evaluation, monitoring, and reflection, are results of cognitive socialization (e.g., Vygotsky, 1978; Wertsch, Tulviste, & Hagstrom, 1993). From a sociocultural perspective, "internal" mechanisms are not properties of the individual. Rather they are imported interactions. Therefore, proactivity can be a socially determined procedure that is enacted in the absence of its social source—another form of compliance. An SRL pedagogical goal is to shift responsibility to individuals, rather than authorities, to maintain constant surveillance and perform self-reformation. If individuals appropriate scripts and adapt them to new situations, external influence does not disappear.

Researchers recognize this problem and suggest that in order to count as self-regulating, individuals must adapt socially learned processes and behaviors in novel ways to new situations (Järvelä & Järvenoja, 2011; McCaslin & Burross, 2011; Schunk & Zimmerman, 1997). That is, they must be adaptable. The association between adaptation, SRL, and agency is of concern, one that is discussed in the chapters on critical pedagogy and neoliberalism. Here, I briefly summarize the concern. The adaptable person reflects a particular subject position, one that happens to align with middle-class conventions and neoliberal subjectivity (Walkerdine, 2003). Becoming effective at adapting requires guidance and dependence on others, as well as reliance on psychological tools and techniques of self-study. In order to be agentic, individuals must have the appropriate self-knowledge, which is developed through calculation and documentation of behaviors, psychology, and environmental contingencies. As a result, pedagogical interventions include tools for measurements, documenting techniques, and changing, if necessary, individuals' efficacy beliefs. The logic is that through calculation and documentation of these beliefs, individuals can develop information about themselves and their worlds that serve as the foundation for regulatory behavior.

Scales, logs, and charts are part of the scientific management of people. This type of management, which is supported by psychological discourse, is about recognizing and disciplining difference so that individuals can operate in alignment with some normative aim. Rose (1999) states:

> Psychologists were to claim a particular expertise in the disciplining of the uniqueness and idiosyncrasies of childhood, individualizing children by categorizing them, calibrating their aptitudes, inscribing their peculiarities in an ordered form, managing their variability conceptually, and governing it practically. (p. 135)

Visibility of the person is required to determine what needs to be reformed and which pedagogical strategies are going to most efficiently and effectively produce the targeted change. Psychological instruments are used to normalize individuals, inscribe their differences, and invite reformative action. Rose (1999) points out that monitoring, calculating, and documenting oneself is tied to humanistic concerns related to responsibility and freedom, and such techniques are double-edged. He states:

> They institute [techniques of self-scrutiny], as the other side of their promises of autonomy and success, a constant self doubt [sic], a constant scrutiny and evaluation of how one performs, the construction of one's personal part in social existence as something to be calibrated and judged in its minute particulars. (p. 239)

Gergen (2009) adds that this kind of a self-relationship can produce low esteem, stress, and isolation. Gergen and Rose do not explicitly state that self-scrutiny is not agentic. They agree that self-scrutiny can support the operation of certain thoughts and actions. However, those actions and behaviors are only agentic because they align with a narrow set of practices, norms, and conventions. If teachers assume that SRL is agentic, and that agency is made possible by studying the self, there might be a steadfast commitment to teach SRL, without recognition of the angst, constraints, and obligations that are associated with such pedagogy. And agency may not be recognized unless it resembles adherence to this narrow kind of self-relationship.

Although SRL researchers treat self-observational techniques as a way and means to exercise human agency, they do not consider that these practices may disaffirm agency. There are some key questions for considering this possibility:

(1) What type of self is endorsed in this view of agency? (2) What are the techniques used to know the self? (3) How are self-knowledge and techniques tied to political contexts? (4) What effects do these forms and techniques of knowledge have on people? The self that underpins the social cognitive view of agency aligns closely with both the expressive and scientific selves. If one treats selfhood as emergent, evolving, historically constituted, and undetermined, then teaching students to monitor and calculate themselves encourages the formation of a particular kind of self, one that is rooted in the Western Enlightenment, classical liberal political philosophy, neoliberalism, and middle-class conventions—arguments made in the upcoming chapters. A fundamental assumption is that selfhood is not neutral, value-free, ahistorical, and disconnected from power. Validating and inscribing a particular kind of self can be subordinating, constraining, obligatory, and stressful.

Agency in Co-regulation and Socially Shared Regulation

Ideas about agency in co-regulation and socially shared regulation depart in some respects from the social cognitive perspective of SRL. Researchers who draw from sociocultural theory conceptualize the social and individual in particular ways that highlight the social world in agency. The contributions of sociocultural theory have pushed researchers to account for the role that social and contextual influences have on a variety of phases of academic regulation and the exercise of agency. Although sociocultural views of academic regulation seemingly depart from internalist views of agency, there are points of overlap between all three concepts of regulatory learning theory that reflect internalist commitments. These include the naturalization of self-regulatory capacities, separation of individuals from the world, and the reliance on goal setting, self-reflection, and planning. These commitments provide the justification for the association and affirmation of agency across accounts of regulatory theory. That is, proponents of co-regulation and socially shared regulation also affirm and associate regulatory learning with agency.

Agency in Co-Regulation

Co-regulation is grounded in Vygotskian and neo-Vygotskian theory (Hadwin & Oshige, 2011; McCaslin & Hickey, 2001; McCaslin, 2009). Hadwin and Oshige (2011) define co-regulation as "a transitional process in a learner's acquisition of self-regulated learning, within which learners and others share a common problem-solving plane, and SRL is gradually appropriated by the individual learner through interactions" (p. 247). The term "appropriate" is used to suggest conceptual problems with the notion of internalization. Many sociocultural theorists believe in the nonpassivity of individuals, who are believed to bring their own expertise, experience, and history to relationships and interactions. Sociocultural theorists are less likely to use the notion of internalization because it connotes transmission of an external interaction that directly corresponds to a mental imprint. The logic is that although interactions give form to mental material, what happens on a social plane does not directly correspond to a mental structure. The assumption is that there is an individual mediating social and environmental information; the learner constructs knowledge, albeit within a social and cultural context.

Construing individuals as having a priori cognitive structures that are used to construct knowledge and mediate information assumes SRL and agency. As Winne (2005) states, "Learners are agents. Learners construct knowledge. Whether scaffolding is available or not, these paradigmatic stances necessitate that learners can and do self-regulate learning" (p. 559). There is an assumed agentic self-regulated learner underpinning co-regulation. Some sociocultural theorists who study SRL presume that individuals are inherently self-regulated or at least have the capacity to self-regulate (Hadwin, 2012; Järvelä & Järvenoja, 2011). Järvelä and Järvenoja (2011) state, "In collaborative learning, individual group members represent interdependent self-regulating agents (cognitive angle) who at the same time constitute a social entity that creates affordances and constraints for group and individual engagement (situative angle)" (p. 351). The notions of cognitive and situative angles preserve the mediating role of individual cognition, reflection, and interpretation, while attempting to situate them within particular environments.

Although preserving the concept of the preontological mediating individual, sociocultural theorists emphasize SRL and agency as emergent. Co-regulation can be thought about as socially coordinated actions and interactions that lead to the emergence of independent action. Hadwin and Oshige (2011) describe it as "the temporary sharing or distributing of self-regulatory processes and thinking between a learner and a more capable other (peer or teacher), where the learner transitions toward self-regulatory practice" (p. 248). In this sense, co-regulation is an instrument to agency, and the mark of the self-regulated learner is when socially learned practices are implemented independently and automatically. While moving toward this end, individuals exert control over themselves and environments while moving toward mastery of self-regulatory activity.

A key feature of co-regulation is that environments are viewed as mutable, dynamic, and influenced by individual contributors. McCaslin and Burross (2011) state:

> Cultural influences set norms and challenges that define what is *probable* for persons and social and cultural institutions. *Probable is malleable* [emphasis added] nonetheless because personal and social influences can resist or work to change cultural norms and expectations. (p. 327)

Viewing the self and environment as dynamic and emerging is key for agency. Although the environment is recognized to both constrain and afford certain possibilities for behaviors and outcomes, individuals are believed to construct those environments and are believed to make choices that can shape environmental influences on individual actors and the group. In other words, individuals are presumed to already be self-regulated, and when joined with other self-regulated individuals, give form to contexts that influence thoughts and action of individual contributors and the group as a whole.

Similar to the social cognitive view of SRL, agency from a co-regulation perspective has to do with adaptive learning (McCaslin, 2009). Adaptive learning is agentic because individuals recognize that their actions influence outcomes and they can strategically direct outcomes by adjusting actions and the situation. In this sense, proponents of co-regulation believe that individuals can strategically and intentionally change themselves and their environments in order to influence academic performance.

Agency in Socially Shared Regulation

The notion of socially shared regulation refers to collective activity in which the regulatory processes and products are shared (Hadwin & Oshige, 2011). Hadwin and Oshige (2011) describe two lines of theorizing related to this perspective. The first involves an ecological understanding in which social configurations interact in reciprocal and coordinated fashion, whereby individual and social changes are both products and mechanisms of interactions. Hadwin and Oshige explain this line in the following way:

> When people set goals and take actions toward them, their behaviors are not based on individual standards, but on socially accepted notions. Their behaviors are affected by the opinions, comments, and behaviors of other people within the same social network. . . . personal goals are inseparable from social goals and are achieved through social interactions. Thus, people's behaviors are influenced by communal regulation. Even

when people self-regulate their affective modes, they also do so in a way that cultural standards allow them to do. (p. 255)

From this perspective, activities such as setting goals and self-evaluations are understood against a backdrop of institutional practices and normative standards. What is most notable about his account is that individual goals are treated as inseparable from social goals. One of the primary justifications for associating SRL with agency relates to the attribution of goals to internal sources. This perspective pushes against a neat separation between internal and external goals and opens up a line of questioning related to whether or not adopting and pursuing goals are unequivocally agentic.

The second line of theorizing highlights a collective entity and movement toward a social good. In this line of theorizing, the distinction between personal and cultural goals is dissolved more so than the line discussed above. From this view, transformations of the social practices of the entire group cannot be reduced to an analysis of what any one participant in the group does or knows. This line of thinking about socially shared regulation not only emphasizes the importance of relationships, it also speaks to the importance of the social good, which Martin (2004a, 2007) argues has been a missing element in SRL research. This view of SRL aligns in part with the notion of, what Martin (2007) calls, a communal agent.

Both lines of theorizing emphasize interdependent and collective regulatory processes that are orchestrated in service of a shared outcome (Hadwin, Järvelä, & Miller, 2011). Not unlike the concept of co-regulation, individuals are constructed as interdependent, regulated individuals. A primary difference, however, is that socially shared regulation involves a co-construction and synthesis of "strategies, monitoring, evaluation, goal-setting, planning, and belief towards shared outcomes" (Hadwin, Järvelä, & Miller, 2011, pp. 69–70). From this perspective, agency resides in the preservation of individuals as regulated beings and their capacity and opportunity to contribute to the production of shared processes and goals. Although this perspective has a great deal of promise for shifting regulatory learning theory away from internalist commitments, there are some limitations.

Maintaining the conception of individuals as self-regulated beings endorses the naturalization and decontextualization of the self and agency. In addition, socially shared regulation, as well as co-regulation, fails to account for power dynamics in the construction of so-called shared processes and outcomes. Work needs to be done to explore what "sharing" means. If sharing involves adopting processes and goals that are institutionally sanctioned and culturally prescriptive, then the association between collective action and agency is problematized. Furthermore, although theorists of co-regulation and socially shared regulation give prominence to the social in theorizing about agency and academic regulation, many of the thought processes and actions that characterize SRL from the social cognitive perspective are the same. Hadwin, Järvelä, and Miller (2011) state, "Understanding processes by which learners set goals, plan, execute, and reflectively adapt learning is a primary focus of regulated learning theory" (p. 66). Although some differences exist in relation to the ontology and mechanisms of academic regulation, researchers across accounts agree that academic regulation involves intentional and goal-directed behaviors, metacognition, and the regulation of behavior, cognition, and affect—processes and mechanisms that are presumed as preontological certainties.

Agentive Externalism: Sociocultural Constitution

Commitments to agency in co-regulation and socially shared regulation seemingly depart from agentive internalism and are reflected in what Sugarman and Sokol (2010) call "agentive externalism" (p. 5). Although agentive externalist views exist on a spectrum, they share a common commitment to construe agency as involving processes and structures that extend beyond personal physical boundaries. From this group of perspectives, agency is inseparable from interactions, context, and a historical moment. Sugarman and Sokol explain:

> The source of agency, according to the externalist view, is shared between individuals and their environments, and cannot be reduced entirely to one or the other. Thus, where internalists consider context as correlative, but nonetheless only contingent in shaping the deliberations and actions of human agents, externalists hold that context has a more profound role in providing conditions necessary for, and constitutive of, agentive choice and action. (p. 3)

The social world is not a factor that influences the direction of individuals' actions or a force to be studied and countercontrolled—an understanding that is fundamental to both social cognitive and sociocultural perspectives. Although proponents of co-regulation and socially shared regulation share some commonalities with agentive externalism, they tend to construe the social as influential and, to some degree, controllable.

Martin (2007) argues that just because social and cultural contexts assume a strong presence does not necessarily mean a departure from agentive internalism. Martin, Sugarman, and Thompson (2003) argue that "culture is more than influential communications and interactions. It consists in conceptual and symbolic systems that furnish routines, frames, and other resources for thought and action—resources that once appropriated and internalized help to constitute psychological persons" (p. 62). These authors warn against the treatment of the social as distinct and influential, and agency as an internal mechanism that mediates that influence. As Wertsch, Tulviste, and Hagstrom (1993) believe, this view of agency, the individual, and the social world makes it "difficult, if not impossible, to deal adequately with how sociocultural forces shape or constitute individuals" (p. 338).

The construal of the social world is one way that co-regulation and socially shared regulation resemble agentive internalism and limit the efficacy of these theories from adequately addressing the limitations and dangers of the social cognitive view of SRL. Like in the social cognitive perspective, there is a clear separation between the social and individual in co-regulation and socially shared regulation. As a separate and distinct entity, the social world is considered "influential" in the exercise of agency as opposed to constitutive. Some sociocultural researchers use the concept of constitutive to discuss ideas about persons, agency, and the world (Wertsch, Tulviste, & Hagstrom, 1993; Kirschner & Martin, 2010; Sugarman & Sokol, 2010). From a constitutive sociocultural perspective, psychological phenomena are made up from interactions, coordinated conduct, and historical and cultural practices. Capturing this view, Sugarman and Sokol (2010) write:

> Agentive constitution necessarily includes context, and not, as the internalist account would hold, as simply some accidental or arbitrary factor that may influence the direction of individuals' actions. The source of agency . . . is shared between individuals and their environments, and cannot be reduced entirely to one or the other. (p. 3)

From a constitutive perspective, the self, and other cognitive and motivational mechanisms, emerge from interactions among biology, historical context, and culture. Agentic capabilities are not universal, a priori characteristics of human beings. Rather, agency is made possible from our interactions with the world and is understood against a backdrop that shapes what counts as agentic actions.

Sugarman and Sokol (2010) reference the work of George Herbert Mead as an example of constitutive thinking. They state that Mead's philosophy is based on the idea that through immersion and participation in socially dynamic interactions, people "are positioned in a matrix of coordinated perspectives and come to learn and act within them with increasing psychological sophistication and complexity" (p. 6). From this perspective, individuals are socially and culturally constituted, as well as self-interpreting and self-determining. The idea of perspective is essential for this theory. Perspective means a particular role in a matrix of subject positions and not merely a mental schema. Sugarman and Sokol state, "We come to occupy, manifest, and enact perspectives first through interactivity with others who direct and support the social activities of which perspectives are part" (p. 7). Agency comes from a combination of perspectives from a reconstructed past and an anticipated future that intersect at the perspective of the immediate present. Martin and Gillespie (2010) explain:

> Recalled pasts and imagined futures are woven into our perception of immediately present situations such that we can act not on the basis of what is, but on the basis of what might be, or even, what might happen if we don't act a certain way. It is, according to Mead, by inhabiting this extended environment . . . that humans find their agency. (p. 256)

Mead does not assign rational control over behavioral, psychological, and social functioning—especially given the fact that his theory is not characterized by such fragmentation. Nor does he subscribe to static circumstances that reproduce conditions of existence. From activity and interactivity in a particular time and place, individuals emerge as agents by synthesizing perspectives and constructing possibilities for thinking and acting.

A constitutive perspective is one way to escape individual and world dualism and the oversimplification of control. However, some researchers may raise concern that a constitutive sociocultural perspective challenges an essential element of regulatory learning theory, namely that individuals through their own personal efforts can strategically influence themselves, their worlds, and learning outcomes. Butler (2002) suggests that relying too much on the social world for theorizing SRL contradicts notions such as autonomy, independence, and agency. It makes sense, therefore, that SRL researchers who draw from sociocultural theory construct a social world while construing individuals as self-regulated agents who mediate social influences and give form to environments. By holding on to that commitment, sociocultural theories of SRL resemble agentive internalism.

Another limitation of sociocultural views of agency and SRL is the absence of the consideration of power. In all concepts of regulatory learning theory, though more explicit in co-regulation and socially shared regulation, researchers emphasize the malleability and co-constitution of contexts, an important justification for agency. In influencing the environment, even if the environment is influencing oneself, one is believed to be exercising personal control because they have contributed to the production of the environment. According to proponents of co-regulation, individuals are independent SRL agents who come together with other agents to constitute an environment. Although the environment can impose constraints on agentic action, individuals can exercise control by changing themselves and the environment. These assumptions are not unlike those in the social cognitive perspective of SRL. Like the social cognitive perspective, proponents of co-regulation and socially shared regulation pay little attention to the role of power in the formation of environments (cf. McCaslin & Burross, 2011). There are three concerns: (1) individuals may only be able to influence environments in ways that are aligned with institutional mandates and norms; (2) the production of environments may merely be compliance to institutional mandates and orders; and (3) there are forces that protect and reproduce particular arrangements.

I am not suggesting that environments do not change and that individuals do not have a role. Sugarman (2011) helps to explain:

> The forms and meanings conveyed by sociocultural orders and practices are not fixed and static. They change over history. The ongoing change evinced in individual and collective life would not be possible if sociocultural structures and practices were fully determinate of human action and experience. In order for sociocultural structures and practices to change, they must be at least partially open-ended in ways that permit individuals to develop new descriptions, classifications, and possibilities for action and experience that can contribute to social and cultural transformation. (p. 21)

Sugarman suggests the mutability of oneself and the world makes agency possible. However, unlike proponents of co-regulation and socially shared regulation, Sugarman does not assign a priori agentic status to individuals. In addition, he argues that what counts as agency itself can change. Sugarman writes, "Our conceptions of agency vary in degree and type, are influenced by specific cultural conceptions, and are always open to revision and change" (pp. 21–22). This point captures a fundamental concern with agency. There are particular norms, conventions, practices, and values that give shape to particular social arrangements. The structure of these arrangements provides the basis for recognizing agency. For this reason, Sugarman does not suggest that individuals are furnished with the psychological capacity and disposition to be agentic. Rather, there are specific discourses that provide the lens to recognize actions and thoughts as agentic. Sugarman's claim aligns with a poststructural approach to the question of agency. Fendler (2010) contends that this approach is guided by two questions: (1) What are the historical circumstances that tend to favor belief in determinism and what circumstances tend to support belief in agency? (2) What effects do these beliefs (determinism and agency) have on people? These questions shift the focus away from whether or not individuals are agentic and what forces play a role in their agency. Instead, the focus is on what institutional discourses inform interpretations about what counts as agency.

Conclusion

The goal for this chapter is not to argue which treatment of agency makes sense, offer a different definition of agency, or attempt to integrate disparate views into a coherent and operational conception. Rather, the goal is to highlight assumptions and complexities related to notions of agency that inform theories of regulated learning. This exploration is important because agency remains implicit and assumed in research on SRL and divorced from its ethical, ideological, and philosophical roots. My intention is not to affirm or disaffirm the association between SRL and agency. Rather, my intention is to highlight and point out limitations and dangers of this association. For example, the discourse of SRL can heighten attention to personal control and responsibility for changing self and the environment to strategically achieve particular goals. Overstating the degree of personal control can invite student blame, personal stress, social isolation, and communal disconnectedness. Furthermore, if researchers and practitioners assume that students can exercise personal control over their learning, then pedagogical interventions that are intended to address inequality will be designed to reform individuals—an instantiation of ideological individualism. Such interventions involve shaping perceptions so that individuals recognize that what they do and think is causally related to their outcomes, helping students develop scripts to make choices that enable them to meet situational challenges, and encouraging techniques of self-study. Although these processes and practices might be conducive to school learning, there is question about whether or not they unequivocally signify agency.

As will be discussed throughout this book, making choices, pursuing goals, studying the self, and adapting to meet situational demands are features of people who function well within neoliberal environments. In this regard, those thought processes and practices that signify agency could simultaneously signify subordination to a particular economic and cultural logic.

The complexity surrounding personal control is related to the question about what counts as agency. In the discourse of SRL, what must one do and think to count as agentic? As was noted, SRL researchers contend that all individuals are agentic. Thus, if one believes that, then the question changes: what counts as the realization and exercise of agentic capabilities? The criteria associated with agency are entangled in politics, power, institutional norms, and particular ways of seeing the world. That which counts as agency is no simple or neutral matter. Although regulating learning is viewed as an expression and form of agency, I suggest that regulating learning can also run counter to agency. The arguments that I make in this book are that SRL reflects middle-class conventions, aligns with neoliberalism, and renders individuals adaptable. Therefore, regulating learning is tied to privileging one set of cultural practices, endorsing a problematic economic logic, and subordinating individuals to oppressive structures; regulating learning is not unequivocally an expression of agency. There must be a consideration of what makes it possible to construe some thoughts and behaviors as agentic, and not others.

Chapter 4
Efficiency, Productivity, and Adaptability: Neoliberal Subjectivity

Introduction

Neoliberalism increasingly shapes education policy and practice (Apple, 2006; Cavieres, 2011; Harvey, 2006; Hursh, 2000; Lakes & Carter, 2011). The central tenet of neoliberalism is a belief that all economic and social arrangements operate best when structured as if there were a free market. Therefore, objectives are to transform institutions to maximize choice, deregulate activity, and support competition. As critical theorists contend, such a structure requires a specific subjectivity (Apple, 2006; Fitzsimons, 2011; Foucault, 2008; Rose, 1998), which is referred to as an entrepreneurial self (Rose, 1998), a managerial self (Fitzsimons, 2011) or *homo economicus* (Foucault, 2008). Here, it will be referred to as the neoliberal self. This self is characterized by the commitment to maximize personal autonomy and freedom of choice in the pursuit of happiness, wisdom, success, and personal fulfillment, which are rationalized in terms of economic value. The neoliberal self is construed in terms of human capital and is guided by an ethic of efficiency and productivity. With the spread of neoliberalism in all areas of life, institutions, such as schools, are continuously transformed to inscribe and validate neoliberal selfhood.

The discourse of self-regulated learning (SRL) aligns closely with neoliberalism. The conceptualization of the neoliberal self and the self-regulating learner bear striking resemblance. SRL involves a commitment to make strategic choices in order to efficiently and productively pursue academic enhancement and to increase personal value (Boekaerts & Cascallar, 2006; Järvelä, 2011; McCaslin et al., 2006; Zimmerman, 2002). The purposes of SRL are steeped in the language of efficiency, productivity, and identity development—all features of the discourse related to neoliberal selfhood. Additionally, educational psychologists emphasize the importance of maximizing choice and control for academic success, in general, and particularly for the development and enactment of SRL. The emphasis on structuring environments to maximize choice and personal control is not unlike neoliberal efforts to produce market structures in public institutions. The discourse of SRL is aligned with a neoliberal objective to shape subjectivity in ways that enable individuals to be productive and efficient in environments that maximize choice and competition.

The discourse of neoliberalism and SRL are aligned to the degree that supporting the development and enactment of SRL is necessary for success within neoliberal environments, and the spread of neoliberal environments makes it necessary to support SRL. Entangled in neoliberal logic, the empowerment and agency that is associated with SRL is suspect because neoliberalism is a contentious ideology that is implicated in subjugating individuals to a free-market rationality, endorsing intense self-interest, eroding civic virtue, and reproducing inequality (Biesta, 2009; Briscoe, 2012; Martin, 2004a; Matusov, 2011). By articulating an alignment to neoliberalism, SRL becomes subject to similar critical scrutiny and invites critical reflections on the value of SRL for democratic engagement and student empowerment. Similar to neoliberal selfhood, SRL contradicts empowerment and civic virtue because (1) individuals must learn to manage themselves in relation to a particularly contentious logic; (2) operating within neoliberal environments requires certain kinds of discipline and constraints; (3) individuals are bound to disciplinary norms and authorities who are responsible for shaping a particular subjectivity; and (4) adherence to a particular ethic of personhood is required.

Neoliberalism and Schooling

Neoliberalism is well known as an economic logic that is underpinned by the idea that the best way to ensure prosperity and equal opportunity is to transform all economic and social arrangements to operate as a free market. Although this logic had been influential for several decades, Hursh (2000) contends that neoliberalism began to explicitly and forcefully shape educational reform in the United States following the Reagan administration's 1987 report, *A Nation at Risk* (ANR). Most significant about the ANR report was that the public education system was conceptualized as being in crisis, a caricature that largely remains unquestioned today. Establishing a crisis that puts the United States "at risk" creates panic and intensifies neoliberal reform efforts (Apple, 2006; Klein, 2007). Apple (2006) writes:

In the United States the "panic" over falling standards, dropouts, and illiteracy; the fear of violence in schools; and the concern over the destruction of traditional values have had a major effect and have led to attacks on teachers and teacher unions and to increasing support of marketisation and tighter control through centralised curricula and national testing. These fears are exacerbated and used by dominant groups in the politico-economic arena who have been able to shift the debate on education (and all things social) onto their own terrain—the terrain of *traditionalism, standardisation, productivity, marketisation, and economic needs* [emphasis added]. (p. 22)

Proponents of neoliberalism suggest that a free-market logic based on competition and freedom for innovation is needed to address the so-called crisis (i.e., achievement gap between students and standing in global rankings) in public schools.

According to neoliberal logic, an infrastructure must exist as a referee to ensure unfettered competition by maximizing choice and liberating entrepreneurial freedoms. Proponents of neoliberalism view competition as serving the common good, a logic that can be understood in relation to public charter schools. Some charter school advocates believe that traditional public schools are failing because a lack of competition renders them lethargic and centralized control stifles creativity and innovation. Public charter schools are believed to have a competitive advantage because they operate independently of centralized district control over teacher hiring, curricula decision making, and administration. The assumption is that such independence and freedom allows for innovative pedagogical programs and the structuring of an effective teaching body. Given that public schools and charter schools compete for students, and the public funding that follows them, a major assumption is that all schools are encouraged to improve academic outcomes by adopting policies or practices of charters schools, or look to surpass them by developing their own efficient, productive, and innovative curricula.

A number of contemporary school policies, practices, and reforms are underpinned by neoliberalism. Examples include the Bush administration's No Child Left Behind Act, the Obama administration's Race to the Top, and the expansion of charter schools, as well as explicit efforts to weaken and eradicate teacher unions. In addition, Lakes and Carter (2011) identify a number of products and by-products of neoliberal reforms. These include publicly supported vouchers for private school tuition, high-stakes standardized testing, public and private charters, single-sex schooling, scripted curricula, the deskilling of teachers, alternative teacher training, outsourcing of tutoring, and the underfunding of public education. These practices, commitments, and reforms are rationalized as supporting global competition and economic prosperity for both the nation and individuals (Hursh, 2000; Lakes & Carter, 2011).

Hursh (2000) argues that since the time of the Reagan administration, education in the United States has been increasingly transformed to meet the competitive needs of corporations within globalized markets. Educational reform efforts, debates, and conversations are no longer about social equity, character development, or citizenship. Rather, conversations about ways schooling can best serve the economy and global competition have achieved hegemonic status (Bartlett, Frederick, Gulbrandsen, & Murillo, 2002). As President Obama (2009a) recently stated, "It's time to prepare every child, everywhere in America, to out-compete any worker, anywhere in the world." It is largely unquestioned that the primary role of schooling is to support the economy by cultivating the knowledge, skills, and dispositions that prepare students for the workforce and improve global competitiveness. Becker (1993) believes that the increasing reliance on industry enhances the value of all forms of education. He views education purely in terms of its contribution to economic growth.

If education is reformed in service of the economy, then it is essential to have an image of what that economy is or a projection of what it will be. Researchers argue that in the 21st century few occupations will require individuals to perform repetitive tasks but rather require individuals to problem solve, adapt, create, self-direct, work with others, and innovate (Ellis & Folley, 2010; Gee, 2004; Gorlewski, 2011; Walkerdine, 2003). The transmission of technical knowledge is no longer adequate, as the economy shifts rapidly and many occupations require more than the application of technical knowledge. The new requirements for functioning within contemporary environments can be grouped under 21st-century competencies (21CC) (see, e.g., Organisation for Economic Co-operation and Development [OECD] Competencies, 2005; Partnership for 21st-Century Skills [P21], 2009). The assumption is that to support a modern economy and students' ability to compete for social and economic positions, schools must cultivate 21CC. Otherwise, students may be relegated to employment with low wages, instability, and minimal benefits (Gorlewski, 2011; Walkerdine, 2003).

The Neoliberal Self

For neoliberalism to work, individuals need to embody neoliberal selfhood (Apple, 2006; Read, 2009). The neoliberal self competes in the marketplace and is driven by self-interest as rationalized through an economic logic of productivity and efficiency. The neoliberal self manages freedom of choice by calculating interests, costs and benefits, beliefs, desires, and past experiences. Rose (1998) states:

> [The neoliberal self will] make an enterprise of its life, seek to maximize its own human capital, project itself a future, and seek to shape itself in order to become that which it wishes to be. The enterprising self is thus both an active self and a calculating self, a self that calculates about itself and that acts upon itself in order to better itself. (p. 154)

Calculations of self are used to chart courses of action that are designed to achieve personal improvement and enhancement (Brown, 2003; Read, 2009; Rose, 1998). Personal evaluations, calculations, and management are necessary to maximize advantage in an environment of deregulation and choice. Neoliberal contexts favor students who have the knowledge, skills, and dispositions to evaluate and adapt themselves, make "appropriate" choices, implement plans, and take risks. Freedom of choice requires that students develop and learn to use personal and social resources to pursue a goal.

The notion of human capital is associated with neoliberal selfhood. Foucault (2008) writes, "[*Homo economicus* is an] entrepreneur of himself, being for himself his own capital, being for himself his own producer, being for himself the source of [his] earnings" (p. 226). The emphasis on human capital is one feature that distinguishes neoliberalism from other subjectivities (Fitzsimons, 2011; Read, 2009). Becker (1993) defines human capital as the knowledge, skills, values, and dispositions that enable individuals to perform functions that raise their personal value. He treats human capital as a bank account or shares of stock that are exchangeable for a monetary worth. Becker considers schooling and training to be the most important investments in human capital because of the potential for raising income and productivity. From a neoliberal perspective, individuals are construed as human capital—with schooling as a key source for its development, acquisition, and accumulation (Apple, 2006; Fitzsimons, 2011; Peters, 2001; Read, 2009; Rose, 1998).

The frameworks for 21CC are clear examples of neoliberal selfhood. According to an OECD (2005) report, a competency is "more than just knowledge and skills. It involves the ability to meet complex demands, by drawing on and mobilizing psychosocial resources (including skills and attitudes) in a particular context" (p. 4). Some of the competencies include initiation, self-direction, capacity for change (adaptability and flexibility), ability to execute (productivity resulting from self-management or the management of others), problem solving (goal-directed thinking and action), interpersonal skills (communicating with others to solve problems), and information literacy (the ability to access, analyze, evaluate, and create information). In an OECD (1988) report, ideal selfhood is described in the following way:

> An enterprising individual has a positive, flexible, and adaptable disposition towards change, seeing it as normal rather than a problem. To see change in this way an enterprising individual has a security borne of self-confidence, and is at ease when dealing with insecurity, risk, difficulty, and the unknown. An enterprising individual has the capacity to initiate creative ideas, develop them, either individually or in collaboration with others, and see them through. An enterprising individual is able, even anxious, to take responsibility and is an effective communicator, negotiator, influencer, planner, and organizer. An enterprising individual is active, confident and purposeful, not passive, uncertain, and dependent. (p. 33)

Proponents of 21st-century education contend that developing these skills is necessary to prepare students for success as future workers and citizens. In environments characterized by choice, competition, and rapid change, the neoliberal self makes strategic efforts to achieve a particular goal—one that is recognized to increase personal value. Those who adapt, innovate, create, plan, execute, and remain confident can operate within, benefit from, and take advantage of neoliberal environments.

Self-Regulated Learning and Neoliberalism: Conceptual Alignments

There are a number of points of alignment between neoliberalism and the discourse on SRL. First, the conception of the self-regulated learner resembles the neoliberal self. From this alignment, SRL can be viewed as an example of the kind of subjectivity that is required for and instrumental to neoliberal environments. Second, the purposes of SRL map onto neoliberal objectives. These purposes include efficient production, pursuit of identity, and social participation. Third, like proponents of neoliberalism, SRL researchers strongly endorse efforts to structure environments in ways that optimize opportunities for choice and personal control, which furthers the need for neoliberal subjectivity and SRL. In general, the discourse of SRL is aligned with a neoliberal objective to shape subjectivity in ways that enable individuals to act in accordance with neoliberal logic and worlds. The maximization of choice, requirement for risk taking, increase in competition, and seemingly rapid changes to the material world all create a need for SRL, which concomitantly serves as a form of subjectivity that endorses neoliberal structures.

Choice and Shifting Environments

Like proponents of neoliberalism, SRL researchers argue that environments must maximize choice and emphasize personalized learning in order to support students' academic success (e.g., Bednall & Kehoe, 2011; Dabbagh & Kitsantas, 2012; Perry, VandeKamp, Mercer, & Nordby, 2002; Zimmerman, 1998, 2002). Researchers argue that choice and personal control increase students' motivation (Bandura, 2001; Perry et al., 2002; Wolters & Taylor, 2012; Zimmerman, 1998). Cleary and Zimmerman (2004) state, "When students are given less choices about curriculum activities and are given less opportunities to assume personal responsibility, they may develop self-defeating cycles of self-motivational beliefs" (p. 537). Perry and colleagues (2002) describe choice as selecting among various learning strategies, academic materials, perspectives to advocate, with whom to work, and how to spend time. Ostensibly, choice is the availability of options, and opportunities to select among those options, in order to shape one's learning.

Zimmerman (2002) suggests that giving students choices is essential because of certain contemporary educational conditions, such as student diversity and large class sizes. With assumptions about individual learning differences, accompanied by large classes, Zimmerman reasons that it is difficult for teachers to tend to the learning needs of all students. Providing choices and opportunities for personalized learning, along with teaching students how to monitor and direct themselves, is more efficient and effective than teachers adjusting their instruction for all students. This reasoning makes sense; after all, having 30 students voluntarily monitor and direct themselves to achieve learning goals is much more efficient than a teacher making several pedagogical adjustments. Even if it were possible for teachers to meet the needs of all students through differentiation, according to Zimmerman, a key purpose of schooling is undermined as students may not develop self-regulatory skills.

Zimmerman (2002) argues that both in and outside of school, individuals are inundated with choices for possible behaviors and various technologies, such as computers, television, phones, and video games. Some researchers suggest that contemporary economic demands require individuals to be able to manage themselves by making choices that enable them to adapt to situational demands. For example, Järvelä (2011), an authority in the field, states (all emphases are added):

> As we progress into the 21st century the importance of *learning competence* is growing. At school and in their free time students are surrounded by *competing demands for their*

attention. In their working life adults experience increasingly *strong pressure to innovate and solve problems*. What, then, enables us to meet these demands? Both students at school and adults at work have to *make appropriate choices, prioritise and plan their work and lives strategically*. They need to *focus and adapt* their behaviours and actions to fit each situation's demands. *Improving academic, professional and personal efficiency* requires repeated efforts. Successful students regulate their learning. They use a repertoire of strategies—cognitive, behavioural and motivational—to guide and *enhance* their learning process toward completing academic tasks. (p. 297)

According to Järvelä, the environmental conditions and purposes for which SRL has value reflects a neoliberal world. SRL is designated as a form of engagement that supports successful functioning within environments whereby individuals work to "improve" and "enhance" all areas of their lives (academic, professional, and personal) through strategic efforts and "appropriate" choices. In order to make those choices that support innovation, problem solving, and adaptation to shifting situational demands, individuals must use a number of key processes and practices that are associated with making good choices, such as planning, strategizing, evaluating situations, self-monitoring, reflection, self-evaluation, and self-observation.

Competencies, Skills, and Dispositions for 21st-Century Environments

The logic of neoliberalism is that in competitive environments that are characterized by choices, individuals must have certain dispositions, competencies, and a cache of learning strategies. Organizations such as P21 and OECD, which operate with and endorse neoliberalism, have developed overlapping frameworks that list key 21st-Century Competencies (21CC). These competencies include problem solving, adaptability, creativity, self-direction, interpersonal management, and innovation. There is significant overlap with the neoliberal discourse of 21CC and SRL. Frameworks for 21CC and notions of SRL emphasize adaptability, self-direction and goal pursuit, and interpersonal management. Aside from paralleling 21CC, SRL can also be viewed as a skill that further supports the development of them. In these regards, SRL is deeply aligned with 21CC.

Self-Direction

In conducting an analysis of the conceptual commonalities between 21CC and SRL, Wolters (2010) contends that self-direction is the strongest link. All models of 21CC emphasize the need for individuals to set and balance their own goals, to initiate and self-direct their own activities, and to work independently. A hallmark of SRL is setting and managing goals, in addition to initiating activity that is independent of an external source. Some researchers use the notion of proactivity to capture this feature of SRL (e.g., Cleary & Zimmerman, 2004; McInerney, 2011; Zimmerman, 2000). Proaction means setting goals, evaluating tasks, and developing plans without being prompted to do so or reacting to an environmental consequence, such as a bad grade. McInerney (2011) states that SRL involves activities that "students do for themselves in a proactive way, rather than as a covert event that happens to them reactively as a result of teaching experiences; self-regulated learners are self-starters" (p. 442). Proactivity is associated with setting and seeking challenging tasks in order to improve skill and performance.

Reactivity also has a role in self-direction. Reactivity involves reflecting on environmental consequences (e.g., score on an exam) to evaluate goals and strategies (Zimmerman, 2000). That is, self-regulating learners treat feedback as valuable pieces of information that can prompt a reevaluation of themselves in order to enact changes, if necessary and desired. According to Zimmerman (2000), reactivity is a problem only when it predominates and occurs independent of proaction. The belief is that individuals must take action that is independent of external cues (e.g., teacher prompt) and consequences (e.g., bad grade); yet, they must remain attuned to external messages for information about the effectiveness of their regulatory processes and strategies.

Self-direction is conceptually aligned with neoliberalism. This alignment is clear in the emphasis on 21CC. More generally, a fundamental feature of neoliberal selfhood is self-direction (e.g., Clarke, 2005; Davies & Bansel, 2007). In neoliberal discourse, self-direction may be discussed as taking initiative. The model neoliberal citizen uses all resources and information to (1) set goals; (2) operate with as little oversight as possible; (3) respond to environmental changes; (4) commit actions to a purpose; and (5) strive for improvement. Self-direction is a fundamental element to a neoliberal logic of accountability and individual responsibility. Clarke (2005) describes the neoliberal subject as "responsibilized" (p. 447). Davies and Bansel (2007) argue that schools are continuously configured to produce highly individualized, responsibilized subjects. By "responsibilized," the authors mean that individuals are construed as accountable for their own success and failures by virtue of their choices. Those who are successful make appropriate choices for which goals to pursue, plans for actions, strategies to use, personal adjustments, and how much to persist.

Adaptation

All frameworks for 21CC emphasize the importance of being flexible and adaptable, which involves working effectively within ambiguous and shifting environments by being attuned to external demands, incorporating feedback, understanding diverse views, adjusting goals, altering strategies, and being inventive. Adaptability is a defining element of SRL (Boekaerts & Corno, 2005; Chong, 2006; Järvelä, 2011; McCaslin et al., 2006; Schunk & Zimmerman, 1997; Wolters, 2010; Zimmerman, 2002). Boekaerts and Corno (2005) state, "All theorists assume that students who self-regulate their learning . . . *adapt* [emphasis added] their thoughts, feelings, and actions as needed to affect their learning and motivation" (p. 201). To restate part of an earlier quotation, Järvelä (2011) asserts that "students . . . have to make appropriate choices, prioritise and plan their work and lives strategically. They need to focus and adapt their behaviours and actions to fit each situation's demands" (p. 297). Researchers tend to agree that effective and productive self-regulated learners do not adopt a habit or a routine set of skills or strategies, but rather respond to new learning challenges in productive ways by strategically changing tasks, task perceptions, goals, plans, beliefs, and strategies. Wolters (2010) contends that self-regulating learners adapt well because they are skilled at creating and using different forms of feedback in relation to learning tasks. In addition, he argues that these learners maintain an active and ongoing awareness of task demands, the effectiveness of learning strategies, and their progress toward task completion.

An essential requirement for neoliberalism is adaptability. As environments rapidly shift, being competitive and functional requires that individuals continuously change to meet new demands. Walkerdine (2003) describes this process as involving "self-invention" (p. 240). She states:

> It is the flexible and autonomous subject who negotiates, chooses, succeeds in the array of education and retraining forms that form the new "lifelong learning" and the "multiple career trajectories" that have replaced the linear hierarchies of the education system of the past and the jobs for life of the old economy. It is argued that these times demand a subject who is capable of constant self-invention. (p. 240)

The neoliberal self remains in constant evaluation and judgment of self in all its minute particulars in order to make adjustments to thoughts, actions, goals, and strategies that are responsive to changing situational demands. The neoliberal self is intensely attuned to the environment and its demands, and it has the wherewithal to mobilize personal resources to respond appropriately to those demands. The neoliberal self sees adaptability as a normal process rather than a problem.

Interpersonal Management

Models of 21CC stress the importance of communication and interpersonal management. This competency means that individuals must be able to work with others to achieve both common and individual goals; individuals must be able to interpret messages communicated by others and, in turn, effectively articulate their own perspectives. Working with others is a feature of those with effective self-regulated learning. Wolters (2010) writes:

> Because they [self-regulated learners] are motivated and effective at managing their environment, self-regulated learners are able to work with others in the academic context in a way that will aid them in the achievement of their personal learning goals. To the extent that it will serve to further these learning goals, SRL would include effective collaboration with others. (p. 9)

Interpersonal management can also be tied to help-seeking, which is an important skill for SRL. Effective self-regulated learners evaluate the limitations of their knowledge and skill and strategically evaluate how others can be instrumental in the pursuit of personal and shared learning goals.

Although interpersonal management connotes dialogue and mutual engagement, in neoliberal contexts there is a danger that such management can encourage individuals to strategically form relationships that serve a personal aim. The neoliberal self sees social connections and life activities as worthwhile to the extent that they are instrumentally tied to the goal of enhancing personal value and advancing a personal agenda. In this regard, other people are instruments for personal gain, competing with possibilities for solidarity and the pursuit of a social good. To illustrate, consider the importance of networking. Individuals must be strategic about where they are and how they can form relationships with those who can improve their chances of gaining access to certain social and economic positions. Cultivating interpersonal management in instrumental terms invites an intense self-interest and attention to how others can be used to serve needs, regardless of how the help might affect the help-giver, others in the context, or the reproduction of problematic social structures.

As an example of neoliberal subjectivity, 21CC are conceptually similar and compatible with SRL. Self-direction, personal responsibility, adaptability, and interpersonal management are important features of SRL, 21CC, and neoliberal subjectivity. Although Wolters (2010) contends that there are some possible points of ambiguity between 21CC and SRL, he concludes that in general these discourses are aligned. It makes sense to foster SRL in order to promote student success within neoliberal environments that require individuals to be adaptable, strategic, inventive, effective at executing plans, and collaborative.

Purposes of Self-Regulated Learning

Other points of alignment between the discourse of SRL and neoliberalism relates to the purposes. McCaslin and colleagues (2006) distinguish between SRL theoretical theses that emphasize efficient production, pursuit of self, and social participation. The first purpose combines two fundamental features of neoliberalism: efficiency and productivity. In terms of SRL, efficient production means achieving a learning goal in a designated amount of time by limiting competition to goal achievement. Pursuit of self involves forming an understanding of and asserting one's identity. Social participation involves learning how to be part of and contribute to a community. The first two purposes, more than the third, closely align with the logic of neoliberalism. However, the third purpose is steeped in language of individualism, efficiency, optimization, and effectiveness, suggesting a connection to neoliberalism as well.

Efficient Production

One of the defining features of neoliberalism, and perhaps most problematic, is the emphasis on efficiency and productivity. These notions are frequently referenced in SRL literature and reflect the clearest alignment with neoliberalism (e.g., Corno, 1986; McCaslin et al., 2006; Zimmerman, 2000). Efficiency refers to setting and prioritizing goals, staying focused on a task, ignoring competing demands, and enacting strategic behaviors—all in service of adapting to situational demands with as little misdirection, meandering, and "waste" as possible. The expansion of and access to diverse technologies requires students to prioritize activities and suppress impulses that compete with the pursuit of academic goals. For example, given the vast and distracting elements of the Internet, which has become an important source of information dissemination, students must suppress impulses to move off-task and pursue unproductive avenues. One's perceptual and navigational fields must be tightly focused with the proper monitoring mechanisms to ensure that seemingly extraneous information is ignored, while suppressing all impulses that compete with achieving a set goal.

Efficient production reflects a life ethic that is guided by instrumentalism and the economy of activity. It is about ways that everyday actions, thoughts, and activities have maximum value for achieving a particular objective. In other words, relationships and activities are valuable to the degree that they can increase personal value with as little cost as possible. This commitment ensures that behaviors, thoughts, and activities are mobilized to quickly produce an intended effect. In environments that are characterized by choice and competition—and a goal to maximize personal value—efficient production is essential.

Pursuit of Self

McCaslin and colleagues (2006) contend that a second wave of research emerged at the end of the 20th century. This wave is characterized by an emphasis on the importance of identity assertion, confirmation, and development. Researchers emphasized gathering ideas about identity, social role, strengths, weaknesses, and aspirations in order to establish one's place in the world. The assumption is that each individual will construct an identity based on experiences, choices, possible futures, and desires. McCaslin and associates argue that constructing identity is foundational to second-wave perspectives of SRL because identity furnishes individuals with the necessary self-knowledge to set goals and plan courses of action. Researchers suggest several ways to pursue the development and assertion of self. Referring back to the importance of optimizing choice, McCaslin and colleagues reason that choice enables learners to reflect on interest and self-knowledge, as well as deliberate over possible selves. That is, self is made possible by giving students choices, helping them construe their choices as indications of self, using that knowledge to perform strategic actions, and recognizing that they have personal responsibility for their outcomes.

In addition to providing choices, researchers suggest that there are formal ways to pursue and develop the self. These include assessing thoughts, behaviors, tendencies, and beliefs by using journals (e.g., Du Bois & Staley, 1997), graphs (e.g., Kitsantis & Zimmerman, 2006), logs (e.g., Zimmerman, Bonner, & Kovach, 1996), and computer technology (e.g., Azevedo, Johnson, Chauncey, & Graesser, 2011). The metaphor of the individual as a scientist who investigates oneself underpins this commitment. Individuals investigate themselves by recording and analyzing personal data, using certain techniques to change thought patterns or surroundings, and examining the data to see whether the desired change has occurred. With such knowledge, individuals are believed to develop the capacity to exert countercontrol on themselves and their environments by drawing upon a repertoire of effective thoughts and behaviors. The idea that the self is a project—something to be known, studied, and improved—directly correlates with neoliberalism.

The pursuit of self is a key goal of neoliberalism and is not mutually exclusive of efficient production. Efficiency and productivity require intense self-evaluations and judgments, as they provide the foundation for goals and for which thoughts and behaviors can support goal attainment. If individuals are required to make personal choices that efficiently and productively maximize value, they must have a firm understanding of their interests, aspirations, strengths, thoughts processes, dispositions, and weaknesses. This self-knowledge serves as a crucial resource for making strategic decisions about how to achieve a particular goal. For example, a commitment to efficient production encourages a focus on discerning individual strengths so that they can be harnessed for producing maximum benefit. Neoliberalism emphasizes a profound interiority by encouraging individuals to pursue their interests and focus on what they can do. Neoliberal selves manage choices by considering interests, beliefs, desires, and past experiences to chart courses of action designed to achieve personal improvement and enhancement (Read, 2009; Rose, 1998). The pursuit of self in neoliberal discourse is not just about the instrumentalism of self-knowledge, it is also about producing a particular kind of self. That is, the neoliberal self is, or works toward being, confident, adaptable, creative, inventive, productive, and purposeful.

Societal Participation

Societal participation, informed by sociocultural perspectives of SRL, involves contributing to a community, pursuing a shared goal, and producing shared ways of thinking. Arguably, this last purpose does not align as neatly with neoliberalism as the previous two. It is not surprising that this last purpose receives the least amount of attention in SRL literature. The misalignment between this purpose and neoliberalism stems from the emphasis on a shared communal goal, as opposed to an individualistic one. Although there is a strong emphasis on shared goals and cognition, researchers who endorse this view contend that individuals do not necessarily think the same way, form the same identity, or pursue the same objective. There is an individualist component to this purpose. McCaslin and colleagues (2006) maintain that the individuals are distinct actors who must strategically work with others to shape their environment in order to efficiently contribute to a shared purpose. Individuals recognize themselves as having distinct identities and must pursue a sense of self, but they recognize that identity as relational and embedded within a particular context.

Despite the seeming departure from neoliberal discourse, McCaslin and associates (2006) steep their language of social participation in individualism, optimization, productivity, and efficiency. For example, sociocultural perspectives of SRL invite questions about the role of environments in students' academic success. The focus on environments challenges assumptions about individual accountability and responsibility. However, McCaslin and colleagues contend that such a focus pushes researchers and educators to consider how social contexts can be optimized to support students' success. Although judgments about individuals are discouraged from this perspective, McCaslin and associates suggest that the goal is to shape environments to encourage efficient and productive pursuit of a communal goal. Although neoliberal discourse is seldom accused of focusing on the social good or a communal goal, there is concern for socially shared cognition that is underpinned by a commitment to be efficient, productive, and committed to the development of self.

Critical Reflections: Management of Self in a Neoliberal Context

The discourse of SRL aligns with, complements, and endorses neoliberalism. The emphases on self-direction, adaptability, efficiency, productivity, interpersonal management, pursuit of identity, choice, and personal enhancement bind these discourses. This association is problematic because neoliberalism is highly contentious. Educational theorists and practitioners argue that neoliberal educational policy and practice contribute to the erosion of the social, moral, and democratic fabric of United States citizenry (Apple, 2006; Biesta, 2009; Lakes & Carter, 2011; Ravitch, 2010). Apple (2006) writes:

> Behind much of these neoliberal . . . "reforms" is a clear sense of loss of control over a number of things: economic and personal security, the traditional knowledge and values that should be passed on to children, what counts as important texts and authority, and social relations of gender, race, and class in the larger society. (p. 22)

Harvey (2007) argues that instead of growth, stability, and the narrowing of income gaps, neoliberal structural arrangements continue to produce stagnation, volatility, and increased inequality. Ravitch (2010), one of the political architects of neoliberal education reform who served in the Department of Education under George H. W. Bush, has become a vocal critic of neoliberal educational policies in the last few years. She is highly suspicious of an educational reform movement focused on competition and deregulation. Ravitch has come to the conclusion that public education policy has become fundamentally undemocratic, and that vouchers, school choice, and charters do little or nothing to alter inequalities in educational performance in the face of segregation and economic inequality. Ravitch is also opposed to what she sees as a corporate-driven focus on test scores that treat students as consumers of knowledge, as she believes that the central mission of public schools should be the promotion of democratic citizenship.

Aside from broad problems with social inequalities, neoliberalism is implicated in endorsing and inscribing a self that is (1) radically internalized, self-interested, and individualistic; (2) tied instrumentality to oneself and others; (3) committed to self-enhancement; (4) rational and an autonomous chooser; and (5) calculable and intelligible (Apple, 2006; Biesta, 2009; Fitzsimons, 2011; Martin, 2007; Smith, 2011). Apple (2006) contends that the success of neoliberalism depends on shaping selfhood in this way. Critics of neoliberalism charge that this self is dehumanized, undemocratic, radically self-interested, and attuned to personal desires (Apple, 2006; Lakes, 2008; Rose, 1998). Fitzsimons (2011) links neoliberal education to a managerial philosophy that treats students as "autonomous choosers" who must be driven primarily by economic goals in the pursuit of knowledge. The student is part of a market-driven world in which the interests of enterprise are universalized. Fitzsimons argues that this educational direction is fundamentally changing and demeaning the notion of human being. He argues for a social-democratic response to (re)humanize education as well as addressing the general crisis of public service in the modern welfare state.

Aside from contributing to broad inequalities and endorsing a narrow sense of self, there are a number of contradictions in general with neoliberalism, but specifically surrounding ideas of personhood. For example, rather than freeing individuals from constraints by inscribing competencies to function within neoliberal environments, individuals are bound to a specific set of rules and techniques for everyday living that are organized around efficiency, productivity, self-direction, calculation, and personal responsibility. This contradiction can be understood by exploring issues with adaptability. The adaptable person is not free or autonomous but one who is bound to environmental configurations.

The adaptable person can be managed through psychological tools and techniques to evaluate, measure, and monitor the self, environment, and outcomes. Adaptability is supported by a discourse that is entangled in surveillance and normalization. Being adaptable entails the establishment of limitations, controls, coercion, and obligations—as well as adherence to a particular ethic of personhood—that render individuals easily inserted into neoliberal structures.

Given the association with neoliberalism, SRL is subject to similar critiques and concerns. SRL can support functioning and success within neoliberal environments. In this regard, SRL is validated. However, the association with agency and empowerment is called into serious question. Operating in seemingly free-market structures is not freedom from power but a form of discipline in which subjective capacities are constructed in narrow ways to produce manageable people. SRL does not mean autonomy from power but subjection to it. Martin and McLellan (2008) capture this issue by stating:

> In pursuing individual freedom, we may adopt technologies of the self that actually reduce our freedom. When reading representative selections from the research and intervention literature on self-regulation, one cannot help but be struck by the obvious degree of researcher and/or teacher control exercised over students' self-regulation. (p. 444)

By "technologies of the self," the authors mean the knowledge and practices of the self that enable people to govern themselves. Control over SRL is not always direct but manifests in defining and defending SRL with neoliberal emphases. To function and operate within neoliberal environments, individuals must understand themselves in particular ways and play by certain rules—ways not unlike SRL.

The Adaptive Worker

A common feature of SRL and neoliberal selfhood is adaptability, also referred to as flexibility in the literature on 21CC. Adaptability is the capacity and skill to efficiently and effectively make personal adjustments to meet situational demands. In these discourses, adaptability frees individuals from environmental determinism and enables self-driven improvements in contexts that rapidly change and increasingly provide opportunities for choice, control, and personalized learning. Adapting is believed to be self-directed and self-controlled, evidence of one's autonomy and freedom. However, there are some critical concerns. The adaptable person must (1) be attuned to environmental configurations and dependent on them for prompting actions; (2) have the knowledge, skills, and dispositions to implement appropriate personal changes; and (3) rely on others to ensure environmental demands are read appropriately and personal changes are adequate to meet those demands.

As Fendler (2001) contends, adapting is tied to various forms of self-discipline. One of them involves the discipline to remain attuned to environmental demands and to be ready to respond to them. She explains:

> The definition of flexible has come to mean response-ready and response-able; and the definition of *freedom* has come to mean the capacity and responsibility for self discipline [sic]. Obviously, response-ready cannot be an autonomous state; there must be a "stimulus" to prompt the response. In current discourses, however, the stimuli are also flexible, meaning various and changing. There is no fixed or specified source or pattern of stimuli; if there were, the corresponding subject would not have to be response-ready, just obedient to some designated authority. (p. 122)

Think about a runner at the starting line of a race. They are set, tense, and focused; they are also waiting for an environmental trigger to set them in motion. The runner is not unlike the adaptable person who is attuned to and relies on prompts for setting a course of action. Unlike races, however, prompts can change and courses of action are not well defined. However, that variability is not a condition for autonomy: cues prompt responses, configurations provide a compass to evaluate responses, and consequences invite reflections about those responses. If adaptations were not made in relation to cues and configurations, then responses may seem maladaptive, incoherent, inefficient, and willy-nilly. Although individuals may seem to independently make personal changes, they are guided by their assessments of the context to decide to act, deliberate over what to do, and figure out if what they are doing is effective.

Recognizing adaptation as dependent on an external prompt problematizes assertions about proactivity and autonomy. As Dilts (2011) argues:

> [The person] who responds systematically to modifications in the variables of the environment, appears precisely as someone manageable, someone who responds systematically to systematic modifications *artificially introduced* [emphasis added] into the environment . . . *homo economicus* will act on the environment and systematically modify its variables. (pp. 270–71)

The key term in this quotation is "artificial." Dilts suggests that authorities no longer have to govern individuals directly. Rather, they can shift and structure environments to govern from a distance, allowing for the perceived self-determination of actions, thoughts, and changes. If individuals perceive themselves as being proactive, and not obedient to some predetermined social order, then they are more likely to be motivated than when perceived to be explicitly and immediately directed by an external source (e.g., Ryan & Deci, 2000; Zimmerman, 2000).

Shifting environments to invite particular responses works only if individuals are attuned to those environments, and if they have the knowledge, skills, and dispositions to institute appropriate responses, evaluate the consequences of responses and adjust personal variables if necessary. Thus, to be proactive and adaptive requires an array of psychological supports (Fendler, 2001; Rose, 1998; Walkerdine, 2003). Being adaptable requires the use of what Rose (1998) refers to as the "psy" disciplines, which includes psychology and other disciplines that are psychologized. Regardless if certain processes and dispositions, such as adaptability, planning, help-seeking, and reflection, are naturalized, researchers agree that they must be worked on; not all individuals suppress impulses to move off task, set appropriate goals, initiate learning activity, or adapt themselves in accordance with situational demands. The tools, concepts, and techniques of psychology support efforts to teach students to adapt themselves effectively to situational demands.

Psychological Tools and Techniques: Surveillance and Normalization

Adaptability is made possible by evaluating, measuring, and monitoring the self, environment, and outcomes. Judgments are made about strengths, weaknesses, preferences, desires, beliefs, and interests. Such scrutiny is necessary to plan, evaluate the efficacy of actions and thoughts for attaining a desired goal, and responding to environmental shifts. Evaluating and calculating the self is assumed to support the management of risks, planning of appropriate courses of action, making of "good" choices, and implementation of personal changes. The underlying assumption is that self-knowledge is an essential element of adaptive skill. The tools, instruments, and language of educational psychology contribute to ways of knowing the self.

Porter (2001) contends that the Enlightenment was characterized by the emergence of the scientific study of people, in which philosophers and scientists were interested in discerning (or perhaps constructing) laws that governed thoughts, behaviors, and the production of social environments. With the production of such self-knowledge, scientific techniques, and disciplines such as psychology, some Enlightenment thinkers, for example, Immanuel Kant, believed that individuals could control themselves and give shape to their worlds. These assumptions are foundational for the neoliberal self and SRL. In these discourses, individuals are believed to be capable of knowing, studying, forming, and reforming themselves in order to produce a desired effect. Both the capability and desire to know and control oneself is treated as a natural and adaptable human function that is developed through education.

The kind of self-scrutiny that is needed for adaptation is an example of what Rose (1999) calls a "regime of visibility" (p. 136). That is, one's "inner self" must be codified and made visible using various techniques and concepts. Although a form of individualization of self, such visibility is made possible within a network of norms in which features of the self are judged in relation to institutional and disciplinary standards. In other words, concepts such as self-efficacy, metacognition, interests, and strengths are used to make selfhood intelligible and visible, and there are norms for what these should look like. Consider self-efficacy, for example. Having a high and accurate understanding of self-efficacy is essential for SRL. Bandura (1989) argues, "The stronger the perceived self-efficacy, the higher the goals that people set for themselves and the firmer their commitment to those goals" (p. 730). The logic is that if students believe that they can influence their educational outcomes, they are more likely to enact behaviors to do so and continue to seek and overcome new challenges. If students believe they cannot be successful on a specific task, social cognitive theorists reason that they will be less likely to engage with the task and persist in the face of challenge.

The accuracy of perceptions of self-efficacy is equally important for SRL. If students over- or underestimate what they can do, the result can be lack of preparation or task avoidance, respectively. Zimmerman, Bonner, and Kovach (1996) state, "Pessimism can lead to poor motivation, and over-optimism can lead to insufficient preparation" (p. 30). Inaccurate self-efficacy, whether too high or low, can also create mismanagement of learning. To support adaptable SRL, teachers, guardians, and students themselves must be aware of the importance of self-efficacy, how to measure it, what levels are appropriate, and how to support those levels. There are a number of strategies that teachers and students themselves can use to measure self-efficacy: scales, verbal interactions, behaviors, and the evaluation of predictions for performance in relation to actual outcomes. There are similar discourses surrounding the measurement, evaluation, and reformation of other psychological elements, such as identity, metacognition, strengths, weaknesses, goals, thought processes, and beliefs.

Within the educational psychology discourse of SRL, the self is compartmentalized into a number of different features, all of which must be measured, evaluated, and shaped in particular ways that support efforts to take advantage of environments that emphasize choice, efficiency, and productivity. The production of this type of self is not autonomous. Individuals are bound by the norms of disciplinary psychology, which promote a specific kind of self and self-relationship. The assumption is that individuals must study themselves as accurately as possible to measure their strengths, weaknesses, beliefs, thought processes, behaviors, desires, interests, and goals. These self-truths are not just about psychological states but also about how environments interact to shape behaviors and thoughts, and also about how thoughts and beliefs shape behaviors. Being adaptable requires intense scrutiny and construction of subjectivity using psychological tools, concepts, and techniques.

There are several issues with this type of self-relationship. Rose (1999) argues that engaging in self-scrutiny to form accurate representations renders individuals susceptible to having things done to them. Rose (1999) states, "In rendering subjectivity calculable it makes persons amenable to having things done to them—and doing things to themselves—in the name of their subjective capacities" (p. 8). For example, knowing one's level of self-efficacy makes it possible to know if an intervention is needed. Additional knowledge of individuals must be ascertained to judge which strategies might work best to shape the appropriate levels of self-efficacy that support adaptive SRL. The assumption is that the more that is known about people, the more specific and targeted (and potentially effective) the reformative practices. Although teachers can implement interventions, individuals count as proactive when they know, evaluate, monitor, and reform, if necessary, their own states.

Self-knowledge not only renders individuals amenable to having things done to them and doing things to themselves, it also works to ensure that whatever is done has maximum benefit. Foucault (1988) refers to this practice as "truth therapy." The underlying assumption of truth therapies is that individuals know exactly who they are in order to achieve a particular outcome, whether it is salvation, wisdom, educational credentials, happiness, or well-being. Truth about the self must have some basis in reality; otherwise one might not display the necessary levels of motivation, exert the right amount of effort, pursue the correct goals, or implement the right learning strategies. In some sense, self-representations are dependent on the validation and recognition of sources of authority, which is not an autonomous act. As self-perceptions and self-knowledge can be inaccurate, and the tools for self-scrutiny are appropriated from psychology, learning to accurately evaluate and measure the self requires help from others. For these reasons, Walkerdine (2003) argues that adaptability requires psychological support. The author suggests that there is a great deal of dependence on others and the environment to adapt.

Another issue with self-evaluations and self-scrutiny relates to consumption. The purpose of evaluating, measuring, and monitoring the self is to recognize incompleteness, adequacy, and inadequacy. The recognition of incompleteness and inadequacy can invite the consumption of activities and credentials to move toward a normative standard. This kind of self is what Cushman (1990) refers to as an empty self, which is a disengaged and unencumbered self that is disconnected from its historical and cultural background. It is a self that experiences a significant absence of community, tradition, and shared meaning. The empty self seeks fulfillment through consumption and the pursuit of self-interested goals. As Rose (1999) argues, any production of self is an act of violence, because certain arguments, evidence, theories, and beliefs about selfhood and reality are not allowed to enter the "true." In neoliberal contexts, Apple (2006) argues that:

> The educational task . . . is to change people's understanding of themselves as members of collective groups. Instead, to support a market economy we need to encourage everyone to think of themselves as individuals who always act in ways that maximize their own interests. (p. 23)

There is a real concern that this particular selfhood undermines civic virtue and responsibility, as well as being tied to obligations and constraints.

Although monitoring, judging, and reforming oneself is tied to humanistic concerns of responsibility, freedom, and adaptability, there is an often-ignored unintended consequence. Rose (1998) states:

> Promises of self-assertion and self-control offer each of us access to those qualities that ensured the success of those we envy. But these progressive principles are double edged. They institute, as the other side of their promises of autonomy and success, a constant self doubt [sic], a constant scrutiny and evaluation of how one performs, the construction of one's personal part in social existence as something to be calibrated and judged in its minute particulars. (p. 239)

In addition to self-doubt, Gergen (2009) contends that the examined life can produce low esteem, stress, and isolation. In her meta-analysis on anxiety and birth cohorts, Twenge (2000) validates these possibilities by suggesting that contemporarily there are more problems with anxiety than several years ago.

An important point made by Sugarman (2011) is that the visibility of psychology is not a process of making known that which already exists, but constructing the psychological phenomena through discursive acts. Sugarman argues that those who participate in the construction and management of psychological states fail to recognize how their tools, concepts, and interventions contribute to the production of those states. That is, they assume that measurements of self-efficacy, for example, are mere depictions of states that already exist, not constructions of phenomena that are made possible through concepts, instruments, and disciplinary commitments. Psychological concepts, tools for measurement, and interventions reflect a specific way to render people thinkable—a way that is not given, universal, or natural. In rendering individuals thinkable, visible, calculable, and intelligible, certain justifications and strategies for interventions are made possible.

To summarize this line of thinking, being adaptable is not unequivocally autonomous and empowering because (1) being adaptable binds individuals to situational demands and requires them to be disposed to respond to them; (2) individuals must learn to interpret and respond to those demands by relying on psychological discourse to study and scrutinize themselves; and (3) individuals must rely on consequences and authorities to learn how to evaluate and interpret their responses. Relying on the help of others to use psychological discourse to change oneself in ways that enable one to respond to environmental shifts is aligned with a neoliberal objective. Being an adaptable person is made possible by harnessing and shaping subjectivity to produce individuals who resemble the ideal neoliberal self. Theorists suggest that the adaptable person is manageable and fit for neoliberal structures (Dilts, 2011; Fendler, 2001; Walkerdine, 2003).

Efficiency and Productivity: Institutional Compliance, Dehumanization, and Social Reproduction

Adapting oneself, being flexible, and measuring and evaluating selfhood are tied to the commitment to make learning efficient and productive. Although this commitment may seem to promote humanistic practices of self-actualization and self-control, there is another way to think about it. Efficient production is primarily about promoting knowledge, skills, and dispositions that can support individuals' compliance to institutional orders and mandates (e.g., Apple, 2006; Hursh & Martina, 2003). For example, the concept of and what counts as waste makes sense only in relation to particular values and institutional structures. Ostensibly raising expectations via standardized test performance helps to produce well-defined learning goals and increases the requirement to figure out how to rapidly and effectively pursue those goals. Schools designate valid and valued learning goals and normalize timelines for achieving them. Failure to reach those benchmarks—as likely measured by some normative assessment—can direct focus on students' problems with their self-management. Hence, the increase interest in research on supporting students' ability to regulate learning. Efficient production in schools may be understood as a commitment to achieve institutionally validated standards; activities, thoughts, and behaviors that do not support these objectives can be designated as wasteful. The ethic of efficiency, designated learning goals, or timelines are not viewed as a source of educational problems but rather students' ability to exercise the appropriate self-management.

On a related point, efficient production is underpinned by an intensely rational view of learning whereby individuals unequivocally know what activities, experiences, knowledge, thoughts, and behaviors can lead to the attainment of a particular goal. Efficient production is about making choices, suppressing impulses, implementing strategies, and evaluating oneself in order to ensure a learning goal is met. A key assumption of this commitment is that students can know what is needed to attain a learning goal, or at least they must remain constantly evaluative of themselves in order to make judgments about their movement toward goal achievement. Even if students could exercise the kind of self-management that makes efficient production possible, there is a question about whether learning should be this way. Navigating ideas in unpredictable and unprotected ways can store the element of surprise in learning, which does not always need to be efficiently pursued. Serendipity in learning competes with efficient production because direction may not always be well defined, a strategic rationalization does not underpin learning, what counts as waste becomes fuzzy, and a preset time does not constrain the learning activity. A certain amount of caution must accompany a commitment to serendipity, as if it were something controllable. With the value of creativity and innovation in 21CC frameworks, as well as the value of risk taking and entrepreneurialism, it seems reasonable that in a neoliberal climate, policymakers, researchers, and educators will strategically seek to structure learning environments to manufacture serendipitous experiences.

Another issue with efficiency and productivity relates to a social efficiency model of education, which is closely aligned with neoliberalism. Historically, social efficiency models of education were based on the transmission of the kinds of technical knowledge that were deemed appropriate for certain socioeconomic positions. The assumption underpinning this model is that society has diverse needs and must have people to fill those needs. It is inefficient to train all individuals for the same social and economic positions. Thus, people need certain kinds of knowledge and skills in order to function well within a particular social and economic order. This model makes sense in an ethos in which education is primarily an economic instrument. Today, some researchers and policymakers suggest that in the 21st century, individuals across all strata require similar kinds of knowledge, skills, and dispositions—albeit they are not being taught across strata. Notwithstanding calls to homogenize educational objectives, individuals continue to be exposed to hidden and explicit curricula that prepare them for different rungs of society (Anyon, 1981; Bernstein, 1971; Bowles & Gintis, 1976; Finn, 2009; Gorlewski, 2011; Journell, 2011; Miller, Heafner & Massey, 2009; Willis, 1977).

Some believe that all individuals have the opportunities to learn and demonstrate their mastery of the kinds of knowledge and skills that are required for positions with high economic compensation and social prestige. A fundamental assumption is that there are no direct oppressive regimes that limit students' opportunities to compete for particular positions—a view of schooling and society known as "meritocracy." Those who believe in meritocracy assume that schools first socialize individuals and then sort them according to merit. If this caricature of schooling is correct, then SRL can be a means to level the playing field. If no direct oppressive regimes are limiting opportunity, then students must learn the skills and techniques to master school learning, which will open up opportunity for them. Being efficient can support the attainment of learning objectives, and qualify individuals to compete with others.

Researchers repeatedly problematize the characterization of schooling as a meritocracy.

Bowles and Gintis (1976) argue that schools socialize individuals to function within their respective and expected socioeconomic positions. They characterize school as a disciplining body that controls and modifies the behavior of certain classes of children to produce a subordinate work force and a managerial class. They suggest that the class to which individuals are born will shape the quality of their education and ultimately decide which positions they will be socialized to fill. In this regard, schooling is reproductive in different ways for individuals across social class backgrounds. It is reproductive because individuals are exposed to implicit and explicit curricula and pedagogy that are associated with particular social and economic positions. For example, Anyon (1981) observed that children attending a school primarily comprised of working-class youth were exposed to curriculum and pedagogy that emphasized acquiring facts and simple skills, which were to be memorized, not analyzed or used for analysis. Knowledge consisted of fragmented facts that were isolated from context and wide bodies of meaning and activity. Additionally, there was an emphasis on technical procedures. Researchers continue to make these types of observations, and conclude that children from working-class backgrounds are exposed to curricula that emphasize discipline (i.e., following rules), performance goals (i.e., a focus on products and not processes), rote procedures, and conformity (Finn, 2009; Gorlewski, 2011; Miller, Heafner, & Massey, 2009; Willis, 1977). In Anyon's research study, schools that served students from affluent and elite backgrounds had curricula centered on promoting autonomous thinking, creative projects, personal development, and producing knowledge through discovery and direct experience.

Despite efforts to homogenize curricula as a way to level the playing field, individuals continue to be exposed to curricula and practice that reproduce class position. Considering the reproductive role of schooling, SRL becomes suspect. If schools serving children from working-class backgrounds are focused on obedience, receiving monetary incentives for work, and thinking in basic ways, then fostering SRL can be tied to the rapid and efficient operation of power by creating people who can be good workers. Neoliberalism is associated with the increased militarization of schools that serve individuals from economically disadvantaged backgrounds. The assumptions are that students do not have the professionalism, discipline, and work ethic to succeed in neoliberal worlds. Therefore, certain pedagogical practices are adopted—under the guise of social justice—that focus on disciplining individuals to follow orders, adhere to neoliberal institutional mandates, and perform rote tasks. Integrating SRL into this educational structure may only serve to shift surveillance techniques to individuals to exercise militaristic discipline on themselves, realize neoliberal objectives, and become workers who do not need oversight. Also socialized in accordance with an economic hierarchy, individuals from middle and upper classes may learn to regulate themselves in ways that are well suited for managerial positions. Given curricula differences, a danger of institutionalizing SRL is that it can be an efficient and productive way to reproduce a social and economic order by enlisting individuals in their own subjection to a hierarchical order.

Conclusion

Although some theorists trace the emergence of neoliberalism to the mid-20th century, the 1980s mark a significant thrust of neoliberal reform, especially in the area of education. It is not surprising that also during this time SRL emerged as an object of study. As the last couple of decades have witnessed an increased attention to SRL, neoliberal reform efforts have increasingly shaped education. From a self-regulation standpoint, this concurrence makes sense because in neoliberal educational environments in which choice, personal management, problem solving, innovation, and risk taking are valued, SRL can support academic success. Thus, in reference to a new social and economic world—a neoliberal one at that—SRL has strong appeal as a pedagogical goal, student outcome, and means for achieving personal goals. Although SRL is viewed as a source of empowerment and agency, the association with neoliberalism provides ways to reflect on how SRL is entangled in a set of problematic rules for living. One of the concerns related to neoliberalism is that the conditions of freedom entail the establishment of limitations, controls, forms of coercion, and obligations.

In addition, neoliberalism has been implicated in the erosion of civic responsibility, intensifying individual interest, producing workers that fit within modern corporate structures, and limiting the possibilities for personhood. Critical theorists suggest that one of the most effective forms of power involves the solicitation of people's voluntary participation in efforts to mold them into the right kinds of people. In the case of SRL and neoliberalism, individuals must be molded to be self-sufficient, self-interested, strategic, and adaptable. SRL is entangled in a form of government in which the logic is to harness self-regulatory capacities and mold them in ways that align with a neoliberal goal. Contrary to the discourse of SRL and neoliberalism, the regulation of learning does not mean autonomy from power, but subjection to it.

Chapter 5
Social Class in Self-Regulated Learning

> Until models of human learning and motivation are developed and validated with students from a range of economic backgrounds, we risk being unable to inform the development of appropriate educational practices for a large percentage of our population. (Murdock, 2000, p. 113)

Introduction

There tends to be an absence of social class in conversations about self-regulated learning (SRL) (Martin, 2004a). Typically considered a universal human characteristic of which all individuals are capable and attempt to enact, SRL researchers suggest that there is nothing historical, social, or cultural about setting goals and employing strategic action to achieve those goals. Therefore, conceptions of and pedagogical models for supporting SRL are intended to apply across social classifications and realities. However, by comparing research on children and guardians from working- and middle-class backgrounds, the discourse related to SRL can be implicated in class-based discrimination. There are two foci of this analysis: guardian involvement in SRL development and characteristics of effective SRL. The form of guardian involvement and conditions of home environments that are identified as necessary to support SRL development resemble middle-class homes. The second focus relates to representations of effective SRL. That which counts as effective academic self-regulation in contemporary educational environments reflects the knowledge, skills, and dispositions associated with middle-class children. I suggest that the discourse of SRL aligns with middle-class norms, economic conditions, practices, and values for selfhood. Thus, teaching and rewarding SRL in the classroom has the danger of marginalizing and disadvantaging individuals from working-class backgrounds.

By analyzing an alignment between middle-class conventions and SRL, I do not intend to invite or encourage deficit thinking. It is a mistake to conclude that working-class children lack the necessary knowledge, skills, and dispositions to self-regulate their learning. It is also a mistake to conclude that working-class guardians lack the necessary knowledge, skills, and dispositions to support their children's SRL. Further, I do not suggest that guardians and children from working-class backgrounds need to change; teaching SRL may just be another way to propagate middle-class norms. My intention is to invite a conversation not about whether individuals across class backgrounds are self-regulated but about how the discourse on SRL is entangled in class norms, assumptions, and practices.

This analysis is important because it reveals another way in which schooling environments that are structured to teach SRL can contribute to the protection and maintenance of schooling as a middle-class enterprise. For working-class children, schooling can be a site of misfortune and violence, which can play out in subtle and unintended ways (e.g., Fine & Burns, 2003; Gorlewski, 2011; Willis, 1977). The point of this analysis is to expose class norms in the discourse on SRL and illuminate ways it contributes to a set of institutional rules that maintain middle-class advantage and perpetuate misfortune.

Socioeconomic Class

Although class is part of everyday discourse, there is not always agreement about what it is and whether or not it is relevant in contemporary conversations about opportunity. Notwithstanding, researchers continue to illustrate the relevance of class for shaping experiences with schooling (e.g., Bourdieu & Passeron, 1990; Brantlinger, 2003; Fine & Burns, 2003; Gorlewski, 2011; Hardaway & McLoyd, 2009; Hill & Torres, 2010; Weis, 2004; Wright, 2008). The notion of class is defined as the identity of a group of individuals that exists in a matrix and is constituted in relation to material worlds and everyday practices (Bourdieu & Passeron, 1990; Gorlewski, 2011; Weis, 2004; Wright, 2008). Class designates identity, practices, tastes, desires, and aspirations, which are tied to economic conditions such as property ownership, income, ownership of assets, consumptive patterns, consumptive power, and labor power (i.e., skills and expertise). Class is not only what people have (e.g., income, homes, and degrees), but also what they do, consume, believe, and desire. The assumption is that those with similar material circumstances share motivational, cognitive, behavioral, and psychological characteristics (e.g., Bernstein, 1971; Bourdieu,

1977, 1984; Brice-Heath, 1983; Lareau, 2003; Luttrell, 1989; Schutz, 2008; Weis, 2004).

Bourdieu (1984) uses three concepts in his theory of capital to explain this understanding of class: cultural capital, social capital, and habitus. Cultural capital is the knowledge and skills that are exchanged for material and immaterial goods. For example, Brice-Heath (1983) associates specific language practices, such as choice of words, logic of expression, and accent, with individuals from specific class backgrounds. She argues that within schools certain ways of speaking—ones that reflect white middle-class conventions—have value and can be exchanged for grades. In general, researchers contend that middle-class cultural capital is valued, rewarded, and validated in schools (Bernstein; 1971; Brantlinger, 2003; Gorlewski, 2011; Lareau, 2003; Willis, 1977). Social capital is the resources that exist within networks and to which individuals who by virtue of their membership in the network have access (Coleman, 1988; Bourdieu, 1984; Putnam, 2001). Similar to cultural capital, the contents of and the available resources within networks are shaped by class. For example, a network of individuals may have power over employment, information about organizations, and knowledge of schooling. Those who are members of this network have access to those resources. Social capital can shape the accumulation of cultural capital and vice versa. The notion of disposition is well suited to understand the habitus (Bourdieu, 2004). Bourdieu (2004) defines disposition as "an organizing action, with a meaning close to that of words such as structure; it also designates a way of being, a habitual state (especially of the body) and, in particular, a predisposition, tendency, propensity, or inclination" (p. 214). According to Bourdieu, there is homogeneity in class habitus without any direct, explicit, or intentional coordination of practice. That is, there is regularity in the dispositions of those individuals who share similar material realities without a central social force orchestrating that regularity.

Although particular forms of social capital, cultural capital, and habitus are associated with class groups, categorization is messy. Schutz (2008) identifies several challenges with class categorization: (1) there are shifts in occupational structures; (2) groups are fragmented; (3) there is social and economic movement; (4) class may not constitute an essential identity; and (5) individuals may not neatly fit into one particular category. Schutz warns that too often class categories refer to neatly packaged systems of values, beliefs, dispositions, and knowledge. Therefore, not unlike some sociological and philosophical traditions, critical approaches in educational psychology are cautious of oversimplifying, homogenizing, and essentializing group and individual characteristics. Notwithstanding, the importance of research on class cannot be overstated.

As a result of the complexities with grouping, Weber (1997) proposes a theory of ideal types. Explaining this concept, Schutz (2008) states, "[Ideal types] draw together a set of related social tendencies into a coherent model [because] class categories exist nowhere in the world in any 'pure' form" (p. 408). The class categories mainly referred to in this analysis are middle-class and working-class, as there is a great deal of scholarship that describes features of these groups. Schutz (2008) states that those individuals who are likely to be categorized as middle-class are professionals, managers, and analysts, and, in general, people who operate independently within and outside the major corporations that dominate economic life. Lareau (2000) states that teachers, lawyers, doctors, professors, and computer technicians, to name a few, are some middle-class occupations. The middle-class can also include those with economic security, home ownership, and college degrees (Bullock & Limbert, 2009; Wright, 2008).

Those who occupy skilled labor positions are likely to be characterized as working-class (Schutz, 2008). These positions can include industrial jobs, such as manufacturing, construction, industrial transport, and even lower-level administrative positions. Freie (2007) characterizes working-class jobs as those in which an employee has little authority or autonomy at work. This parallels some of the criteria used in the characterization of jobs governed by the federal Fair Labor Standards Act as either exempt or nonexempt, such as many of those that fall outside of management and professional occupations. Although those from the working-class are typically thought about as not having a tertiary degree, individuals in these positions have credentials and specialization that are earned on the job and from technical school. There is also some measure of job security compared to many service jobs, even if only due to union affiliation.

By using middle- and working-class groups as ideal types to capture dispositions, knowledge, and skills it is possible to detect class-based norms, conventions, and values within the discourse of SRL. In particular, the conditions recognized as important for SRL development and features of self-regulating learners map onto the middle-class. To restate, I am not suggesting that working-class guardians cannot foster SRL or that working-class children cannot regulate their learning. In agreement with Hadwin (2012), all individuals have the opportunity to regulate their learning by drawing on their experiences, cultural practices, dispositions, and knowledge. However, that which is recognized as effective SRL for schooling aligns with features of middle-class people.

In this regard, the literature on SRL endorses and aligns the middle-class, making explicit efforts to teach SRL a component of class-based discrimination.

Guardian Involvement, Self-Regulated Learning Development, and Class

I use the term "guardian" to be inclusive of diverse familial configurations. A child's guardian is not necessarily his or her biological parent, but typically assumes the majority of responsibility associated with raising the child. It is well documented that guardians play an important role in their children's academic success. Among many ways to influence academic success, researchers suggest that guardians play a key role in the development and enactment of students' SRL (e.g., Corno & Xu, 2004; Huang & Prochner, 2004; Martinez-Pons, 2002; Neitzel & Stright, 2003; Perry, Nordby, & VandeKamp, 2003; Strage, 1998; Swalander & Karin, 2007; Zimmerman, 1998). In this literature, researchers identify specific conditions, interactions, guardian dispositions, and structures in the home that foster SRL. These include, but are not limited to, working with teachers to cultivate school-valued capital, modeling self-regulatory learning behaviors, adopting authoritative parenting, and evaluating and measuring children's emotions, beliefs, and thought processes.

This research is significant because it is well documented that guardians from certain class backgrounds have specific knowledge, skills, dispositions, and material realities that shape their involvement in children's schooling (Brice-Heath, 1983; Kusserow, 2004; Lareau, 2000, 2003; Lee & Bowen, 2006; Schutz, 2008; Lamont, 2000; Linkon, 1999). By juxtaposing the literature on SRL development and class differences in guardian involvement, it is possible to align middle-class home conditions, guardian and child interactions, and guardian dispositions with SRL development.

Self-Regulated Learning Development

Researchers argue that classroom instruction alone is insufficient to foster SRL (Cleary & Zimmerman, 2004; Martinez-Pons, 2002; Stoeger & Ziegler, 2011; Zimmerman, 1998). Zimmerman, Bonner, and Kovach (1996) argue that SRL instruction works best when conducted in broad contexts. They suggest that SRL development not only requires the support of teachers across grade levels and suitable curricula but also home practices that are appropriately aligned with school activities. Stoeger and Ziegler (2011) state, "To maximize students' self-regulated learning, it is important to carry out training in home settings as well as in regular classrooms. When self-regulation occurs in both of these places it increases their likelihood of transfer" (p. 88). Researchers emphasize the importance of enlisting guardians in cultivating the knowledge, skills, and dispositions necessary for their children's SRL at school and for school-related activities.

Researchers suggest that there are specific conditions, practices, and interactions that contribute to the development of SRL in the home. For example, guardians who consistently work with their children on homework are said to invite key self-regulatory behaviors and processes, such as managing work space, monitoring and controlling emotions, controlling impulses, and self-motivating (Xu & Corno, 2003, 2006). A correlation is made between family help with homework and important self-regulatory processes and conditions. Although important, homework support is insufficient for fostering SRL. Researchers argue that there must be certain types of interactions between guardians and children during homework and other events surrounding school learning.

In SRL literature, guardians who work with children on academic tasks in ways that are responsive (Salonen, Lepola, & Vauras, 2007), adaptable (Mattanah, Pratt, Cowan, & Cowan, 2005), warm (Pino-Pasternak, Whitebread, &Tolmie, 2010), and democratic (Steinberg, Lamborn, Dornbusch, & Darling, 1992) are likely to promote behaviors and psychological conditions that are associated with SRL. These features of guardian interactions are associated with an authoritative parenting style, which is explicitly associated with SRL (Puustinen, Lyyra, Metsäpelto, & Pulkkinen, 2008; Steinberg, Mounts, Lamborn, & Dornbusch, 1991). Describing the ways in which this style is of benefit to girls, Puustinen, Lyyra, Metsäpelto, and Pulkkinen (2008) state:

> It appears as if a warm, child-centered parenting style contributes to the development of emotionally stable and self-confident girls who dare to face difficult problem-solving tasks calmly: they do not hesitate to take time to think about the problems by themselves before deciding to ask for help, and when seeking assistance, they do not ask questions that avoid the problem-solving situation (i.e., ready-made answers, irrelevant questions) or that reflect a lack of self-confidence (i.e., confirmations). (p. 168)

Although these researchers focus on girls, educational psychologists argue that authoritative parenting, as opposed to passive or authoritarian, is likely to foster those dispositions, behaviors, self-perceptions, and thought processes that are associated with SRL.

As part of this parenting style, Pino-Pasternak, Whitebread, and Tolmie (2010) argue that guardians use scaffolding to either decrease or increase task challenges in ways that are responsive to children's affect while balancing the requirements of school tasks. These kinds of interactions are like an orchestrated dance in which evaluations of children and tasks are conducted in order to strategically adjust interactions in ways that support task completion while preserving particular psychological states, such as high self-efficacy, interest, and motivation. Making a similar argument, Stright, Neitzel, Sears, and Hoke-Sinex (2001) argue that guardians who evaluate their children's learning needs and provide instructions in flexible steps promote effective self-regulatory help-seeking behaviors. From these research studies, supporting SRL in the home involves guardians evaluating children's psychological characteristics concomitant with task conditions in order to design and adapt interactions that are designed to support learning objectives.

Although researchers identify guardians as an important source for SRL, they argue that not all guardians understand the importance of SRL for schooling, rely on practices to support this engagement, or have knowledge of strategic learning techniques (Corno, 1989; Perry, Nordby, & VandeKamp, 2003). This claim led Corno (1989) to suggest that guardians need to become informed about SRL classrooms. Echoing this idea, Perry, Nordby, and VandeKamp (2003) note, "For some parents and students, high-SRL teaching practices are unfamiliar. They need to learn the routines and participation structures in high-SRL classrooms" (p. 320). These statements point to the importance for guardians to have familiarity with a particular kind of classroom structure and for them to be able to support this structure in the home. That is, they endorse the ideas that structural continuity between home and school is needed to support SRL. To gain familiarity with SRL classrooms and structure home environments accordingly, guardians need to have relationships with others who have that knowledge.

In addition to learning about and supporting SRL classrooms, Martinez-Pons (2002) suggests that guardians themselves need to be self-regulated learners in order to support it in the home. Martinez-Pons contends that guardians who model and support self-regulatory behavior have children who enact similar behaviors. He describes this support as the "hidden curriculum of the home" (p. 128). Martinez-Pons argues that guardians' self-regulatory behaviors precede their children's development of regulatory skills. He argues that guardians need to be aware that their learning methods and problem solving strategies influence how their children study. Therefore, guardians must be explicit and intentional with their modeling of and interactions that support SRL. Martinez-Pons concludes that children who are left to develop SRL through self-discovery—without guardian support and modeling—are at a significant disadvantage.

Among other factors, researchers identify guardians and home practices as important sources of SRL. Researchers suggest that guardians foster SRL when they work with children on their homework, adopt an authoritative parenting style, model regulatory behaviors, evaluate children's psychological states, understand how to appropriately adjust tasks in relation to children's states, collaborate with teachers, learn about SRL classrooms, and structure home interactions in accordance with these classrooms. Comparing representations of middle- and working-class homes (Kusserow, 2004; Lareau, 2000, 2003; Schutz, 2008), the guardian dispositions, patterns of interactions, types of interactions, and home conditions that are associated with SRL development validate middle-class conventions and realities.

Class-Based Guardian Dispositions and Home Conditions

Researchers observe differences in commitments to child rearing across class groups (Kusserow, 2004; Lareau, 2000, 2003; Schutz, 2008). Lareau (2003) characterizes middle-class child rearing as guided by concerted cultivation, which is a commitment to support the development of school-related knowledge and the acquisition of credentials that are valued and rewarded in schools. Colloquially, this kind of involvement can be referred to as "helicopter parenting," as guardians are characterized as "hovering over" their children. Those who are committed to concerted cultivation work with others by enlisting their children in a variety of curricular and extracurricular activities, such as sports teams and afterschool classes, including music, dance, art, and swimming, that support academically based cognitive socialization. Guardians who are committed to this logic use every opportunity to teach their children the knowledge, skills, and dispositions that are rewarded, validated, and valued in schools. For middle-class guardians, concerted cultivation is part of the habitus of everyday life (Lareau, 2003). As part of this cultural logic, researchers assert that guardians reason with children, ask their opinions, continuously assess their talents and skills, intervene on their behalf, and make deliberate and sustained efforts to stimulate their children's development (Lareau, 2003; Schutz, 2008).

Inherent in and necessary for the logic of concerted cultivation is fluidity and continuity between home and school spheres, another feature of middle-class homes (Lareau, 2000; Schutz, 2008). Guardians from middle-class backgrounds dissolve boundaries between home and school by actively shaping these spheres in ways that produce consistency and continuity. They work to ensure that the knowledge, activities, and forms of engagement across home and school are complementary and similar. Researchers suggest that such fluidity is made possible because of occupational conditions, educational history, dispositions, and perceptions. In terms of the former, Lareau (2000, 2003) observes that middle-class guardians bring their work home, and by the nature of their occupations, they have opportunities to model organization, time management, and perseverance. Occupational conditions serve as a model for school and home relationships and provide guardians with the opportunity to model self-regulatory strategies. Lareau (2000) argues that the dissolution between home and school is also made possible because of educational history and guardian perceptions. Middle-class guardians may be familiar with the discourse of schooling and, therefore, be comfortable with supporting and cultivating school learning.

Dissolving the boundaries between home and school is also made possible by social networks. Researchers observe that middle-class guardians tend to have networks comprised of school personnel and other guardians who have access to the kinds of cultural capital rewarded in schools (Coleman, 1988; Lareau, 2000; Schutz, 2008). Schutz (2008) notes that middle-class guardians are more likely than working-class guardians to make connections with relative strangers (e.g., teachers). Schutz adds that because middle-class guardians are considered more or less equals to those in the network, they are likely to have access to collective resources. Benefitting from the resources of a network requires others to concede to membership and when others expect reciprocal benefit in the network.

Lareau (2003) observes that in contrast to middle-class families, guardians from working-class backgrounds organize their child rearing around what she calls "natural growth," which she characterizes as a laissez-faire commitment to cognitive development. The assumption is that children's cognitive development will naturally unfold. According to Lareau, this means that as long as children have food, shelter, and comfort, their development is viewed as "unfolding spontaneously" (p. 238). From this logic, children's academic development is not viewed as a part of everyday life for which guardians are responsible. As a consequence, researchers observe that working-class children are given more autonomy during their leisure time than children from middle-class backgrounds (Lareau, 2003; Schutz, 2008). Schutz (2008) describes working-class children as engaged in more child-directed play than middle-class children.

Another characteristic of the logic of natural growth includes maintaining clear boundaries between adults and children (Lareau, 2003). This feature shapes guardian and child interactions in specific ways. Schutz (2008) notes that working-class guardians have little tolerance for "back-talk" (p. 415). Lareau (2003) observes that working-class guardians negotiate little with children. As a consequence, researchers suggest that working-class children develop neither a general sense of entitlement nor a sense that contextual conditions should and could change to meet their needs (Kusserow, 2004; Lareau, 2003; Schutz, 2008). Unlike their middle-class counterparts, working-class guardians do not treat their children as being on an equal plane.

Lareau (2000, 2003) contends that working-class families tend to treat school and home as separate spheres. The separation may involve leaving documents such as papers and report cards in school, conducting institutionally validated education between school hours, deferring schooling to professionals, reading little to or with children, valuing knowledge that is incongruent with schooling, and interacting little with school personnel. Lareau (2000) argues that the separation between home and school that characterizes families from working-class backgrounds reflects occupational structures. Lareau suggests that these guardians tend to experience little continuity between their work and homes. Lareau (2003) states, "Working-class guardians never carried out work tasks in the home. . . . Their children never observed them at home doing labor linked to their occupational success" (p. 115). Employment conditions are implicated in shoring up the boundaries between home and school. For example, Lareau (2000) argues that long, variable, and inflexible hours preclude some guardians from engaging consistently with their children in homework, attending school events, and supporting extracurricular activities. In addition, income can affect guardian involvement via transportation. Lack of access to transportation, both public and private, can preclude some guardians from meaningfully participating in their children's schooling.

Even if the boundaries between home and work for working-class guardians were fluid, the demands of employment may not necessarily require guardians to use learning strategies in the home that are related to their work. Lareau (2000, p. 115) states, "The content of the work was more routine, closely supervised, and far less complex than the labor process in upper-middle-class jobs." Therefore, guardians from working-class backgrounds may not display time management, organization, or problem solving in their homes in relation to their employment. Although Schutz (2008) disagrees with Lareau about the complexity of the labor required for working-class positions, he agrees that the quality of labor between working- and middle-class employment is implicated in variations of guardians' opportunities for cognitive socialization.

Guardians' perceptions also influence the production and maintenance of a boundary between home and school (Lareau, 2000; Purcell-Gates, 1997). As Lareau (2000) observes, working-class guardians are more likely than middle-class guardians to resist schooling involvement because of perceptions of academic competence. These guardians tend to defer education to professionals because they do not perceive themselves as having the experience or knowledge of schooling to support their children's school-based learning.

Dissimilar to middle-class families, Lareau (2003) observes that guardians from working-class backgrounds have networks comprised of kin and individuals who do not always have experience with formal schooling. Schutz (2008) contends that working-class guardians tend to form strong ties with family and those embedded in their communities. Therefore, the resources to which they have access are from others from similar socioeconomic backgrounds and who share similar histories. Teachers, administrators, and school officials are typically not included in their networks. Lareau (2000) argues that working-class guardians resist forming relationships with teachers because they do not perceive themselves as experienced enough in schooling to participate in sustained dialogue about their children's formal education.

Endorsing Middle-Class Logic, Practices, and Conditions

Research on guardian involvement and SRL development endorses, validates, and complements middle-class norms, practices, and material realities. The requirement that SRL be developed within broad, supportive, and fluid contexts favors middle-class guardians. Many of the practices, conditions, and interactions associated with supporting SRL reflect middle-class homes. These include working consistently with children on homework, developing relationships with teachers, modeling school-valued behavioral and thought processes, and evaluating children's learning needs to adjust academic interventions in the home. The expectation that guardians explicitly cultivate SRL aligns with a middle-class child rearing logic of concerted cultivation. The suggestion that guardians interact with teachers to structure their homes in accordance with SRL favors middle-class social capital. If middle-class guardians are not already fostering SRL, they may have the networks in place to learn about and have access to resources that enable them to support SRL in the home. Committed to concerted cultivation, they might do some research to find out about SRL. Middle-class guardians may end up realizing that either they have been fostering SRL all along or they can tighten up their routine.

If SRL is part of the equation for school success, and schools are channels for mobility and possibility, then enlisting guardians in the effort to develop SRL can, in theory, level the playing field. However, guardian practices and dispositions are entangled in economic and cultural conditions that complicate these assumptions. The dissolution between home and schools for middle-class families is made possible because of guardians' experience with schooling, occupational conditions, and a commitment to concerted cultivation. In addition, middle-class guardians are more likely to be familiar with the discourse of schooling and have the knowledge to evaluate their children and adjust tasks accordingly. By virtue of their occupational conditions, middle-class guardians might facilitate SRL through everyday situational demands by working in their home and modeling organization, time management, and strategies for perseverance. Given that these work habits are important for SRL, it is possible that children from a middle-class background will have observed and acquired these habits at home—a suggested precursor for developing and enacting SRL in schools. The demands and conditions of middle-class occupations lend themselves not only to dissolving the boundaries between home and schools but also to encouraging guardians to model valued and rewarded forms of self-regulatory behaviors.

Adopting the strategies, dispositions, and networks to support SRL in the home may be difficult for working-class guardians. It may not always be possible for working-class guardians to dissolve boundaries, form certain networks, familiarize themselves with the discourse of schooling, and evaluate their children using psychological tools. Spontaneous expansions and alterations of social and cultural networks are not always possible. Social capital is tied to occupational conditions, personal history, geography, and education level (Bourdieu, 1984; Coleman, 1988). Networks are formed and expanded based upon reciprocity and trust. Benefitting from the resources of any given network requires others conceding to group membership (Putnam, 2001). Requiring guardians to learn about SRL classrooms can privilege middle-class families because the necessary social relationships across home and school may already be in place. Forming new networks may also mean changing perceptions about academic competence and the role of guardians in formal schooling. If SRL is taught, valued, and rewarded in schools and SRL development requires guardian involvement, then working-class guardians are at a disadvantage, one that might be difficult to overcome.

Characteristics of Self-Regulated Learning

Although researchers argue that SRL is a universal human characteristic, representations of effective SRL map onto features of middle-class children. I draw from a number of research studies in order to construct profiles of middle- and working-class children. The foci are self and personhood, help-seeking, and goal orientations, which are important components of SRL. The conception of self that underpins SRL aligns with the self that is endorsed in middle-class homes and embodied by middle-class children. Likewise, the form of help-seeking that is recognized as self-regulatory aligns with and complements the behavioral dispositions of children from the middle-class. Finally, children from middle-class backgrounds have certain opportunities and experiences that invite a mastery goal orientation, which is correlated with effective SRL.

Selfhood, Class, and Self-Regulated Learning

The Selves of Self-Regulated Learning

The self is an essential component to conceptions of SRL, even in co-regulated and socially shared regulated learning. Yet, few researchers explicitly consider the assumptions of self that underpin the literature on regulatory learning (Martin & McLellan, 2008). The lack of attention is problematic given that conceptions of self in SRL are in line with those fostered in middle-class children. Martin (2007) argues that there is a common conception of self across the various accounts of regulatory learning theory. He states:

> The self that lies behind research . . . on self-regulation . . . is an inner bastion of individual experience and existence that surveys the exterior landscape for *signs of affirmation and possibilities for expression* [emphasis added] on the one hand, and *clues to strategic action* [emphasis added] on the other. Its most vital resources are located within itself, as it acts as final arbiter over whether or not its strategies are effective or its appraisals self-sustaining. Academic tasks and social experience both can be accomplished and controlled by this *masterful* [emphasis in original] self's attention to its own basic organismic tendencies and potentials, and/or its metacognitive, strategic ruminations. (p. 82)

In this quotation, Martin alludes to two types of self that are naturalized in and foundational to SRL, expressive and scientific. The latter is oriented toward self-mastery through its commitment to understand its psychological characteristics and employing strategies to harness or change itself in the pursuit of personal goals. This self is called scientific because it is characterized by a commitment to study and control thoughts and behaviors for the purpose of personal improvement. The expressive self is guided by the imperative to identify the uniqueness and importance of emotional experiences. This self is called expressive because it is guided by a commitment to identify, validate, develop, and express psychological states. Not unlike the scientific self, the expressive self is orientated toward self-improvement, but with a humanistic rationalization.

The expressive and managerial selves both implicitly and explicitly underpin the conceptions of SRL. The scientific self is clearly foundational for SRL. The importance of the expressive self is less obvious but equally important. One of the primary purposes of SRL is the pursuit of self and identity, which means learning about who one is and taking action to assert that identity within learning contexts (McCaslin et al., 2006). To regulate learning requires individuals to construct and express their unique qualities and characteristics, and use that information to achieve personal goals. The logic is that to know the self is to be able to control the self.

Although these features of selfhood are naturalized within and underpin the discourse of SRL, a foundational assumption in this book is that the self is constituted and reflects a particular kind of understanding. Treating the self as constitutive means that it forms and continuously evolves as a result of interactions between biology, history, culture, and politics (Martin & Sugarman, 2001; Mead, 1934). Thinking about the self as constitutive makes it possible to conceive of a self that can take different forms in relation to a number of class-related factors, such as occupational conditions, material constraints, culture, geography, history, and community. Researchers contend that there are different kinds of self across middle- and working-class backgrounds (Bourdieu & Passeron, 1990; Delpit, 1996; Jackson, Mackenzie, & Hobfoll, 2000; Kusserow, 2004; Lareau, 2003; Schutz, 2008). The conception of self that characterizes middle-class culture is self-interested, unique, expressive, individualistic, and managerial; whereas, the self of working-class culture is socially mediated, tough, resistant, and action based. Considering this distinction, the conception of self that underpins SRL complements and validates the self of middle-class children.

Class-Based Conceptions and Practices of Selfhood

Researchers observe that soft individualism is the province of middle-class families (Kusserow, 2004; Schutz, 2008). Kusserow (2004) describes soft individualism as encouraging self-expression, pursuing self-interest, recognizing uniqueness, and understanding how psychological states are causally related to actions. A feature of soft individualism is that children learn to associate emotions and thoughts as responsible for setting certain behaviors in motion. Schutz (2008) affirms this picture of middle-class commitments to selfhood. He states that middle-class families celebrate children's unique characteristics and capabilities, helping them develop a sense of themselves as discrete and unique individuals. Although a clear alignment to the expressive self, middle-class selfhood is characterized by a composite of psychological features that must be monitored and controlled in ways that support the achievement of learning goals. Schutz contends that middle-class children learn at an early age to monitor themselves and use techniques of surveillance to achieve personal learning goals. Weininger and Lareau (2009) argue that middle-class guardians work closely with children to develop their dispositions and skills for this type of self-management. Consequently, Lareau (2003) asserts that in relation to schooling, middle-class children have an understanding of their learning needs and the strategies to negotiate with others to ensure their needs are met. Middle-class selfhood is constructed in relation to a number of psychological features, such as intentions, attitudes, strengths, weaknesses, and beliefs.

Schutz (2008) argues that individuals from working-class backgrounds treat the kind of self of middle-class culture as "wasteful indulgence" (p. 411). Working-class children are not oriented toward identifying and expressing their unique characteristics. They do not use psychological language to describe their actions. For example, Miller (1986) studied working-class individuals from Baltimore and contends that her participants were more likely to express themselves by stating, "I kicked the table" instead of "I was angry." Action, as opposed to psychological evaluations and descriptions, defines selfhood. In contrast to soft individualism, Kusserow (2004) argues that individuals from working-class backgrounds are committed to what she calls "hard individualism," which is characterized by protection, toughness, and action. There is a component of expression in hard individualism. However, Kusserow argues that such expression is not organized around psychological descriptions, evaluations, and measurements. Rather, expression is through the recollection of narratives that reflect personal class-based struggles. Echoing this finding, Schutz (2008) argues that because working-class children's dramatic storytelling reflects narratives about struggle and long-term relational ties, the kind of expression for working-class children is less about the unique and distinct psychological qualities of themselves, and more about one's narrative in relation to others and collective struggle.

In addition to a tough, relational, and action-oriented self, researchers describe children from working-class backgrounds as having a self that is oriented toward community and family, rather than driven by individual betterment and the pursuit of self-interested goals (Eckert, 1989; Jackson, Mackenzie, & Hobfoll, 2000; Kusserow, 2004; Schutz, 2008). Although Fine and Burns (2003) argue that it is dangerous to overstate the degree to which the self of working-class culture is community oriented, researchers contend that working-class children tend to have selves that are far more socially mediated than their middle-class counterparts (Eckert, 1989; Jackson, Mackenzie, & Hobfoll, 2000; Lareau, 2003; Schutz, 2008).

Middle-class selfhood is described as individualistic (e.g., Eckert, 1989), pushy (e.g., Walkerdine, 2003), and entitled (e.g., Lareau, 2003). In Eckert's (1989) research study comparing a group of middle- and working-class students, who were referred to as Jocks and Burnouts, respectively, she found that the former group was far more individualistic than their counterparts. Middle-class selfhood is not unlike the neoliberal self with an emphasis on personal responsibility, self-reliance, individual freedom, and competition. In competitive and individualistic environments, self-management is an important skill for maintaining and reproducing advantage. The self that characterizes working-class culture is associated with communal selfhood. The communal self recognizes itself as inseparable from the social context of its emergence. It is a social-mediated self that is committed to solidarity, civic responsibility, and democratic equality. The communal self is not primarily guided by efforts to improve itself via personal goals. Although working-class selfhood is associated with a brand of individualism, the composition of the self is more strongly tied to community then middle-class selfhood.

The selves of middle-class culture reflect expressive and managerial selves. The representation of SRL complements the kind of self that is associated with middle-class children and the self that is valued and inscribed in middle-class homes. Middle-class selfhood is characterized by commitments to self-evaluation, monitoring, and self-knowledge in the pursuit of achieving personal goals. In contexts wherein SRL is valued, individuals are expected to reflect on their beliefs, knowledge, emotions, and intentions as part of task conditions. In these contexts, middle-class children may experience congruence between their already existing self and the self that is valued in that kind of environment. Those who do not embody the selfhood that is aligned with SRL are at a disadvantage. Environments that value and validate scientific and expressive selves encourage individuals to see themselves in ways that reflect middle-class culture. Therefore, an environment that is designed to teach SRL can exclude certain ways of being, add unfair learning burdens, confuse students, create a chasm with home culture, produce personal tensions, and invite resistance to teachers and classrooms.

Help-Seeking: Negotiation and Comfort

Although arguably something that all individuals do, self-regulatory help-seeking is tied to class-specific dispositions, behaviors, self, and goals. Self-regulatory help-seeking involves (1) working independently by exhausting all resources to complete a task; (2) recognizing the limitations in personal knowledge, skill, and efficacy to complete tasks; (3) asking others only those questions that serve to facilitate progress toward independent task completion; and (4) interacting and negotiating with individuals who are seen as having the resources to complete tasks. Students must seek help only after extensive thought, reflection, and for the purpose of completing tasks on their own. Regulatory help-seeking involves psychological evaluations: what is known, what could be known through personal efforts (e.g., learning strategies, strengths, weaknesses, abilities, and capabilities), and how others could support task completion. Like selfhood, regulatory help-seeking is entangled in class as the knowledge, skills, and dispositions required for such engagement are aligned with and endorse middle-class children's behaviors, selves, dispositions, and goals.

Class-Based Patterns of Help-Seeking

Researchers observe differences in patterns of help-seeking across children from middle- and working-class backgrounds (Calarco, 2011; Lareau, 2003; Streib, 2011; Weininger & Lareau, 2009). Calarco (2011) conducted a longitudinal ethnographic study in a suburban elementary school to compare patterns of help-seeking across white middle-class and working-class students. She observed that middle-class children made more requests for help from teachers and used different strategies than did their working-class peers. Rather than wait for assistance, middle-class students called out or approached teachers directly, even interrupting to make requests. Calarco observed that those teachers valued and rewarded middle-class students' help-seeking strategies and behaviors by helping them more frequently and instantly than their working-class counterparts. Teachers also provided middle-class students with the necessary support to complete assignments. According to Calarco, teachers viewed middle-class students as proactive and engaged in the learning process.

Researchers argue middle-class guardians explicitly coach their children on the language and strategies for help-seeking (Calarco, 2011; Lareau, 2003; Streib, 2011). Resulting from concerted cultivation, Lareau (2003) argues that middle-class children develop better verbal agility, strategies for negotiation, interactive patterns with adults, and comfort when negotiating with adults than children from working-class backgrounds. Lareau asserts that middle-class children internalize the idea that it is legitimate and reasonable for others to adjust their actions to suit their preferences. Studying four-year-olds, Streib (2011) observes that children from middle-class backgrounds are more willing to speak, interrupt, and talk to adults as conversational equals than working-class children. Streib asserts that these students use these behaviors and dispositions to gain teachers' attention, improve their negotiation skills, and win the bulk of class disputes. A result, Streib contends, is that working-class preschoolers are inadvertently but effectively silenced.

On the other hand, Lareau (2003) argues that children from working-class backgrounds are less likely to negotiate with adults, operate with a sense of entitlement, and shape external conditions to meet learning needs. Weininger and Lareau (2009) contend that children from working-class backgrounds are less likely to argue with adults and more likely to silently comply with external demands than middle-class children. According to Calarco (2011), when working-class students seek help they do so in subtle ways, such as sitting back on their chairs. She contends that working-class students are less likely to approach the teacher for help than their middle-class counterparts. Streib (2011) observes that working-class children use fewer words when talking with adults, do not use language to call attention to themselves, and do not talk to adults as they talk to each other. Researchers attribute the emergence of these characteristics to disciplinary practices, status distinctions between adults and children, guardian dispositions, structures of working-class employment, and adult modeling (Calarco, 2011; Lareau, 2003; Weininger & Lareau, 2009).

Although some researchers suggest that working-class children are socialized to silently comply, others suggest that working-class children tend to resist schooling, in general, and school authorities, specifically (Anyon, 1981; Eckert,

1989; Finn, 2009; Gorlewski, 2011; MacLeod, 1987; Willis, 1977). This resistance is tied to the structure of working-class occupations, which can be characterized as struggles between managers and workers. Individuals from working-class backgrounds may operate with a sense of distrust and resistance to managers, who might be viewed as enforcers trying to exploit workers by maximizing their labor power without fair compensation. Although these relationships can shape patterns of interactions between students and teachers, there are other factors that contribute to working-class resistance to schooling. Kohl (1992) argues that resistance may not be a result of deficiencies with children from working-class backgrounds, but from challenges to personal and family loyalties, integrity, and identity. Given that schools are middle-class enterprises, working-class children are confronted with the choice of cultural preservation or academic success (Fine & Burns, 2003). The conflict with teachers, schooling, and identity can invite resistance to schooling, making it less likely that working-class students will seek help with academic tasks.

Self-Regulatory Help-Seeking and Class

There are differences in patterns of interactions across children from middle and working-class backgrounds. Self-regulatory help-seeking aligns with and endorses norms, practices, and dispositions of individuals from middle-class backgrounds. These include striving for independent and self-interested engagement, intensely scrutinizing oneself, negotiating task conditions, pursuing personal preferences, being comfortable with asking for help, and knowing how to ask for help. Middle-class guardians invite their children to reflect on their strengths, weaknesses, beliefs, and opinions. Neitzel and Stright (2003) found that when mothers provided their children with this metacognitive information, their children were likely to ask teachers for help in regulatory ways. The requirement that students monitor and measure personal conditions and states, such as knowledge, self-efficacy, goals, and strategies, to count as self-regulatory help-seeking favors middle-class children. The expressive and scientific selves can be associated with cultivating the disposition to seek help in self-regulatory ways.

Help-seeking can also be regarded as pushiness, another middle-class convention (Walkerdine, 2003). Buttressed by a sense of entitlement, middle-class children have little problem with interrupting the class and silencing others in order to support their learning. Identity, personal preferences, and perceived needs are asserted into the classroom. Although educational psychologists do not associate entitlement, negotiation, comfort, and assertiveness with SRL, these dispositions and practices can have an impact on children's help-seeking, which can be interpreted as indicative of SRL—inviting teachers to respond favorably to such behaviors. Metacognitive reflections, comfort when engaging with teachers, identity assertion, and task negotiation are foundational to self-regulatory help-seeking. Guardians' schooling interventions serve as models for children to learn the skills and dispositions to interact and negotiate with teachers to ensure their learning needs are met. Working-class guardians are less likely to collaborate and negotiate with teachers.

Another way self-regulatory help-seeking is tied to middle-class norms of selfhood relates to neoliberalism and instrumentalism. The neoliberal self, which reflects the middle-class self more than the working-class self (Lakes, 2008; Walkerdine, 2003), construes all relationships as part of a strategic endeavor to maximize the acquisition of credentials and capital. The neoliberal self sees social connections worthwhile to the extent that they are instrumentally tied to the goal of enhancing personal value. Driven by competition, self-enhancement, and the attainment of credentials, relationships are treated in instrumental terms whereby others serve personal needs. Although educational psychologists do not explicitly endorse such instrumentalism, the conditions of self-regulatory help-seeking reflect this form of engagement. That is, individuals must contemplate how others can serve their personal learning needs and employ strategies to solicit help from others in ways that enable them to achieve personal goals. This commitment reflects the self-interest that is often associated with middle-class selfhood.

Goal Orientations

Self-regulatory help-seeking also requires that individuals buy into learning tasks and are oriented toward task mastery. Researchers link self-regulatory help-seeking with a mastery goal orientation (Boekaerts & Corno, 2005; Greene & Azevedo, 2007; Karabenick, 2003; Newman, 1994; Perry et al., 2002). A "mastery orientation" is defined by an intrinsic interest to pursue learning for understanding and improving competence. Being mastery oriented can shape the qualities and quantities of SRL, in general, and help-seeking, in particular. My argument is that working- and middle-class children have different opportunities and choices in relation to the pursuit of academic mastery. There are socializing agents that shape individuals' relationships and orientations to schooling that make it less likely for working-class children than middle-class counterparts to pursue task mastery. That is, school curricula look different across schools serving individuals across class backgrounds. These differences can be implicated in inviting different goal orientations. In addition to curricula differences, working-class resistance to schooling can shape goal orientation. Given the importance of a mastery orientation for SRL, working-class children are less likely to pursue mastery in schools.

Mastery, Performance, and Avoidance

There are two primary classifications for goal orientation: mastery and performance. A performance orientation involves the mobilization of thoughts and behaviors in pursuit of some normative standard. Individuals with this orientation might work diligently to understand a topic in order to be seen as competent to their peers, teachers, or guardians. The focus is on the product and the social value of that product. A mastery orientation is characterized as the motivation to master tasks, display positive affect, and use solution-oriented strategies. With this orientation, individuals focus more on the process than the product. The product is important to the extent that mastery for the sake of mastery is achieved. A mastery orientation is associated with task focus, resilience, perseverance, positive self-views, and process orientation. Individuals can regulate their learning effectively with both orientations, though a mastery orientation is more highly correlated with SRL (Greene & Azevedo, 2007). There are other goal orientations that shape academic engagement; these include work-avoidance and helpless orientations. The former is characterized by motivation to avoid doing work altogether or do the least amount of work possible. The latter is characterized by a focus on personal inadequacies, lack of ability, and the display of negative affect, such as boredom and anxiety.

Educational psychologists tend to avoid treating goal orientations as stable features of individuals. The assumption is that one can operate with a mastery orientation in one context and not another. This variability is shaped by a number of factors, such as teachers, subject matter, self-efficacy beliefs, peers, academic history, and curricula. Given variations in curricula in schools across class backgrounds, students will be invited to pursue goals in different ways. Schools serving children from middle-class backgrounds are exposed to curricula that emphasize problem solving, creativity, critical thinking, and producing knowledge, as these characteristics are required for middle-class occupations. Schools serving children from working-class backgrounds emphasize rote learning, obedience, and knowledge transmission. From these differences, middle-class children are invited to pursue mastery, whereas working-class children are invited to be product oriented and learn rote procedures. Although arguably working-class children have opportunities to master tasks regardless of the curricula, the outcomes that are valued in working-class schools render a mastery orientation a means to reproduce a class hierarchy.

Curricula Differences and Mastery Orientation

Researchers continue to show that children from different class backgrounds are exposed to pedagogical conditions in the home and at school that teach the knowledge, skills, and dispositions needed for employment in their respective occupational strata (e.g., Bowles & Gintis, 1976; Finn, 2009; Gorlewski, 2011; Journell, 2011; Miller, Heafner, & Massey, 2009; Willis, 1977). Although there is variability within class groups, there are generalizable features related to occupational requirements. The conditions of employment for individuals from working-class backgrounds require complicity to authority, routine actions, and the use of external skills for material production. At the same time, working-class positions are also characterized by antagonism with authorities. In contrast, middle-class occupations are said to require emotional investment, problem solving, critical thinking, and independence (Gorlewski, 2011; Hochschild, 1979; Kusserow, 2004; Lareau, 2003). Although middle-class occupations can involve antagonism with authorities, there tends to be independence from authorities, in addition to a valorization of them. Researchers link these differences to variability in curricula and expectations for student engagement.

In one often-referenced study, Anyon (1981) compared implicit and explicit curricula across five schools serving students from different socioeconomic strata: two working-class, one middle-class, one affluent professional, and one elite. In these schools, individuals were exposed to curricula, both implicit and explicit, that reflected preparation for occupations that corresponded to their class backgrounds. In the working-class schools, the curricula and pedagogy emphasized acquiring facts and simple skills, which were to be memorized and not analyzed. Anyon contends that the texts in these schools contained less information as compared to those texts used in other schools. Learning was about technical and rote procedures, with a focus on performance outcomes. Anyon describes the curricula in the following way:

> What constitutes school knowledge here is (1) fragmented *facts*, isolated from context and connection to each other or to wider bodies of meaning, or to activity or biography of the students; and (2) knowledge of "practical" rule-governed *behaviors*—procedures

by which the students carry out tasks that are largely mechanical. Sustained conceptual or "academic" knowledge has only occasional, symbolic presence here. (p. 12)

Anyon alludes to a pattern that others have found, namely children from working-class backgrounds are exposed to curricula that emphasize discipline (i.e., following rules), performance goals, rote procedures, and conformity (Finn, 2009; Gorlewski, 2011; Journell, 2011; Miller, Heafner, & Massey, 2009). Abstract thinking and broad systems of meaning were not part of the curricula.

In schools serving students from affluent and elite backgrounds, Anyon (1981) observed that curricula were significantly different. For example, in the affluent school serving children whose parents were highly paid doctors, cardiologists, television and advertising executives, interior designers, or other affluent professionals, the curriculum centered on promoting autonomous thinking, creative projects, personal development, and producing knowledge through discovery and direct experience. In the so-called elite school, in which the majority of students' fathers in this school were vice presidents or more advanced corporate executives in multinational corporations or financial firms on Wall Street, the teachers and the curriculum stressed reasoning and problem solving. As Anyon describes, there was a theme of excellence—the necessity of preparation for being the best, for top-quality performance. Students were responsible for their work, and they felt as though they needed to know existing knowledge and to do well, to understand, explain, and answer correctly (and quickly) in order to address the most pressing problems discussed.

Researchers continue to make these kinds of observations (Finn, 2009; Gorlewski, 2011; Journell, 2011; Miller, Heafner, & Massey, 2009). The underlying assumption is that curricula differences contribute to the socialization of individuals to fill roles that correspond to their existing positions. Schooling is not alone in reproducing class position. Researchers suggest that families and communities act as integral socializing agents that prepare children for work within occupations that correspond to class position (Hochschild, 1979; Kusserow, 2004; Weininger & Lareau, 2009). Hochschild (1979) suggests that each class tends to prepare its children with the necessary skills, knowledge, and dispositions that are necessary for their expected work environments. Schutz (2008) states, "People's life histories tend to prepare them to engage more skillfully in the practices more common in their milieu or social field" (p. 413). Replicating for their children, the perceived social reality has been described as a "powerful human urge" (Kusserow, 2004, p. 93). Whether intentional or not, or from guardians or school, children are socialized in ways that reflect particular socioeconomic contexts and such socialization can shape orientations to work.

Based on these curricula and socializing differences, middle-class children may be invited to pursue mastery more than their working-class counterparts. In fact, the emphasis on rote procedures, obedience, and products is implicated in the reinforcement of working-class resistance to schooling (Miller, Heafner, & Massey, 2009). Miller, Heafner, and Massey (2009) argue that children are less likely to pursue mastery when the curriculum emphasizes obedience and rote procedures. Such curricula can communicate low expectations and students can infer negative messages about their intellectual worth. Thus, working-class children may be less likely to pursue mastery in schools. However, even if they pursued mastery of curricula goals, such an orientation may only serve to reproduce a class hierarchy as mastery may involve developing proficiency for working-class positions.

Conclusion

Although critical approaches in educational psychology are cautious of oversimplifying, homogenizing, and essentializing group and individual characteristics, there is evidence to suggest that the discourse related to SRL endorses and aligns with middle-class conventions. Therefore, teaching SRL serves as another example of the ways middle-class homes are aligned with schooling. The cognitive structure of employment, time constraints, resources for concerted cultivation, resistance to authority, curricula differences, behavioral dispositions, economic resources, child-rearing logic, and forms of selfhood are implicated in shaping different opportunities for developing and enacting SRL. Thus, if working-class children are to succeed in environments that reward, validate, value, and teach SRL, then both children and guardians must overcome limitations that result from socioeconomic conditions.

In addition to mitigating the effects of socioeconomic conditions for SRL, individuals from working-class backgrounds must recondition dispositions, alter selfhood, learn new behaviors, and acquire certain forms of knowledge. Children must embody scientific and expressive selves, help-seek in a particular way, trust teachers, and pursue mastery. Guardians must change their child-rearing logic, learn school-related knowledge, intentionally problem solve in the home, communicate with teachers, and view schooling as their responsibility. All of this occurs at the same time that children learn academic content. Although arguably all children can benefit from SRL instruction (Winne, 2005), there are features of working-class subjectivity that are not complementary and in alignment with SRL. Thus, regulating one's learning in schools may require a fundamental shift in cultural identity for individuals from working-class backgrounds.

The expectation to mediate socioeconomic conditions and reshape subjectivity in order to support the development and enactment of SRL is a concern. These additional requirements can place unfair cognitive and cultural burdens on working-class individuals. If environments are set up to teach SRL, working-class students and guardians are faced with a fundamentally different set of choices from their middle-class counterparts. As Gee (1992) argues, those whose home and school spheres align experience less tension, conflict, and fragmentation within schools than whose spheres misalign. Those with matching spheres may generalize and adapt learning strategies across spheres, as there is less emotional, cultural, and cognitive conflict. The alignment between school and home discourses might mean less socialization, learning about new norms, rules for engagement, and ways of knowing. Therefore, for working-class guardians and children, taking up the aim to cultivate and enact SRL, respectively, can involve making a choice between identity and attempts at academic success.

It is important to avoid viewing middle-class subjectivity as inherently more valuable than working-class subjectivity. The seeming deficit in working-class culture is not innate. The value of capital exists in a matrix and becomes more or less valuable in relation to other capitals within institutional discourses. If the matrix shifts, then the value of capital and habitus shifts. The key point is that educational contexts that value, validate, reward, and teach SRL can favor particular kinds of people. Issues with SRL are not just about the cognitive burden and constraints, but also about values for subjectivity that can produce different advantages and opportunities. Middle-class subjectivity (and the practices associated with it) is not inherently more desirable or better than working-class subjectivity. I am not suggesting that if guardians and children mitigate the effects of class, then all children and guardians can and should be effective self-regulated learners. To suggest this normalizes and naturalizes features of middle-class subjectivity and SRL.

The selfhood of SRL and middle-class culture is underpinned by individualism, freedom of choice, independence, and the pursuit of self-betterment. As Jackson, Mackenzie, and Hobfoll (2000) argue, these values are rooted in an economically privileged, Western, male perspective. Fox, Prilleltensky, and Austin (2009a) argue that such selfhood blinds people to the impact of their actions and lifestyles on those who are oppressed. They also argue that embodying a self that is based on individualism disproportionately hurts members of relatively marginalized groups. Although a conversation about the relative merits of particular brands of selfhood is important for thinking about the kinds of citizenship that support the functioning of a democracy, the point here is that SRL endorses a particular selfhood and can be implicated in the exclusion and invalidation of diverse ways of being. Shaping environments to teach SRL can marginalize identities, add cognitive burdens, produce interpersonal tensions, and reinforce a cultural hierarchy by making it seem as if middle-class subjectivity is better.

Chapter 6
Adaptation, Prescription, and Dependency: Critical Pedagogical Reflections on the Ethics of Teaching Self-Regulated Learning

> Education is not about the insertion of the individual into the existing order but entails an orientation toward autonomy and freedom. (Biesta, 2010, p. 43)

Introduction

Self-regulated learning (SRL) is almost exclusively associated with empowerment, agency, and democratic participation. There is little consideration of the ways in which SRL pedagogy is entangled in politics of control, conformity, obedience, and oppression. As a result of this lack of attention, researchers and practitioners may be driven by humanistic concerns to empower their students, while ignoring the possibility that SRL is entangled in what Ayers and Ayers (2011) refer to as the "hidden curriculum of obedience" (p. 104). Drawing from the educational philosophy of Paulo Freire (1987, 2000), teaching students to academically self-regulate can be tied to adaptation, prescription, and dependence, which characterize relationships of subordination. Respectively, I suggest that self-regulated learning (1) targets individual psychological changes that render individuals adaptable to existing social orders; (2) is guided by a logic to prescribe a certain kind of self; and (3) produces a relationship of dependence as learners depend on teachers for learning the necessary scripts to regulate their learning.

Adaptation, prescription, and dependency are problems for the following reasons. First, educational environments can stubbornly resist change, making it difficult for individuals to transform their realities in socially just ways. Second, SRL involves homogenized and normalized behavioral and psychological scripts.

Although educational psychologists contend that students regulate themselves in different ways, SRL is a prescribed form of engagement. In other words, students may use different strategies and thought processes, but SRL pedagogical efforts encourage certain ways of being, doing, and relating that support adaptive functioning within schools. Contrary to assumptions about autonomy and independence, students become dependent on teachers and environmental configurations to regulate themselves in effective ways. In sum, a consideration of Freire's critical pedagogical philosophy makes it possible to tie SRL to dehumanization and oppression because students become dependent on external sources to learn prescribed ways of engagement that encourage adaptation to an existing order—a problem especially given the influence of neoliberalism on forming environments.

Critical Pedagogy: An Introduction

Freire's (1987, 2000) pedagogical philosophy is tied to a democratic view of schooling. Capturing this view, Dewey (1938) posits that the responsibility of a democratic society is to develop in children the ability to question the status quo in order to create better processes and functions within society. To achieve this democratic purpose, individuals must perceive the mutability and continual development of themselves and their realities. Freire (2000) states, "[Children are] unfinished, uncompleted beings in and with a likewise unfinished reality" (p. 92). This incompleteness does not mean encouraging individuals to see themselves as falling short of some ideal and in need of reformation. Incompleteness is not about consuming images, products, and information in order to generate the perception of a complete and affirmed identity. Rather, incompleteness is about oneself and the world being in dialogic evolution, and working with others in solidarity to produce practices and functions that mitigate inequality. According to Freire, the purpose of schooling is not about functioning within an existing order, but for giving shape to a reality that affirms the humanity of all.

Although it is in its own right necessary for humanization, transforming self and world is especially important given the inequities in schooling environments. A starting point for critical pedagogical theorists is that the world is rife with unequal, dehumanizing, and oppressive social and institutional arrangements (e.g., Freire, 2000; Giroux, 2009; McLaren, 2009). McLaren (2009) states, "Critical theorists begin with the premise that men and women are essentially unfree and inhabit a world rife with contradictions and asymmetries of power and privilege" (p. 61). From this picture, there are disenfranchised and advantaged individuals and groups who are positioned as such through environmental configurations. Schools are one of the many institutions that are implicated in producing and protecting inequalities. Adapting to existing schooling environments, especially so that one can adapt to a particular order outside of school, not only precludes participation in the transformation of reality but also validates an unjust social order.

Although critical theorists contend that schools are sites of oppression and dehumanization, they also believe that schools can be sites for hope and humanization. Freire (2000) states:

> Education either functions as an instrument which is used to facilitate integration of the younger generation into the logic of the present system and bring about conformity [a pedagogy of dehumanization] or it becomes the practice of freedom, the means by which men and women deal critically and creatively with reality and discover how to participate in the transformation of their world. (p. 34)

A major consideration will be how SRL fits into these possibilities. Does teaching SRL involve encouraging adaptation to an existing social order or does teaching SRL align with a practice of freedom? Contrary to the prevailing assumptions within educational psychology, teaching students to self-regulate can be tied to dehumanization and oppression because students become dependent on external sources to learn prescribed ways of engagement that encourage adaptation to an existing order.

Oppression and Dehumanization

Two fundamental notions in Freire's (2000) work are the oppressor and the oppressed. Though some identify specific groups as oppressed, such as women, persons with disabilities, and African Americans, to name a few, Freire is not as specific in naming groups. For him, the oppressed are people whose humanity is denied, and oppressors are those who deny the humanity of others. Individuals affirm their humanity through participation in the production of themselves and their world in ways that affirm the humanity of others. Thus, one cannot be fully human if his or her consciousness and action reify social configurations that deny the humanity of others. For this reason, Freire argues that those who oppress are also oppressed. He states, "No one can be authentically human while he prevents others from being so" (p. 85). Thought about this way, the distinction between oppressed and oppressor is not always clear. However, what remains clear in critical pedagogical philosophy is that there are institutional structures that serve the interests of those who hold certain kinds of political, economic, cultural, and social capital.

A key feature of oppression and dehumanization is the effort to socialize individuals to adapt to and function within these unjust institutional arrangements. Freire (2000) uses the notion of "banking" to explain this pedagogical aim. Banking is a pedagogical format that is characterized by depositing information into students, who, by this metaphor, are positioned as passive receivers of information. Knowledge is treated as static, predetermined, and possessed by an authority (i.e., teacher) who must bestow it upon others (i.e., students). Freire argues that such a pedagogical relationship is in the interest of the oppressors, who can secure a particular order by regulating the way the world enters into others. Freire states, "The educated individual is the adapted person, because she or he is better 'fit' for the world. . . . this concept is well suited for the purposes of the oppressors, whose tranquility rests on how well people fit the world the oppressors have created, and how little they question it" (p. 76). Banking denies the humanities of others by transmitting static knowledge to students so they adapt to a particular social order that is rife with inequalities. Thus, there is concern that adaptation favors an unjust order and disaffirms humanity.

Adaptation and Integration

Freire (1987) is critical of adaptation. He explains:

> Integration results from the capacity to adapt oneself to reality plus the critical capacity to make choices and to transform that reality. To the extent that man loses his ability to make choices and is subject to the choices of others, to the extent that his decisions are no longer his own because *they result from external prescriptions* [emphasis added], he is no longer integrated. . . . If man is incapable of changing reality, he adjusts himself instead. (p. 4)

If individuals are not shaping their realities, but rather are led to adapt to existing configurations by changing themselves, then their humanity is denied. Freire pointedly states, "Adaptation . . . exhibited by man . . . is symptomatic of his dehumanization" (p. 4). He reasons that the more the oppressed can be led to adapt to a preformulated world, the more easily they can be dominated. For example, teachers encourage adaptation when they focus on and attempt to transmit a static form of knowledge to students that is disconnected from the realities of communities and their struggles. Teachers encourage adaptation when a world is positioned as static, wherein individuals must learn the knowledge, skills, and dispositions to function within that world. Thus, for Freire, adaptation is a mechanism of control, subordination, and domination because the focus of change is on the consciousness of the oppressed, not the situation that oppresses them. Although Freire recognizes adaptation as element in critical engagement, integration is necessary for realizing a democratic and socially just ideal. Integration is participation in the construction of oneself and reality in ways that affirm the humanity of all. The distinction between adaptation and integration is essential for Freire's work and integral for considering ethical complexities related to teaching SRL, as I suggest that SRL aligns more with adaptation than integration.

Dependence

When knowledge is treated as static, predetermined, and deposited, it not only disaffirms humanity by rendering education as a tool for adaptation, it also creates relationships of dependence in which the oppressed are expected to achieve liberation by becoming dependent on those who have mastered that knowledge. For example, if teachers are thought to possess the types and forms of knowledge that are deemed necessary to escape conditions of oppression, then students must depend on teachers for their liberation. Freire (2000) is highly critical of relationships of dependence; he argues that they reify the subordination of the oppressed and create impossibilities for independence. For the former, there is a lack of confidence in people's ability to think, act, and know. For the latter, if the oppressed depend on acquiring the knowledge of the oppressor to mitigate oppression, then the seeming achievement of independence from oppression requires dependence. Biesta (2010) captures this point when he states:

> The one to be emancipated is, after all, dependent upon the intervention of the emancipator, an intervention based upon a knowledge that is fundamentally inaccessible to the one to be emancipated. When there is no intervention, there is, therefore, no emancipation. This raises the question of when this dependency will actually disappear. Is it as soon as emancipation is achieved? Or should the one who is emancipated remain eternally grateful to his or her emancipator for the "gift" of emancipation? (p. 45)

Recognizing this ethical paradox, Freire states, "Not even the best-intentioned leadership can bestow independence as a gift" (p. 66).

Efforts by the oppressor to bestow independence or liberation are considered to be false generosity. Freire (2000) states:

> The generosity of the oppressors is nourished by an unjust order, which must be maintained in order to justify that generosity. Our converts [oppressors who strive to mitigate oppression], on the other hand, truly desire to transform the unjust order; but because of their background they believe that they must be the executors of the transformation. They talk about the people, but they do not trust them; and trusting the people is the indispensable precondition for revolutionary change. A real humanist can be identified more by his trust in the people, which engages him in their struggle, than by a thousand actions in their favor without that trust. (p. 60)

Although some oppressors may be well intentioned, they see liberation as the transmission of their knowledge to others so that the oppressed can also benefit from such an order. Such efforts are false charity because there is a lack of confidence that the oppressed can participate in and guide their own liberation. This lack of confidence justifies the need for prescriptions and the transmission of knowledge. Furthermore, from these efforts a social order is affirmed and naturalized—supporting a justification for adaptation.

Critical Consciousness

As Freire and other critical theorists suggest (Apple, 2000; Giroux, 2009; Greene, 1988; McLaren, 2007), there is hope to mitigate oppressive social arrangements. Power is not limited to the oppressor, or structures that support oppressive relationships. Freire (1987) firmly believes that both the oppressors and oppressed have the power to recognize and resist oppressive social arrangements that (re)inscribe, validate, and (re)produce inequality. Critical consciousness implies both action and reflection, what Freire refers to as "praxis." In Freire's philosophy, critical consciousness is communal and not solipsistic musings. Individuals are critically conscious to the degree that they construct their reality in dialogue and solidarity with others, and to the extent they affirm the humanity of others.

Dialogue

Freire (1987, 2000) rejects adaptation, didactics, static knowledge, prescription, and dependence, and instead, embraces authentic dialogue with a problem posing pedagogy. Freire's view of education relies heavily upon the practice and ethic of shared dialogue in the classroom between teachers and students in which questions or problems emerge via the interactions among classroom participants. Presented as an alternative to banking, problem posing is the questioning of the world rather than its codification. A problem-posing method of education requires dialogue as students and teachers are viewed as partners (both learning from each other), and students' ideas and questions are integral in shaping inquiry. Freire believed the most important component of dialogue was love and that dialogue could not be had without love. Darder (2009) provides a thoughtful consideration of what Freire meant by love. She states that love in his philosophy was not a "liberal, romanticized, or merely feel-good notion" (p. 568). Rather, Darder explains that love is the right and duty to fight, to persistently struggle to be human. Through and with love, authentic dialogue is possible.

From a Freirean perspective, it is essential that pedagogy be committed to dialogue and love, while avoiding commitments to transmitting a static form of knowledge, fixing identity categories, and encouraging adaptation to existing norms and structures. Such an education dehumanizes students by invalidating their knowledge and experiences, silencing their voices and decision-making capacities, affirming an oppressive social order, and rendering individuals in the world not part of its production. Critical pedagogy is committed to affirming humanity through the logic of integration, which means that through dialogue and solidarity, individuals participate in the (trans)formation of their worlds in ways that mitigate oppression and discrimination. These are the key tenets used to consider Freire's pedagogical philosophy in relation to the ethics of teaching SRL.

Self-Regulated Learning from a Freirean Perspective

SRL and critical pedagogy are associated with broad educational goals of empowerment, freedom, liberation, and democratic participation. However, despite these commonalities, the vast literatures are seldom merged. There are some guiding questions for considering their relationship: (1) To what degree is SRL tied to the transformation of social reality for the purposes of mitigating inequality and discrimination? (2) What changes in social configurations are made possible through and from SRL, or in other words, does SRL align with the logic of adaptation or integration? (3) Does SRL support efficient and effective transmission of knowledge? While there is potential for variation in responses, there are compelling justifications for viewing SRL as competing and incompatible with Freire's educational philosophy. I suggest that teaching SRL encourages adaptation, prescription, and dependency.

Although the analysis is focused on the points of incompatibility between the aim of teaching SRL and Freire's pedagogical philosophy, there are possible ways to construct this relationship as compatible. One way is to view teaching SRL as instrumental to supporting integration. The assumption underpinning this possibility is that SRL can lead to the production of knowledge, skills, and dispositions to strategically participate in the transformation of reality. As long as SRL is not guided by self-interested goals, teaching students to self-regulate can be instrumental to the goals of critical pedagogy. Another possible point of compatibility relates to the conceptual alignment between SRL and critical consciousness. Educational psychologists view self-regulated learners as agentic and empowered because they learn how to create the effects they want by strategically making their own choices. Again, as long as those effects are not for self-betterment, but fixed on transforming the world to mitigate inequality, teaching SRL can be conceptually aligned with efforts to foster critical consciousness.

Instrumentalism: Supporting Critical Consciousness

Critical theorists suggest that studying skills and discipline are important elements in empowerment and emancipation (Duncan-Andrade, 2010; McLaren, 2007; Trend, 1994). In a letter written to Freire, Duncan-Andrade (2010) associates studying with revolutionary duty. His argument rests on a quotation by Freire:

> A text to be read is a text to be studied. A text to be studied is a text to be interpreted. We cannot interpret a text if we read it without paying attention, without curiosity; if we stop reading at the first difficulty.... If a text is difficult, you insist on understanding it.... To study demands discipline. To study is not easy, because to study is to create and re-create and not to repeat what others say. To study is a revolutionary duty. (p. 167)

For studying, Duncan-Andrade identifies a number of characteristics of SRL. These include persistence in the face of challenge, sustained attention, and discipline. In this regard, SRL seems to support critical engagement with texts by serving as a means to study, understand, and re-create texts. Trend (1994) makes a similar argument in his discussion of what he describes as the new media literacy movement. He argues that critically reading texts is not about consuming a message, but about examining dominant readings, issues of positionality, and ideological underpinnings. Trend contends that reading texts in this way "can be improved with study and that these skills can be taught to children regardless of age or grade level" (p. 235). Duncan-Andrade and Trend agree that discipline, skill, and persistence with understanding texts are important for critical consciousness. SRL seems to have a reasonable alignment with this agenda and can be instrumental to practicing freedom.

Conceptual Overlap with Critical Consciousness

Most educators see their task not simply as that of modifying or conditioning the behavior of their students. Instead, they want their students to become independent and autonomous, to be able to think for themselves, to make their own judgments and draw their own conclusions. Educational psychologists wholeheartedly associate SRL with these pedagogical goals. As Lapan, Kardash, and Turner (2002) state, "Self-regulated learners do more than just passively consume information that has been presented to them by others" (p. 258). Zimmerman (2000) contends that self-regulated individuals perceive themselves as capable of exerting the will and skill to affect the outcomes of their lives. As part of this perceived agency for SRL, individuals learn the way the environment affects thinking and behavior and, therefore, can develop the tools to control the environment to support the pursuit and attainment of goals. Researchers reason that part of the humanistic quality of heightened self-control comes from the increased degree of responsibility and control of actions. Roeser and Peck (2009) state, "The cultivation of awareness and willful self-regulation are preconditions for deep learning, freedom of thought, creativity, harmonious social relationships, and myriad forms of personal and social renewal" (p. 119). SRL carries with it connotations of social emancipation and social betterment. If the social world is oppressive, then understanding the ways individuals are influenced in such a system will help to free oneself from that system and potentially change it.

There are issues with these relationships of compatibility. Freire (1987, 2000) is critical of instrumentalism, as it connotes a predetermined end, a fixed goal, and adaptation. In addition, Martin (2004a) contends that improving studying strategies hardly equates to civic virtue, democratic engagement, and strong communal ties. SRL is often treated as a means to pursue self-interested goals with little recourse to the contradictions and asymmetries within social arrangements. Like McLaren (2007), Martin leaves open the possibility for harnessing SRL for different ends. He states:

> While such innovations [development of knowledge about self-regulation] are certainly not irrelevant to the education of citizens and the improvement of human life in general, *they do not, by themselves* [emphasis added], warrant claims to the effect that psy-

chology in education has improved our conceptions of personhood and civic life. (p. 186)

Although Martin recognizes the limitations of focusing solely on teaching SRL, he does not entirely disregard its usefulness. Similarly, McLaren (2007) leaves open a possibility for SRL in critical pedagogy. He states, "Critical pedagogy eschews any approach to pedagogy that would reduce it to the teaching of narrow thinking-skills in isolation from the contentious debates and contexts in which such skills are employed" (p. 31). He seems to suggest that as long as the context in which SRL is employed is critically engaged and open to transformation that thinking skills, such as SRL, has its place. Martin and McLaren, who operate from vastly different philosophical traditions, converge on the possibility that SRL can be integrated into an educational goal that is tied to the mitigation of injustice and democratic ideals.

Although this possibility makes sense, the upcoming discussion reveals sources of tension that problematize these relationships of compatibility. In sum, SRL is not mobilized to consider the asymmetries and contradictions in curricula nor is it mobilized in reflexive ways. SRL reflects what Duncan-Andrade (2010) calls learning to earn (the pursuit of knowledge for personal gain and learning to function well within a capitalist structure), a commitment in contradistinction to learning for freedom (challenging the prevailing logic of injustice and creating a new social order). It is not just the ends toward which SRL is directed that call into question the compatibility between teaching SRL and critical pedagogy. It is also the homogeneity and prescription of selfhood that is endorsed in SRL pedagogy, as well as the commitments to efficiency and productivity, which are foundational neoliberal commitments that are dehumanizing. The underlying assumptions and commitments in the discourse of SRL are not adequate to sustain a conceptual alignment to the tenets of critical pedagogy.

Incompatibility: Adaptation, Prescription, and Dependence

Adaptation: Personal Changes and Structural Resistance

Freire's (2000) concern that adaptation is a process that generates conformity and obedience to an existing social order has particular relevance for SRL. It is not uncommon for the notion of adaptation to be associated with SRL (e.g., Boekaerts & Corno, 2005; Hadwin & Oshige, 2011; McCaslin & Burross, 2011; Post, Boyer, & Brett, 2006; Schunk & Zimmerman, 1997; Zimmerman,

2002). Boekaerts and Corno (2005) state, "All theorists assume that students . . . *adapt their thoughts, feelings, and actions* [emphasis added] as needed to affect their learning and motivation" (p. 201). As these authors state, educational psychologists associate SRL with the adaptation of personal variables. Describing their developmental model, Schunk and Zimmerman (1997) argue that individuals are not self-regulating unless they adaptively use previously learned strategies to meet new situational demands.

Although the emphasis on adapting personal variables is central, researchers also suggest that SRL involves environmental changes (Bandura, 2001; McCaslin & Burross, 2011; Schunk & Zimmerman, 1997). In addition to planning, managing time, concentrating on instruction, organizing, rehearsing, and coding information strategically, Schunk and Zimmerman (1997) argue that successful adaptation includes establishing productive work environments and using social resources effectively. Other ways to influence the environment include, but are not limited to, asking teachers questions (e.g., Newman, 2002), selecting nondistracting peers with whom to collaborate (e.g., Zimmerman, 2002), choosing models to emulate (Martinez-Pons, 2002), and undertaking challenging activities (e.g., Bandura, 2001). All these suggestions for environmental changes are ones that support the achievement of personal learning goals—and arguably assist in better adapting to a broad schooling environment.

Questions about what environments are and how they change is integral for considering critical pedagogical implications of teaching SRL. Not unlike in SRL literature, the broad notion of adaptation in educational psychology connotes both psychological and environmental changes (Piaget, 1952; Vidal, 1994). However, there is not always agreement about what environmental changes mean. From a constructive perspective, adaptation involves a change in mental schemes or a change in external information to conform the world to schema (Piaget, 1952; Vidal, 1994; von Glasersfeld, 1996). From this view, as Jardine (2010) suggests, environments are not "ready-made" organizations that are imposed on a "passive organism-subject" (p. 133). In other words, the environment is not a static preontological entity. Thus, adaptation involves modifying environments by using psychological schema to impose certain structures of its own. Viewing the environment as a perception and schematic production, which stems from a radical constructivist perspective (von Glasersfeld, 1996), endorses the assumption that individuals have the psychological means and mechanisms to transform their worlds.

Others within educational psychology view environments and environmental formations differently. Sociocultural-oriented SRL researchers view environments as social, evolving, and co-constituted (Hadwin & Oshige, 2011; McCaslin & Burross, 2011). McCaslin and Burross (2011) explain:

> Cultural influences set norms and challenges that define what is *probable* for persons and social and cultural institutions. *Probable is malleable* [emphasis added] nonetheless because personal and social influences can resist or work to change cultural norms and expectations. (p. 327)

Although cultural and institutional forces shape environments, the logic underpinning this perspective is that individuals can participate with others to transform those contexts, which are viewed as emergent, dynamic, and malleable. From a sociocultural perspective, adaptation is not individuals changing themselves to "fit" an environment but acting and interacting with others to give form to it. Hadwin and Oshige (2011) acknowledge this point and state that the "notion of adaptive learning extends beyond individual self-regulation and instead to the community of practice—the way learning communities adapt and evolve as personal, social, and cultural influences come together" (p. 249). The emphasis on participation and malleability for environmental configurations brings SRL close to resembling integration.

However, although it makes sense to view environments as co-constituted and malleable, critical pedagogues are skeptical that all environments are infinitely malleable, constituted in a dialogic way, and independent of the workings of power (Apple, 2006; Freire, 1987; McLaren, 2007). A key assumption of critical pedagogical philosophy is that there are structures independent of one's production and constitution of them, and that such structures operate to reproduce inequality by protecting dominant interests. There are existing orders that are protected by school administrators, teachers, curricula, policy (both local and national), and even some parents and students themselves, that shape possibilities and potentialities for environmental configurations. McCaslin and Burross (2011) acknowledge this point by stating, "No source of influence—personal, social, and cultural—is equally distributed. One result, then, is differential opportunity for culturally valued, socially validated, personally desirable adaptive learning" (p. 327). Although some sociocultural researchers emphasize the malleability and co-constitution of environments, aligning in part with the logic of integration, they ignore the power dynamic in that constitution.

Schooling environments are political and ideological places that protect certain structures, ones that are not easy to change. For example, neoliberal logic continues to transform schooling in particular ways that are protected by various organizational, corporate, legislative, cultural, and individual forces. Neoliberal reform is associated with a number of specific policies, practices, and models of education. Both products and by-products of neoliberal reform shape schooling and produce particular pedagogical structures that are difficult to change. Among the many problematic policies (e.g., see Lakes & Carter, 2011), neoliberalism endorses pervasive and intensely consequential high-stakes standardized testing. Some researchers, interested in supporting students' school success, focus on improving performance on standardized assessments by implementing self-regulatory interventions (Miller, Heafner, & Massey, 2009). In this regard, SRL validates the legitimacy of standardized assessments, which becomes a source for prompting personal change.

Neoliberalism also endorses a social efficiency model of education. The simple premise of this model is that society has different needs and schools should prepare individuals with the knowledge, skills, and dispositions to fill those needs. Notwithstanding efforts to homogenize education through the production of national standards, individuals are exposed to curricula, both hidden and explicit, that prepare them to fill roles that correspond to their existing class background. For example, some researchers observe that schools serving children from working-class backgrounds focus on obedience, monetary incentives, and rote thinking. Whereas, schools serving individuals from middle- and upper-class backgrounds focus on preparing students to be managers by cultivating problem-solving skills and creativity. Given the persistence of these curricula differences, adaptation resembles a mechanism to efficiently and effectively reproduce a social and economic order by enlisting individuals in their voluntary participation in the reproduction of class-based norms and practices. Being an adaptable, self-regulated learner can mean that one is manageable and easily inserted into a particular structure, not being part of its transformation.

In thinking about adaptation and SRL, it is important to consider what is supposed to change, what can change, what kind of change is possible, and whose voices inform those changes. The adaptable self-regulated learner is one who can monitor, evaluate, and change, if necessary, personal variables to meet situational demands. Environmental changes are included in SRL, but reflect modest and self-interested ones. The changes that SRL researchers discuss may support adaptation to neoliberal educational structures, rendering individuals better test-takers and efficient workers. For these reasons, McLaren (2007) argues that teaching thinking skills cannot be divorced from their context. Although adaptation (without integration) itself is a problem for Freire, being adaptable is especially problematic within a world increasingly shaped by neoliberalism. Neoliberal schooling environments are implicated in eroding democratic citizenship, producing an intense self-interest, rendering education as an economic instrument, and reproducing inequality (Apple, 2006; Biesta, 2009; Lakes & Carter, 2011; Rose, 1998). Without attention to ideological underpinnings and stubbornness of educational environments, SRL researchers and practitioners may mistake adaptation for integration. One might be making choices and modifying environments in order to achieve learning goals that align with neoliberal educational objectives and not toward mitigating inequalities.

Prescription: Culture and Ideology in Selfhood

Another issue with adaptability, especially as it pertains to functioning within neoliberal environments, is that it requires a specific kind of self, one that proponents of both SRL and neoliberalism naturalize. There have been century-long debates about what the self is, how it develops, and what role it plays in perception, action, and knowing. In contemporary sociocultural theorizing, Martin and Sugarman (2001) argue that the self is a kind of understanding that is embedded in particular historical, social, and cultural circumstances. The self is not a priori, but emerges as individuals relate to others and reflect on those relations, which are embedded in particular times and places. From this perspective, the self is mutable, dynamic, and historically constituted. Teaching SRL involves constituting a particular kind of self, one that aligns with neoliberal subjectivity and middle-class conventions of selfhood. Drawing parallels with the self of SRL, neoliberalism, and the middle-class, teaching SRL entails prescribing culturally and ideologically specific ways to be, think, and act. Freire (1987) is critical of practices of prescription in general because they require predetermined end points, knowledge transmission, and docility. Prescribing selfhood that mirrors neoliberal logic is especially problematic from a Freirean pedagogical standpoint.

Explicit and broad historical analyses have not been conducted on the kinds of self and personhood that underpin SRL pedagogy. However, Martin (2007) provides a framework and essential starting point for such explorations. He discusses three types of self within educational psychology: scientific self, expressive self, and communal self. The scientific self is so termed because it is committed to the control over thoughts and behaviors through careful calculation, evaluation, and monitoring of thoughts, behaviors, and outcomes in order to be efficient and productive. This self is called expressive because it is guided by a commitment to identify, validate, develop, and express psychological states. The expressive self is defined by an imperative to identify the uniqueness and importance of emotional experiences. The scientific and expressive selves are foundational for SRL, in that they emphasize personal control, self-knowledge, efficiency, and productivity for SRL. These selves are rational, componential, controllable, knowable, interior, and oriented toward personal development; they are not unlike neoliberal subjectivity.

Researchers suggest that different cultural groups inscribe selves that are fundamentally at odds with the self of SRL and neoliberalism. Working-class selfhood comes close to resembling the communal self. Martin (2007) characterizes the communal self as embedded within a time and place. It is a relational self. Unlike the scientific and expressive selves, the communal self is not committed to an ethic of self-study and self-improvement. Psychological states are not featured as the source and cause of activity and outcomes. Working-class selfhood does not arguably resemble the ideal communal self. However, there are features of this brand of selfhood that come closer to the communal self than to the other two selves. Researchers argue that in working-class environments the self is socially mediated and part of a collective identity (Jackson, Mackenzie, & Hobfoll, 2000; Kusserow, 2004; Lareau, 2003; Schutz, 2008). As Schutz (2008) argues, individuals from working-class backgrounds are likely to express selfhood in terms of collective struggle. Kusserow (2004) adds that working-class selfhood is not organized around a commitment to understand, study, and identify psychological states as sources of action.

On the other hand, Schutz (2008) argues that middle-class families celebrate children's unique characteristics and capabilities, helping them develop a sense of themselves as discrete and unique individuals. In addition, he contends that middle-class children learn at an early age to monitor themselves and use techniques of surveillance to achieve personal learning goals. This self is constructed in relation to a number of psychological features, such as intentions, attitudes, strengths, weaknesses, and beliefs. Middle-class selfhood is characterized by a composite of psychological features that must be monitored and controlled. Weininger and Lareau (2009) argue that middle-class guardians work closely with children to develop their dispositions and skills for this type of self-management. Middle-class selfhood is individualistic (e.g., Eckert, 1989), pushy (e.g., Walkerdine, 2003), and entitled (e.g., Lareau, 2003).

The working-class self stands in contrast to the kind of self that underpins SRL. However, there is overlap between middle-class selfhood, SRL, and neoliberalism. This brief overview points to the possibilities that teaching SRL involves prescribing a particular kind of self that endorses neoliberalism and validates middle-class conventions. Additional support for this point is detected in the discourse related to those behaviors and thought processes that are considered adaptive self-regulation. For example, help-seeking is identified as an important strategy for SRL (e.g., Bandura, 2001; Hole & Crozier, 2007; Newman, 2002; Puustinen, Lyyra, Metsäpelto, & Pulkkinen, 2008). Bandura (2001) argues that individuals cannot control every part of a social context and, therefore, must use others for the purpose of achieving personal goals. Bandura uses the notion of proxy agency to describe this process, whereas many SRL researchers use help-seeking.

Help-seeking involves particular ways of thinking, dispositions for negotiation, rational deliberations, and perceptions. Newman (2002) explains:

> When students monitor their academic performance, show awareness of difficulty they cannot overcome on their own, and exhibit the wherewithal and self-determination to remedy that difficulty by requesting assistance from a more knowledgeable individual, they are exhibiting mature, strategic behavior. (p. 132)

Puustinen, Lyyra, Metsäpelto, and Pulkkinen (2008) add:

> Self-regulated learners—and help-seekers—do not ask for help needlessly when they are capable of solving the problem by themselves . . . they confine their questions to just those hints and explanations needed to allow them to finish performing the task on their own. (pp. 161–62)

From these descriptions, to effectively help-seek, individuals must (1) work independently by exhausting all their resources to complete a task; (2) recognize the limitations in personal knowledge, skill, and efficacy to complete the task; (3) ask certain questions that serve only to facilitate progress toward task completion; and (4) interact and negotiate with individuals who are seen as having the resources to complete the task. Students must seek help only after extensive thought and reflection (requiring self-knowledge and commitments to reflection and evaluation) and for the purpose of independently completing tasks.

This portrait of the self-regulated learner strongly reflects the neoliberal mandate to make individuals responsible for their own life projects by not only relying on independent personal changes but also by using others as instruments to attain a personal goal. Help-seeking is also tied to the mandate to be productive and execute a plan of action. Furthermore, the representation of help-seeking in SRL literature is entangled in class-based norms. Researchers observe differences in help-seeking behaviors and dispositions across children from middle- and working-class backgrounds (Calarco, 2011; Lareau, 2003; Streib, 2011; Weininger & Lareau, 2009). Middle-class children are described as comfortable interacting with adults as equals, operating with a sense of entitlement, possessing verbal agility, and having a psychologically informed personal learning profile. On the other hand, Lareau (2003) argues that children from working-class backgrounds are less likely to negotiate with adults, operate with a sense of entitlement, and shape external conditions to meet learning needs. According to Calarco (2011), when working-class students seek help, they do so in subtle ways, such as sitting back in their chairs. She contends that working-class students are less likely to approach the teacher for help than their middle-class counterparts. Further, Streib (2011) observes that working-class children use fewer words when talking with adults, do not use language to call attention to themselves, and do not talk to adults as they talk to each other.

Like the requirements for selfhood, there are specific kinds of behaviors, ones that map onto middle-class conventions and align with the logic of neoliberalism, that count as adaptive SRL. Therefore, teaching SRL can normalize, homogenize, and naturalize the features of personhood that are culturally and ideologically narrow. Apple (2006) argues that "the educational task . . . is to change people's understanding of themselves as members of collective groups. Instead, to support a market economy we need to encourage everyone to think of themselves as individuals who always act in ways that maximize their own interests" (p. 23). That is, teaching SRL encourages individuals to think of themselves as (1) radically internalized, self-interested, and individualistic; (2) tied instrumentality to oneself and others; (3) committed to self-enhancement; and (4) disconnected from the kinds of communal involvements that engender strong moral and social ties. In this regard, teaching SRL can be restrictive of ontological possibilities and can be implicated in invalidating, marginalizing, and pathologizing communal identities.

Dependency: Authorities and Environmental Configurations

Researchers argue that all individuals attempt to regulate their learning and that SRL is a universal human feature. Yet, they also contend that not all individuals regulate themselves in the same way, for the same frequency, toward the same ends or in the same contexts. Though all individuals are believed to attempt to regulate their learning and are capable of doing so, there are certain thought processes and behaviors that have been correlated with effective SRL. Researchers think of SRL differences in terms of qualities and quantities (Boekaerts & Cascallar, 2006; Boekaerts & Corno, 2005; Zimmerman, 2000). Although researchers acknowledge that the distinction between adaptive and maladaptive can be interpreted differently, depending on students' goals (Boekaerts & Cascallar, 2006; Boekaerts & Corno, 2005), specific strategies, behaviors, and personhood are considered to be supportive of adaptive SRL. So even if one concludes that SRL is natural, students must be shaped in ways to exercise their SRL in ways that promote adaptive responses to situational demands.

Developing SRL is associated with agency and empowerment because individuals, through their own strategic skill and choices, can operate independently of environmental determination and mitigate limitations that result from behavioral and psychological factors. However, these assumptions come into question by considering the relationships of dependence involved with teaching SRL. Freire (2000) is highly critical of a liberatory goal that is achieved through the production of relationships of dependence. Of course, it is difficult to imagine a pedagogical relationship that does not require dependence of some sort, even in Freire's pedagogical philosophy. As Schutz (2000) contends, even the most individualistic and communal strategies for freedom and empowerment involve learned social practices. There are specific kinds of dependency that are encouraged in SRL pedagogy that warrant attention, especially because educational psychologists treat SRL as unequivocally an expression of human agency and proactive engagement.

Teaching students to regulate their learning involves generating an explicit and sustained attention to environmental configurations as prompts for action and to serve as a compass to evaluate personal adaptations. Being adaptable requires dependency on one's construction of the external world and a commitment to meet situational demands. The fact that environments and responses to them vary is not a condition of autonomy: environmental cues prompt responses and environmental consequences of those responses provide the compass to evaluate choices and actions. If adaptations were not made in relation to cues and configurations, then responses may seem maladaptive. Maladaptive SRL can be those thoughts, behaviors, self-perceptions, emotions, and aspirations that compete with the display of the appropriate levels of compliance to be efficient, productive, responsible, and competitive. Individuals must learn to be adaptive, as opposed to maladaptive, by relying on what Rose (1999) refers to as "engineers of the soul" (p. 6). Engineers of the soul are those authorities who serve to support an individual's effort to attain a particular goal, one that is of course institutionally, socially, or politically endorsed. Psychologists, and those who operate with psychological discourse, are engineers of the soul who use the "psy" disciplines to work with individuals to make them visible and calculable in order to support their efforts to become what they want to be. Dependency is not restricted to experts of the soul; it also involves relationships to instruments. Normalized psychological and behavior assessments come to define various features of oneself. These instruments are held in esteem and given validity for shaping personal evaluations.

The point is that with guidance from others who rely on certain instruments, individuals must learn to be adaptable in ways that support the efficient and productive pursuit of an institutionally validated goal. Teachers are trained to do less direct transmission of knowledge by supporting the development of personalized learning scripts and self-assessments so that students can direct themselves. In this regard, there appears to be an alignment with SRL pedagogical models and Freire's philosophy, as he is highly critical of the transmission model of education. However, it is questionable whether or not SRL pedagogical models endorse transmission and if SRL environments invite true self-determination. For example, Martin and McLellan (2008) state:

> When students are initially learning to self-regulate, teachers must provide antecedent strategies that clearly explain outcomes, use examples and non-examples of problem-solving behaviors (i.e., persistence or improvement) . . . as well as outcome behaviors (i.e., achievement or performance) and self-monitoring accuracy. Even when researchers and teachers recognize the degree of external control typically required to stimulate students' self-regulation and attempt to reduce such supports, they most often compensate for any decrements in direct teacher instruction by strengthening self-regulatory structures in the curriculum offered. (p. 445)

The authors suggest that prescribing behaviors and thought processes includes and extends beyond teachers coaching their students. It includes shaping curricula and intervening in order to ensure students are regulating themselves in adaptable ways. A key concern is that teaching students to regulate their learning either through direct instruction or environmental structuring is underpinned by an effort to homogenize behavioral and psychological scripts so that individuals can guide themselves in the self-directed transmission of institutionally sanctioned knowledge. Reducing the direct transmission of knowledge in favor of SRL relocates the source of knowledge transmission.

Thus, when students direct their learning, it does not contradict a transmission model of education.

Conclusion

Critical pedagogical theory is committed to an emancipatory agenda, which means identifying and resisting oppressive practices and structures in the name of social justice and freedom. In educational psychology literature, SRL is tied to this educational agenda, as it is associated with economic justice, democratic participation, agency, and empowerment. However, when considered from a Freirean perspective, the discourse of SRL is aligned with the logic of adaptation, prescription, and dependency—three processes and practices of which Freire is highly critical. If personal variables are changed, regardless if they are self-initiated or teacher prompted (as if this difference can always be discerned) in order to meet situational demands, then individuals can be easily dominated because they focus on changing themselves rather than problematic situations. Changing personal factors is misaligned with a commitment to integration, which means transforming reality in ways to support the development of processes and functions within any situation that works to mitigate inequality. Although SRL involves some environmental transformations, this form of engagement is often discussed as monitoring and changing oneself to meet situational demands.

Aside from validating and affirming problematic educational environments, being adaptable is a particular subject position that does not come naturally to people, requires guidance from engineers of the soul, and is steeped in middle-class conventions and neoliberal logic. Thus, SRL can be seen as a way to produce narrow and normative ways of engagement that affirm problematic pedagogical arrangements by endorsing a cultural hierarchy and market-based relations. For these reasons, a Freirean perspective provides a framework to associate SRL with disempowerment and dehumanization.

Conclusion
Reject, Embrace, or Reflect

In educational psychology literature, researchers make a strong case for the value of self-regulated learning (SRL) for academic success. In schools, class sizes are growing, there are competing demands for attention, student diversity is increasing, standards are seemingly being raised, and competition for credentials is high stakes. Beyond the classroom, some believe that individuals will need lifelong learning skills, along with 21st-century competencies in order to function and compete in a rapidly changing and unpredictable economy. Educational psychologists treat SRL as a form of engagement that can enable individuals to meet the challenges and demands of modern educational and economic life. Therefore, SRL is tied to social and economic justice (as a way to level the playing field), agency, empowerment, and humanism. Given the purported value of SRL, teachers will likely be expected to shape, if they are not already doing so, their pedagogy to support SRL. Policymakers and teachers may not have to be persuaded to adopt this pedagogical commitment; there is a seductive quality to SRL. Getting a class of students to initiate activity, stay on task, monitor performance, and make adjustments, if necessary, is an effective and efficient way to achieve pedagogical goals.

However, the main point of this book is to explore different sides of this story. Committed to critical educational psychology (CEP), I draw from multiple perspectives to explore ways that SRL is not neutral, unequivocally agentic, value-free, natural, disconnected from issues of power, or a form of engagement that good teachers foster. From a CEP analysis, it is possible to consider ways that SRL is entangled in compliance, governance, and disempowerment. Currently, this story is given inadequate attention. This lack of attention is cause for concern because SRL is implicated in the production and maintenance of a number of unintended, negative consequences. However, researchers assume that SRL is neutral and empowering, therefore, focus on using the scientific method to improve the conceptualization, measurement, and teaching of SRL. Given the potential for SRL to shape policy, pedagogy, and research, critical awareness of the complexities surrounding this notion is important.

If SRL is construed as neutral and value-free, researchers and practitioners may remain committed to SRL without considering the possibility that it may run counter to certain pedagogical beliefs, assumptions, and principles. Educational psychologists express concern that teachers' self-reported beliefs can conflict with interpretations of their practice (e.g., Pajares, 1992; Raymond, 1997; Richardson, Anders, Tidwell, & Lloyd, 1991; Vassallo, 2010). For example, some teachers might believe in a democratic view of education, yet teach in ways that compete with that belief. In these analyses, teaching SRL involves inscribing a certain kind of self, aligns with neoliberal logic, and endorses class conventions. Although educational psychologists associate SRL with democratic engagement, SRL can also be associated with docility, compliance, adaptability, competition, and self-interest. In some ways, teaching SRL might compete with teachers' beliefs about a democratic view of education. Awareness of the complexities surrounding SRL can support efforts to align beliefs and practices and support ethically informed decisions about what to do.

In general, if pedagogical commitments are embraced without critical awareness, there is a danger of producing unintended consequences, construing students narrowly, and misinterpreting student engagement. In the case of SRL, by teaching and rewarding this form of engagement, teachers might unintentionally marginalize working-class students, blame them for their marginalization, and interpret all types of resistance as illegitimate and unnecessary—not recognizing the tension with identity. Of course, rejecting or resisting SRL may produce unintended consequences as well. If neoliberalism continues to transform institutions, then inscribing the kind of subjectivity to navigate these structures can serve as a means to gain access to resources and opportunities. There is no safe position. However, awareness of some of the critical concerns with SRL provides a basis for recognizing various consequences, how SRL contributed to them, and imagining different pedagogical possibilities.

This book is dedicated to filling a void in SRL literature by using different lines of critical reasoning—polyvocalism, emancipation, and sociohistoricism—in order to examine the philosophical, cultural, and ideological contexts that underpin foundational elements of SRL. Polyvocalism involves integrating a variety of voices and perspectives in pedagogical deliberations and research in order to recognize the limitations of foundational concepts, assumptions, and ideas in educational psychology. This commitment is most evident in the analyses on agency and socioeconomic class. Emancipation involves an explicit commitment to change by way of reforming structures and conditions of oppression and discrimination. The analysis of SRL from a critical pedagogical perspective reflects this commitment. Sociohistorical analyses are concerned with understanding the conditions that make ideas, practices, and concepts possible given certain historical circumstances. The analysis of neoliberalism reflects this commitment. Although each chapter reflects a particular strand of critical theorizing, all themes run throughout each chapter and the entire book as a whole. Furthermore, like the foundations of critical psychology, the analyses reflect commitments to include diverse perspectives, question the dominant discourse, express concern about inequality, and raise skepticism toward universalism, neutrality, and radical individualism.

Examining SRL from a CEP perspective provides a starting point for reflecting on important issues with SRL. It is my hope that pedagogical reflections and academic conversations on SRL take seriously these considerations. Foremost among these considerations is agency, a foundational element of SRL and a theme that runs throughout the book. The prevailing assumption is that SRL is agentic because individuals make strategic choices that produce intended effects. By harnessing personal resources, individuals are construed as those who can transform themselves and their worlds through strategic and goal directed activity. However, as discussions throughout this book make clear, the connection between SRL and agency is not so simple.

Regulating learning involves adapting to meet situational demands by relying on a set of homogenized psychological and behavioral scripts and can endorse a narrow kind of personhood. Therefore, SRL can be implicated in adaptation, prescription, and dependence, which are tools of subordination and docility. Regulating learning may render individuals easily dominated by getting them to monitor and control themselves in relation to external demands. Relying on others to change personal variables that enable one to meet situational demands is a problem in general for a democratic view of education, a problem that is exacerbated in a neoliberal context. SRL is associated with neoliberal selfhood, which is defined as a self-interested, rational competitor who makes strategic choices that increase personal value. From a neoliberal perspective, agency is making good choices, which are evaluated in terms of efficiency, productivity, and value.

With the association between neoliberal selfhood and SRL, there are reasons to problematize the assumptions about agency in SRL literature. In neoliberal contexts, making choices is an obligation. These choices are constrained, judged, and evaluated based on a particular economic logic. In classrooms, good choices are those that enable individuals to efficiently and productively achieve a learning goal that is institutionally validated and recognized. Individuals must rely on authorities and norms of psychology in order to evaluate the appropriateness of their choices. Agency is using the expert guidance of others to make strategic choices that support a self-interested goal. Although viewed as agentic, there are constraints in the type of person one must be, subjugation to psychological expertise, and a commitment to efficiency and productivity. SRL and neoliberal selfhood are tied to a particular life ethic that has specific rules, regulations, and codes of conduct—ones that compete with civic virtue, communal involvement, and democratic engagement. If SRL involves changing personal factors in normative ways that enable individuals to adapt to neoliberal contexts, then SRL is arguably not agentic. SRL might be interpreted as making choices that enable individuals to function well within contexts that are oppressive to individuals and groups, as well as devoid of civic responsibility.

The discussion of class also contributes to the conversation on agency. Researchers repeatedly show that middle-class values, practices, and identities are rewarded and validated in schools, contributing to different advantages and unequal opportunities. The educational psychology discourse related to SRL endorses middle-class norms, practices, dispositions, economic conditions, and values. Teaching and rewarding SRL can set up working-class children to fail because their capitals do not mesh with those required to enact the kinds of self-regulatory learning that is valued and rewarded in schools. If values and norms for SRL are representative of individuals from the middle-class, then improving or developing self-regulatory skills for working-class individuals means moving toward ideal middle-class subjectivity. Agency, then, for working-class students, is the degree to which they give up a part of who they are in order to be a different kind of person. Working-class students may have to choose between two particular selves, a choice that may not feel agentic or humanizing.

One could suggest that individuals always have choices to resist institutional expectations to be a particular kind of person and do particular kinds of things. Resistance to SRL can signal agency. If SRL is normalized, homogenized, and treated as necessary for the 21st century, then those who resist SRL may be subject to interventions and reformative practices that pathologize and change their seeming choices to resist. In other words, if SRL is viewed as a natural form of human engagement, with all its associated qualities, then those who do not embody those qualities will be viewed as a problem and reformed in some way. Regardless if we believe all individuals are agentic or not, those who do not academically self-regulate or who do it ineffectively will be subject to a set of pedagogical interventions that are designed to shape them in specific ways. Thus, some people are given a different set of choices, ones that do not signify pathways to empowerment.

Teaching SRL is tied to neoliberalism and the kind of self that it is inscribed and valued in neoliberal arrangements. Therefore, SRL is implicated in inviting an intense self-interest, consumption, and a commitment to efficiency. These practices can invite a perpetual sense of emptiness, ignorance of the social good, and dehumanization. Furthermore, given that neoliberal forms of selfhood and SRL are tangled in middle-class conventions (e.g., Walkerdine, 2003), teaching SRL can marginalize and invalidate certain class identities. In this regard, SRL can be implicated in reproducing structures that reinforce differential advantages. These structures may be ignored, given that SRL invites the potential to overstate the degree of willful control that individuals exercise over their academic outcomes and life circumstances. Not being critically aware of this message and its dangers can lead to individual blame, reforms directed at individuals, and ignorance of ways educational environments contribute to engagement. Commitments to polyvocalism, emancipation, and sociohistoricism provide the lenses to consider different ways of understanding SRL, how it contributes to discrimination, and how it is embedded in a particular ideological context.

Complexities with agency are tied to other key areas of critical concern related to SRL. These include issues of autonomy, self, control, and empowerment. Each chapter contributes to discussions that focus on the complexities with these notions, which, not unlike agency, are assumed and taken for granted. By critically exploring these assumptions, a different picture of SRL emerges. Painting this alternative picture can provide researchers and practitioners with a starting point for considering the ethics of SRL so that they have a philosophical, ideological, and cultural basis for making pedagogical decisions involving SRL. The assumption driving this work is that critical analyses can invite practice that is ethically informed, as well as attuned to the potential effects that certain practices related to SRL can have on people. If teachers are already teaching or expected to shape pedagogy to support students' SRL, then they need to consider these critical foundational elements that underpin this concept.

My intention is not to encourage a wholesale rejection of SRL but rather to provoke critical conversations that invite possibilities for researchers and practitioners to reject, embrace, or reflect on SRL. By reject, I mean not allowing SRL to enter into one's pedagogical purview. This requires being attuned to various ways that SRL pedagogy can manifest in one's teaching and making an explicit effort to eliminate it. Rejecting SRL and its associated pedagogy does not necessarily signal low expectations or a teacher-directed approach. It is a mistake to see an opposing commitment to teaching SRL as teacher controlled. For one, teaching students to self-regulate their learning involves a great deal of teacher control, although at times that control is implicit and exercised only when students fail to engage in ways that align with a particular pedagogical structure. For example, in a student-centered classroom, direct prompts might not be prevalent. However, teacher surveillance remains constant to ensure that students function in accordance with classroom structure. Otherwise, a teacher might intervene in some way in order to preserve the integrity of the structure. Teachers may also spend a great deal of time socializing individuals to operate in environments wherein teachers take a facilitative role. Thus, what counts as teacher- or student-directed is not always clear. It is also a mistake to see an opposing commitment to teaching SRL as teacher controlled because there are other pedagogical possibilities that are not defined by this binary.

An example of a teacher rejecting SRL can be gleaned from a research study that I conducted in 2009 (Vassallo, in press). For one year, I worked with a secondary English teacher who taught in an urban school that served 100% African American students from an economically disadvantaged community. I conducted interviews and observations with one teacher, who is given the pseudonym Ms. Hall, in order to suggest ways for her to integrate SRL pedagogy in her classroom. Ms. Hall rejected suggestions to integrate SRL because she reasoned that it aligned with the logic of efficiency, endorsed the view of society as a meritocracy, and precluded her from developing meaningful relationships with her students—all of which she associated with the effects of neoliberalism in schools. Ms. Hall engaged in a number of pedagogical practices that she constructed in opposition to SRL. She was committed to forming strong relationships with students that were based on trust and a mutual commitment to think critically about the contradictions of schooling. Constructing this relationship and pursuing this pedagogical goal contradicted messages of SRL. Ms. Hall stated, "My students are not dumb, they see, experience, and live inequality . . . inequality that is beyond their control. If I communicate to them that their actions, thought processes, and goals are responsible for their success, my integrity will be in question." Ms. Hall critically engaged with the idea that hard work and discipline will enable students to achieve some normative standard of academic success. Her reasoning was that some life situations are beyond control and present individuals with vastly different choices; therefore, treating SRL as reflective of an agentic life was dishonest.

Ms. Hall did not always set out to achieve institutional learning goals, or work with students to define, structure, or alter their goals. Instead, she was attuned to, recognized, and validated student resistance, which was used as a means to recognize contradictions and inequalities in schooling. Ms. Hall did not see resistance to schooling as unequivocally negative, despite the fact that it contributed to poor school performance. Ms. Hall did not normalize academic success and did not endorse a middle-class life path, which includes college. She did not pursue pedagogical goals that focused on efficiently achieving "raised" standards for achievement (as measure by standardized scores). Ms. Hall described her teaching as organic and dedicated to valuing her students' capital and community.

In most teaching evaluation frameworks, Ms. Hall would be viewed as an ineffective teacher, a categorization that she found favorable. She argued that most teaching evaluations judge the degree to which pedagogy aligns with neoliberalism. Thus, to score high on those evaluations signaled her effectiveness at protecting and endorsing neoliberal assumptions and goals. Although potentially viewed as ineffective, Ms. Hall's rejection of SRL pedagogy was in favor of a focus on creating trusting relationships, her rejection of institutional mandates, a de-emphasis on pursuing predetermined goals, and not making pedagogical adjustments to ensure maximum efficiency and productivity. Rejecting SRL was not done in favor of adopting a teacher directed pedagogical approach, but one based on community, relationships, dialogue, and critical practice. Perhaps SRL can be integrated in such pedagogy. However, Ms. Hall viewed the values, assumptions, and purposes of SRL as in opposition to her pedagogical commitments.

Rejection of SRL pedagogy does not only come in resistance to neoliberalism; it can come in many forms and look significantly different. As in the case of Ms. Hall, she rejected SRL because of her perception of the assumptions that underpin and messages that are communicated in relation to this notion.

Another possible response that can be invited from the analyses in this book is to embrace SRL. One might fully endorse dominant representations of the 21st century and reason that students will be at a significant disadvantage if they do not effectively self-regulate their learning. Some might conclude that, not unlike proponents of neoliberalism, cultivating scientific, expressive, and entrepreneurial selves are in the interest of both individuals and the economy; therefore, SRL can be viewed both a social and personal good. Embracing SRL means not only valuing it and taking it up as a pedagogical goal, it also means endorsing the many assumptions that accompany this discourse. These include ideas about values for selfhood (expressive and scientific selves), what counts as freedom (making good choices by meeting situational demands), what counts as a social good, what the purposes of education are, and which culturally based conventions should be propagated (middle-class culture).

Although teaching SRL and, in effect, endorsing middle-class conventions may seem immediately problematic, there can be value to this commitment. Middle-class culture is referred to as the culture of power (Delpit, 1996). That means it is the dominant cultural and social capital that is required to gain access to resources and take advantage of available opportunities. Teaching the culture of power can serve a social justice goal, one that is strictly based on economic criteria. Especially given the continued influence of neoliberalism, teaching SRL could be considered part of an effort to teach the kind of cultural capital that supports economic justice. If neoliberalism continues to shape private and public life, then teaching SRL can support a goal to level the playing field by ensuring all individuals have the personal resources to compete. SRL can reasonably be tied to empowerment and justice; therefore, embracing SRL seems like a reasonable response. Embracing SRL should be accompanied by an understanding of what exactly is being embraced, how that shapes pedagogical decisions, and the potential effects of SRL pedagogy on students.

Reflection is the third possibility for engaging with SRL. This commitment is not as absolutist as the previous two. Reflection is not about embracing or rejecting SRL, but integrating it into the complex teaching and learning landscape of possibilities to be drawn on during certain pedagogical moments. Reflection involves engaging in a constant evaluation of pedagogy, practice, and student engagement that may or may not be related to SRL. That is, reflection involves a persistent awareness of (1) ways in which SRL implicitly and explicitly shapes pedagogy; (2) the assumptions, messages, and meanings of those pedagogical practices; (3) the affordances and constraints of SRL; (4) possibilities for engagement and pedagogy that are centered on SRL; (5) pedagogical possibilities that are unrelated to SRL; and (6) how pedagogical decisions can be framed in political, historical, and philosophical ways. This commitment may involve the integration of parts of SRL and the rejection of others—all while remaining attuned to the philosophical, cultural, and ideological underpinnings of those parts.

Reflection may involve ephemeral moments of embracing and rejecting. It can be viewed as a strategic deliberation involving an assessment of classroom dynamics, students' dispositions, broad pedagogical goals, goals for the day, activity, and political purpose of the teaching act. These deliberations can inform pedagogical practices that are judged to produce a particular effect. For example, a teacher may find that in one context, endorsing SRL for a particular student makes sense. Based on the effects teachers want to produce, they may rely on the discourse of SRL to inform a pedagogical intervention. The teacher does not necessarily normalize SRL, pathologize possible resistance to it, or view SRL as agentic and, therefore, for students' own good. Therefore, the teacher can remain flexible, but not in the neoliberal sense whereby the goal is to adapt pedagogical strategies to efficiently and productively achieve mandated curricula goals. Reflection is not about personalizing learning, which may involve deliberations about who needs what types of SRL interventions and whether or not those interventions are effective and in need of change. Reflection is about holding the complexities of SRL in mind when deliberating over pedagogical decisions and goals that are intended to produce particular effects.

Regardless if one rejects, embraces, or reflects on SRL, the common denominator is the commitment to frame SRL in political, historical, and philosophical terms. The book is a starting point for this engagement. Although I draw from a variety of perspectives and consider several dimensions of SRL, the analyses in this book do not capture the full range of critical nuances that need to inform conversations on SRL; of course more work needs to be done.

Continuing with a commitment to polyvocalism, the dialogue can be extended to include critical analyses of race, gender, and disability, to name a few. For example, Jackson, McKenzie, and Hobfoll (2000) suggest that conceptions of SRL tend to reflect conventional Western male characteristics. The critical engagement of SRL can benefit immensely from critical analyses of this alignment and how certain conceptions and pedagogical models align with and endorse gendered identities. Educational psychologists have considered differences in SRL across males and females (Pajares, 2002; Yukselturk & Bulut, 2009; Zimmerman & Martinez-Pons, 1990). However, differences are discussed independent of the values for gendered ways of being. Of similar importance, critical analyses of SRL that are dedicated to identity must consider intersections of group affiliations. For example, the analysis of socioeconomic class can be developed by considering the patterns of SRL among white working-class women and possible differences among black working-class women.

To further develop sociohistorical analyses, other philosophical perspectives, concepts, and methods can be applied to further critical dialogue. For example, a genealogical analysis of SRL can contribute to interesting reflections on how the concept of SRL has changed from one moment to another. Inspired by Michel Foucault, such an analysis may involve exploring how the representation of SRL has changed over time. The analysis can be framed using a four-part analytical framework that is characteristic of Foucault's work. The framework includes ontology, deontology, ascetics, and telos. Ontology, also referred to as ethical substance, involves analysis of which part of subjectivity needs to be studied and worked on. Deontology, or the mode of subjection, is about the ways in which individuals establish their relation to ethical substance. Ascetics, also known as ethical work, consists of those self-forming activities that are meant to transform individuals into autonomous ethical agents who recognize themselves as obliged to follow a certain rule and rationality. Finally, telos is the ideal endpoint, what one strives for or aspires to in their ethical work. This framework can be summed up as the substance that individuals need to work on, how they become bound to this substance, what they do to attain it, and what the end point looks like. This analysis is useful not only for denaturalizing concepts but also for considering the political, cultural, and philosophical contexts that are linked to changes in SRL.

The analyses that I conducted and the CEP perspective offered reflect points of critical reflection about educational psychology, in general, and SRL, in particular. Although more work needs to be done, I hope that SRL is treated cautiously and a conversation remains focused on historical, cultural, and philosophical underpinnings of the assumptions that inform this notion.

References

Abar, B., & Loken, E. (2010). Self-regulated learning and self-directed study in a pre-college sample. *Learning and Individual Differences, 20*, 25–29.

Anyon, J. (1981). Social class and school knowledge. *Curriculum Inquiry, 11*, 3–42.

Apple, M. W. (1980). The other side of the hidden curriculum: Correspondence theories and the labor process. *Interchange, 11*, 5–22.

Apple, M. W. (2000). *Official knowledge: Democratic education in a conservative age* (2nd ed.). New York: Routledge.

Apple, M. W. (2006). Understanding and interrupting neoliberalism and neoconservatism in education. *Pedagogies: An International Journal, 1*, 21–26.

Archer, M. S. (2003). *Structure, agency and the internal conversation.* Cambridge, UK: Cambridge University Press.

Atkinson, R. C., & Shiffrin, R. M. (1968). Human memory: A proposed system and its control processes. In K. W. Spence & J. T. Spence (Eds.), *The psychology of learning and motivation: Advances in research and theory* (Vol. 2, pp. 89–195). New York: Academic.

Ayers, R., & Ayers, B. (2011). Living in the gutter: Conflict and contradiction in the neoliberal classroom: A call to action. *Berkeley Review of Education, 2*, 95–108.

Azevedo, R., Johnson, A., Chauncey, A., & Graesser, A. (2011). Use of hypermedia to assess and convey self-regulated learning. In B. J. Zimmerman & D. H. Schunk (Eds.), *Handbook of self-regulation of learning and performance* (pp. 102–121). New York: Routledge.

Bandura, A. (1989). Human agency in social cognitive theory. *American psychologist, 44*, 1175–1183.

Bandura, A. (1997). *Self-efficacy: The exercise of control.* New York: Freeman.

Bandura, A. (2001). Social cognitive theory: An agentic perspective. *Annual Review of Psychology, 52*, 1–26.

Bandura, A. (2006). Toward a psychology of human agency. *Perspectives on Psychological Science, 1*, 164.

Bartlett, L., Frederick, M., Gulbrandsen, T., & Murillo, E. (2002). The marketization of education: Public schools for private ends. *Anthropology & Education Quarterly, 33*, 5–29.

Becker, G. S. (1993). *Human capital: A theoretical and empirical analysis with special reference to education* (3rd ed.). Chicago: University of Chicago Press.

Bednall, T. C., & Kehoe, E. J. (2011). Effects of self-regulatory instructional aids on self-directed study. *Instructional Science, 39*, 205–226.

Bembenutty, H. (2009). Test anxiety and academic delay of gratification. *College Student Journal, 1*, 10–21.

Bembenutty, H., & Karabenick, S. (2004). Inherent association between academic delay of gratification, future time perspective, and self-regulated learning. *Educational Psychology Review, 16*, 35–57.

Berliner, D. C. (1993). The 100-year journey of educational psychology. In T. K. Fagan & G. R. Vanden-Bos (Eds.), *Exploring applied psychology: origins and critical analyses* (pp. 37–78). Washington, DC: American Psychological Association.

Bernstein, B. (1971). *Class, codes and control.* London: Routledge.

Besley, T. (2002). *Counseling youth: foucault, power, and the ethics of subjectivity.* Westport, CT: Greenwood.

Biesta, G. (2009). Good education in an age of measurement: On the need to reconnect with the question of purpose in education. *Educational Assessment, Evaluation and Accountability, 21*, 33–46.

Biesta, G. (2010). A new logic of emancipation: The methodology of Jacques Rancière. *Educational Theory, 60*, 39–59.

Billig, M. (2008). *The hidden roots of critical psychology: Understanding the impact of Locke, Shaftesbury and Reid.* London: Sage.

Bird, L. (1999). Towards a more critical educational psychology. *Annual Review of Critical Psychology, 1*, 21–33.

Boekaerts, M., & Cascallar, E. (2006). How far have we moved toward the integration of theory and practice in self-regulation? *Educational Psychology Review, 18*, 199–210.

Boekaerts, M., & Corno, L. (2005). Self-regulation in the classroom: A perspective on assessment and intervention. *Applied Psychology: An International Review, 54*, 199–231.

Boekaerts, M., Maes, S., & Karoly, P. (2005). Self-regulation across domains of applied psychology: Is there an emerging consensus? *Applied Psychology, 54*, 149–154.

Bourdieu, P. (1977). Cultural reproduction and social reproduction. In J. Karabel & A. H. Halsey (Eds.), *Power and ideology in education* (pp. 487–511). New York: Oxford University Press.

Bourdieu, P. (1984). *Distinction: A social critique of the judgment of taste.* Boston: Harvard University Press.

Bourdieu, P. (2004). *Outline of a theory of practice.* Cambridge, UK: Cambridge University Press.

Bourdieu, P., & Passeron, J. C. (1990). *Reproduction in education, society, and culture.* London: Sage.

Bowles, S., & Gintis, H. (1976). *Schooling in capitalist America.* New York: Basic.

Bradley, B. S. (2005). *Psychology and experience.* New York: Cambridge University Press.

Brantlinger, E. (2003). *Dividing classes: How the middle-class negotiates and rationalizes school advantage.* New York: Routledge.

Brice-Heath, S. (1983). *Ways with words: Language, life and work in communities and classrooms.* Cambridge, UK: Cambridge University Press.

Briscoe, F. M. (2012). Anarchist, neoliberal, & democratic decision-making: Deepening the joy in learning and teaching. *Educational Studies, 48*, 76–102.

Brown, W. (2003). Neo-liberalism and the end of liberal democracy. *Theory & Event, 7*. Retrieved October 15, 2012, from http://muse.jhu.edu/journals/theory_and_event/v007/7.1brown.html

Bruner, J. S. (1990). *Acts of meaning*. Boston: Harvard University Press.

Bruner, J. S. (1996). *The culture of education*. Boston: Harvard University Press.

Bullock, H. E., & Limbert, W. M. (2009). Class. In D. Fox, I. Prilleltensky, & S. Austin (Eds.), *Critical psychology: An introduction* (2nd ed., pp. 215–231). Los Angeles: Sage.

Burman, E. (2008). *Deconstructing developmental psychology* (2nd ed.). New York: Routledge.

Butler, D. L. (2002). Qualitative approaches to investigating self-regulated learning: Contributions and challenges. *Educational Psychologist, 37*, 59–63.

Butler, D. L. (2003). Structuring instruction to promote self-regulated learning by adolescents and adults with learning disabilities. *Exceptionality, 11*(1), 39–60.

Calarco, J. M. (2011). "I need help!" Social class and children's help-seeking in elementary school. *American Sociological Review, 76*, 862–882.

Carver, C. S., & Scheier, M. F. (2000). Autonomy and self-regulation. *Psychological Inquiry, 11*, 284–291.

Cavieres, E. A. (2011). The class and culture-based exclusion of the Chilean neoliberal educational reform. *Educational Studies, 47*, 111–132.

Chong, W. H. (2006). *Personal agency beliefs in self-regulation: The exercise of personal responsibility, choice and control in learning*. Singapore: Marshall Cavendish International.

Clarke, J. (2005). New Labour's citizens: Activated, empowered, responsibilized, abandoned? *Critical Social Policy, 25*, 447–463.

Cleary, T. J., Platten, P., & Nelson, A. (2008). Effectiveness of the Self-Regulation Empowerment Program with urban high school students. *Journal of Advanced Academics, 20*, 70–107.

Cleary, T., & Zimmerman, B. J. (2004). Self-regulation empowerment program: A school-based program to enhance self-regulated and self-motivated cycles of student learning. *Psychology in the Schools, 41*, 537–550.

Coleman, J. S. (1988). Social capital in the creation of human capital. *American Journal of Sociology, 94*, 95–120.

Corcoran, T. (2007). Counselling in a discursive world. *International Journal for the Advancement of Counselling, 29*(2), 111–122.

Corno, L. (1986). The metacognitive control components of self-regulated learning. *Contemporary Educational Psychology, 11*, 333–346.

Corno, L. (1989). Self-regulated learning: A volitional analysis. In B. J. Zimmerman & D. H. Schunk (Eds.), *Self-regulated Learning and academic achievement: Theory, research, and practice* (pp. 111–141). New York: Springer-Verlag.

Corno, L., & Xu, J. (2004). Homework as the job of childhood. *Theory into Practice, 43*, 227–233.

Cushman, P. (1990). Why the self is empty: Toward a historically situated psychology. *American Psychologist, 45*, 599–611.

Dabbagh, N., & Kitsantas, A. (2012). Personal Learning Environments, social media, and self-regulated learning: A natural formula for connecting formal and informal learning. *Internet and Higher Education, 15*, 3–8.

Darder, A. (2009). Teaching as an act of love: Reflections on Paulo Freire and his contributions to our lives and our work. *The critical pedagogy reader* (2nd ed., pp. 567–578). New York: Routledge.

Davies, B., & Bansel, P. (2007). Neoliberalism and education. *International Journal of Qualitative Studies in Education, 20*, 247–259.

Delpit, L. (1996). *Others people's children.* New York: New Press.

Dewey, J. (1938). *Education and experience.* New York: Collier.

Dilts, A. (2011). From "Entrepreneur of the Self" to "Care of the Self": Neo-liberal governmentality and Foucault's ethics. *Foucault Studies, 12,* 130–146.

Du Bois, N. F., & Staley, R. K. (1997). A self-regulated learning approach to teaching educational psychology. *Educational Psychology Review, 9,* 171–197.

Duncan-Andrade, J. (2010). To study is a revolutionary duty. In G. Goodman (Ed.), *Educational psychology reader: The art and science of how people learn* (pp. 165–178). New York: Peter Lang.

Durrheim, K., Hook, D., & Riggs, D. W. (2009). Race and racism. In D. Fox, I. Prilleltensky, & S. Austin (Eds.), *Critical psychology: An introduction* (2nd ed., pp. 197–214). Los Angeles: Sage.

Eckert, P. (1989). *Jocks and burnouts: Social categories and identity in the high school.* New York: Teachers College Press.

Ellis, C., & Folley, S. (2010). Using student assessment choice and eassessment to achieve self-regulated learning. In G. Dettori & D. Persico (Eds.), *Fostering self-regulated learning through ICT* (pp. 89–104). Hershey, PA: Information Science Reference.

Fendler, L. (2001). Educating flexible souls: The construction of subjectivity through developmentality and interaction. In K. Hultqvist & G. Dahlberg (Eds.), *Governing the child in the new millennium* (pp. 119–142). New York: Routledge Falmer.

Fendler, L. (2010). *Michel Foucault.* London: Continuum.

Fine, M., & Burns, A. (2003). Class notes: Toward a critical psychology of class and schooling. *Journal of Social Issues, 59,* 841–860.

Finn, P. J. (2009). *Literacy with an attitude: Educating working-class children in their own self-interest.* Albany State University of New York Press.

Fitzsimons, P. (2011). *Governing the self: A Foucauldian critique of managerialism in education.* New York: Peter Lang.

Foucault, M. (1988). Technologies of the self. In L. H. Martin, H. Gutman, & P. H. Hutton (Eds.), *Technologies of the self: A seminar with Michel Foucault* (pp. 16–49). Amherst: University of Massachusetts Press.

Foucault, M. (2008). *The birth of biopolitics: Lectures at the Collège de France, 1978–1979* (G. Burchell, Trans.). New York: Palgrave Macmillan.

Fox, D., Prilleltensky, I., & Austin, S. (2009a). Critical psychology for social justice: Concerns and dilemmas. In D. Fox, I. Prilleltensky, & S. Austin (Eds.), *Critical psychology: An introduction* (2nd ed., pp. 3–19). Los Angeles: Sage.

Fox, D., Prilleltensky, I., & Austin, S. (2009b). *Critical psychology: An introduction* (2nd ed.). Los Angeles: Sage.

Freie, C. (2007). *Class construction: White working-class student identity in the new millennium.* Lanham, MD: Lexington Books.

Freire, P. (1987). *Education for critical consciousness.* New York: Continuum.
Freire, P. (2000). *Pedagogy of the oppressed.* New York: Continuum.
Gallagher, S. (2003). *Educational psychology: Disrupting the dominant discourse.* New York: Peter Lang.
Gee, J. P. (1992). *The social mind: Language, ideology, and social practice.* New York: Bergin & Garvey.
Gee, J. P. (2004). *Situated language and learning: A critique of traditional schooling.* New York: Routledge.
Gergen, K. J. (2009). *Relational being: Beyond self and community.* New York: Oxford University Press.
Giddens, A. (1984). *The constitution of society: Outline of the theory of structuration.* Berkeley: University of California Press.
Giroux, H. A. (2001). *Theory and resistance in education: Towards a pedagogy for the opposition* (Rev. and exp. ed.). Westport, CT: Greenwood.
Giroux, H. A. (2009). Critical theory and educational practice. In A. Darder, M. P. Baltodano, & R. D. Torres (Eds.), *The critical pedagogy reader* (2nd ed., pp. 27–51). New York: Routledge.
Goodman, G. S. (2008). *Educational psychology: An application of critical constructivism.* New York: Peter Lang.
Gorlewski, J. (2011). *Power, resistance, and literacy: Writing for social justice.* Charlotte, NC: Information Age.
Graham, S., Harris, K. R., & Troia, G. (1998). Writing and self-regulation: Cases from the self-regulated strategy development model. In D. H. Schunk & B. J. Zimmerman (Eds.), *Self-regulated learning: From teaching to self-reflective practice* (pp. 20–41). New York: Guilford.
Greene, J. A., & Azevedo, R. (2007). A theoretical review of Winne and Hadwin's model of self-regulated learning: New perspectives and directions. *Review of Educational Research, 77,* 334–372.
Greene, J. A., Bolick, C. M., & Robertson, J. (2010). Fostering historical knowledge and thinking skills using hypermedia learning environments: The role of self-regulated learning. *Computers & Education, 54,* 230–243.
Greene, M. (1988). *The dialectic of freedom.* New York: Teachers College Press.
Grinder, R. E. (1989). Educational psychology: The master science. In M. C. Wittrock & F. Farley (Eds.), *The future of educational psychology* (pp. 3–18). Hillsdale, NJ: Lawrence Erlbaum.
Hadwin, A. F. (2012). Response to Vassallo's claims from a historically situated view of self-regulated learning as adaptation in the face of challenge. *New Ideas in Psychology.* doi:http://dx.doi.org/10.1016/j.newideapsych.2012.05.001
Hadwin, A., & Järvelä, S. (2011). Introduction to a special issue on social aspects of self-regulated learning: Where social and self meet in the strategic regulation of learning. *Teachers College Record, 113,* 235–239.
Hadwin, A. F., Järvelä, S., & Miller, M. (2011). Self-regulated, co-regulated, and socially shared regulation of learning. In B. J. Zimmerman & D. H. Schunk (Eds.), *Handbook of self-regulation of learning and performance* (pp. 65–86). New York: Routledge.

Hadwin, A., & Oshige, M. (2011). Self-regulation, coregulation, and socially shared regulation: Exploring perspectives of social in self-regulated learning theory. *Teachers College Record, 113*, 240–264.

Hamamura, T., Meijer, Z., Heine, S. J., Kamaya, K., & Hori, I. (2009). Approach–avoidance motivation and information processing: A cross-cultural analysis. *Personality and Social Psychology Bulletin, 35*, 454–462.

Hardaway, C. R., & McLoyd, V. C. (2009). Escaping poverty and securing middle-class status: How race and socioeconomic status shape mobility prospects for African Americans during the transition to adulthood. *Journal of Youth and Adolescence, 38*, 242–256.

Harris, K. R., Graham, S., & Mason, L. H. (2003). Self-regulated strategy development in the classroom: Part of a balanced approach to writing instruction for students with disabilities. *Focus on Exceptional Children, 35*, 1–16.

Harvey, D. (2006). Neo-liberalism as creative destruction. *Geografiska Annaler: Series B, Human Geography, 88*, 145–158.

Harvey, D. (2007). *A brief history of neoliberalism.* New York: Oxford University Press.

Higgins, E. T., & Spiegel, S. (2004). Promotion and prevention strategies for self-regulation: A motivated cognition perspective. In R. F. Baumeister & K. D. Vohs (Eds.), *Handbook of self-regulation: Research, theory and applications* (pp. 171–188). New York: Guilford Press.

Hilden, K. R., & Pressley, M. (2007). Self-regulation through transactional strategies instruction. *Reading & Writing Quarterly, 23*, 51–75.

Hill, N. E., & Torres, K. (2010). Negotiating the American dream: The paradox of aspirations and achievement among Latino students and engagement between their families and schools. *Journal of Social Issues, 66*, 95–112.

Hochschild, A. R. (1979). Emotion work, feeling rules, and social structure. *American Journal of Sociology, 85*, 551–575.

Hole, J., & Crozier, W. (2007). Dispositional and situational learning goals and children's self-regulation. *Journal of Educational Psychology, 77*, 773–86.

Holzman, L. (1997). *Schools for growth: Radical alternatives to current educational models.* Mahwah, NJ: Lawrence Erlbaum.

Housand, A., & Reis, S. M. (2008). Self-regulated learning in reading: Gifted pedagogy and instructional settings. *Journal of Advanced Academics, 20*, 29.

Howse, R. B., Lange, G., Farran, D. C., & Boyles, C. D. (2003). Motivation and self-regulation as predictors of achievement in economically disadvantaged young children. *Journal of Experimental Education, 71*, 151–174.

Huang, J., & Prochner, L. (2004). Chinese parenting styles and children's self-regulated learning. *Journal of Research in Childhood Education, 18*, 227–238.

Hursh, D. (2000). Neoliberalism and the control of teachers, students, and learning: The rise of standards, standardization, and accountability. *Cultural Logic, 4.* Retrieved October 15, 2012, from http://clogic.eserver.org/4-1/hursh.html

Hursh, D., & Martina, C. A. (2003). Neoliberalism and schooling in the US: How state and federal government education policies perpetuate inequality. *Journal for Critical Education Policy Studies, 1*, 1–13.

Jackson, T., Mackenzie, J., & Hobfoll, S. E. (2000). Communal aspects of self-regulation. In M. Boekaerts, P. R. Pintrich, & M. Zeidner (Eds.), *Handbook of self-regulation* (pp. 275–302). San Diego, CA: Academic.

Jardine, D. (2010). Jean Piaget and the origins of intelligence: A return to "life itself." G. Goodman (Ed.), *Educational psychology reader: The art and science of how people learn* (pp. 130–148). New York: Peter Lang.

Järvelä, S. (2011). How does help seeking help?—New prospects in a variety of contexts. *Learning and Instruction, 21*, 297–299.

Järvelä, S., & Järvenoja, H. (2011). Socially constructed self-regulated learning and motivation regulation in collaborative learning groups. *Teachers College Record, 113*, 350–374.

Journell, W. (2011). Teaching the 2008 presidential election at three demographically diverse schools: An exercise in neoliberal governmentality. *Educational Studies, 47*(2), 133–159.

Karabenick, S. A. (2003). Seeking help in large college classes: A person-centered approach. *Contemporary Educational Psychology, 28*, 37–58.

Kincheloe, J. L. (1999a). The foundations of a democratic educational psychology. In J. L. Kincheloe, S. R. Steinberg, & L. Villarde (Eds.), *Rethinking intelligence: Confronting psychological assumptions about teaching and learning* (pp. 1–26). New York: Routledge.

Kincheloe, J. L. (1999b). Trouble ahead, trouble behind: Grounding the post-formal critique of educational psychology. In J. L. Kincheloe, S. Steinberg, & P. H. Hinchey (Eds.), *The post-formal reader: Cognition and education* (pp. 4–54). New York: Falmer.

Kincheloe, J. L. (2005). *Critical constructivism primer*. New York: Peter Lang.

Kincheloe, J. L. (2007). Introduction: Educational psychology—Limitations and possibilities. In J. L. Kincheloe & R. A. Horn (Eds.), *The Praeger handbook of education and psychology* (pp. 3–40). Westport, CT: Praeger.

Kincheloe, J. L., & Horn, R. A. (2008). *The Praeger handbook of education and psychology*. Westport, CT: Praeger.

Kincheloe, J. L., & Steinberg, S. R. (1993). A tentative description of post-formal thinking: The critical confrontation with cognitive theory. *Harvard Educational Review, 63*, 296–321.

King, A. (2009). Overcoming structure and agency: Talcott Parsons, Ludwig Wittgenstein and the theory of social action. *Journal of Classical Sociology, 9*, 260–288.

Kirschner, S. R., & Martin, J. (2010). The sociocultural turn in psychology: An introduction and an invitation. In S. R. Kirschner & J. Martin (Eds.), *The sociocultural turn in psychology: The contextual emergence of mind and self* (pp. 1–27). New York: Columbia University Press.

Kitsantis, A., & Zimmerman, B. J. (2006). Enhancing self-regulation of practice: The influence of graphing and self-evaluative standards. *Metacognition and Learning, 1*, 201–212.

Klein, N. (2007). *The shock doctrine: The rise of disaster capitalism*. New York: Metropolitan Books.

Kohl, H. (1992). I won't learn from you! Thoughts on the role of assent in learning. *Rethinking Schools, 7*, 16–17.

Kusserow, A. (2004). *American individualisms: Child rearing and social class in three neighborhoods*. New York: Palgrave Macmillan.

Lakes, R. (2008). The neoliberal rhetoric of workforce readiness. *Journal for Critical Education Policy Studies, 6*, 1–9.

Lakes, R. D., & Carter, P. A. (2011). Neoliberalism and education: An introduction. *Educational Studies, 47*, 107–110.

Lamont, M. (2000). *The dignity of working men: Morality and the boundaries of race, class, and immigration.* Boston: Harvard University Press.

Lapan, R. T., Kardash, C. A., & Turner, S. (2002). Empowering students to become self-regulated learners. *Professional School Counseling, 5*, 257–265.

Lareau, A. (2000). *Home advantage: Social class and parental intervention in elementary education.* Lanham, MD: Rowman & Littlefield.

Lareau, A. (2003). *Unequal childhoods: Class, race, and family life.* Berkeley: University of California Press.

Latour, B., & Woolgar, S. (1986). *Laboratory life: The construction of scientific facts.* Princeton, NJ: Princeton University Press.

Lee, J. S., & Bowen, N. K. (2006). Parent involvement, cultural capital, and the achievement gap among elementary school children. *American Educational Research Journal, 43*, 193–218.

Lesko, N. (2001). *Act your age!: A cultural construction of adolescence.* New York: Routledge.

Linkon, S. L. (1999). *Teaching working-class.* Boston: University of Massachusetts Press.

Lizardo, O. (2010). Beyond the antinomies of structure: Levi-Strauss, Giddens, Bourdieu, and Sewell. *Theory and Society, 39*, 651–688.

Lodewyk, K. R., Winne, P. H., & Jamieson-Noel, D. L. (2009). Implications of task structure on self-regulated learning and achievement. *Educational Psychology, 29*, 1–25.

Luttrell, W. (1989). Working-class women's ways of knowing: Effects of gender, race and class. *Sociology of Education, 62*, 33–46.

MacLeod, J. (1987). *Ain't no makin' it: Leveled aspirations in a low-income neighborhood.* Boulder, CO: Westview Press.

Malott, C. S. (Ed.). (2011). *Critical pedagogy and cognition: An introduction to postformal educational psychology.* London: Springer-Verlag.

Martin, J. (2004a). The educational inadequacy of conceptions of self in educational psychology. *Interchange, 35*, 185–208.

Martin, J. (2004b). Self-regulated learning, social cognitive theory, and agency. *Educational Psychologist, 39*, 135–145.

Martin, J. (2006). Social cultural perspectives in educational psychology. In P. A. Alexander & P. H. Winne (Eds.), *Handbook of educational psychology* (2nd ed., pp. 595–614). Mahwah, NJ: Routledge.

Martin, J. (2007). The selves of educational psychology: Conceptions, contexts, and critical considerations. *Educational Psychologist, 42*, 79–89.

Martin, J., & Gillespie, A. (2010). A Neo-Meadian approach to human agency: Relating the social and the psychological in the ontogenesis of perspective-coordinating persons. *Integrative Psychological and Behavioral Science, 44*, 252–272.

Martin, J., & McLellan, A. M. (2008). The educational psychology of self-regulation: A conceptual and critical analysis. *Studies in Philosophy and Education, 27*, 433–448.

Martin, J., & Sugarman, J. (2001). Is the self a kind of understanding? *Journal for the Theory of Social Behaviour, 31*, 103–114.

Martin, J., Sugarman, J., & Thompson, J. (2003). *Psychology and the question of agency.* Albany State University of New York Press.

Martinez-Pons, M. (2002). Parental influences on children's academic self-regulatory development. *Theory into Practice, 41*, 126–131.

Mattanah, J. F., Pratt, M. W., Cowan, P. A., & Cowan, C. P. (2005). Authoritative parenting, parental scaffolding of long-division mathematics, and children's academic competence in fourth grade. *Journal of Applied Developmental Psychology, 26*, 85–106.

Matusov, E. (2011). Imagining No Child Left Behind freed from neoliberal hijackers. *Democracy and Education, 19*, 1–8.

McCaslin, M. (2009). Co-regulation of student motivation and emergent identity. *Educational Psychologist, 44*, 137–146.

McCaslin, M., Bozack, A. R., Napolean, L., Thomas, A., Vasquez, V., Wayman, V., & Zhang, J. (2006). Self-regulated learning and classroom management: Theory, research and considerations for classroom practice. In C. M. Evertson & C. S. Weinstein (Eds.), *Handbook of classroom management: Research, practice, and contemporary issues* (pp. 232–252). Mahwah, NJ: Lawrence Erlbaum.

McCaslin, M., & Burross, H. L. (2011). Research on individual differences within a sociocultural perspective: Co-regulation and adaptive learning. *Teachers College Record, 113*, 325–349.

McCaslin, M., & Hickey, D. T. (2001). Self-regulated learning and academic achievement: A Vygotskian view. In B. J. Zimmerman & D. H. Schunk (Eds.), *Self-regulated learning and academic achievement: Theoretical perspectives* (2nd ed., pp. 227–252). Mahwah, NJ: Lawrence Erlbaum.

McInerney, D. M. (2011). Culture and self-regulation in educational contexts: Assessing the relationship of cultural group to self-regulation. In B. J. Zimmerman & D. H. Schunk (Eds.), *Handbook of self-regulation of learning and performance* (pp. 442–464). New York: Routledge.

McLaren, P. (2007). *Life in schools. An introduction to critical pedagogy in the foundations of education* (5th ed.). Reading, MA: Addison Wesley Longman.

McLaren, P. (2009). Critical pedagogy: A look at the major concepts. In A. Darder, M. P. Baltodano, & R. D. Torres (Eds.), *The critical pedagogy reader* (2nd ed., pp. 61–83). New York: Routledge.

Mead, G. H. (1934). *Mind, self and society*. Chicago: University of Chicago Press.

Miller, G. A., Galanter, E., & Pribram, K. H. (1960). *Plans and the structure of behavior*. New York: Holt, Rinehart, & Winston.

Miller, P. (1986). Teasing as language socialization and verbal play in a white working-class community. In B. B. Schieffelin & E. Ochs (Eds.), *Language socialization across cultures* (Vol. 3, pp. 165–181). Cambridge, UK: Cambridge University Press.

Miller, S., Heafner, T., & Massey, D. (2009). High-school teachers' attempts to promote self-regulated learning: "I may learn from you, yet how do I do it." *Urban Review: Issues and Ideas in Public Education, 4*, 121–140.

Mischel, W., Shoda, Y., & Rodriguez, M. I. (1989). Delay of gratification in children. *Science, 244*, 933–938.

Murdock, T. B. (2000). Incorporating economic context into educational psychology: Methodological and conceptual challenges. *Educational Psychologist, 35*, 113–124.

Myrseth, K. O. R., & Fishbach, A. (2009). Self-control a function of knowing when and how to exercise restraint. *Current Directions in Psychological Science, 18*, 247–252.

Neitzel, C., & Stright, A. D. (2003). Relations between mothers' scaffolding and children's academic self-regulation: Establishing a foundation of self-regulatory competence. *Journal of Family Psychology, 17*, 147–159.

Nelson, G., & Prilleltensky, I. (2005). *Community psychology: In pursuit of liberation and wellbeing.* New York: Palgrave Macmillan.

Newman, R. S. (1994). Adaptive help seeking: A strategy of self-regulated learning. In D. H. Schunk & B. J. Zimmerman (Eds.), *Self-regulation of learning and performance: Issues and educational applications* (pp. 283–301). Hillsdale, NJ: Lawrence Erlbaum.

Newman, R. S. (2002). How self-regulated learners cope with academic difficulty: The role of adaptive help seeking. *Theory into Practice, 41*, 132–138.

Obama, B. (2009a). *Remarks by the President to the Hispanic Chamber of Commerce on a complete and competitive American education.* Retrieved October 12, 2012, from http://www.whitehouse.gov/the-press-office/remarks-president-united-states-hispanic-chamber-commerce

Obama, B. (2009b). *Prepared remarks of President Barack Obama: Back to school event.* Retrieved August 8, 2012, from http://www.whitehouse.gov/MediaResources/PreparedSchoolRemarks/

Ogbu, J. (1993). Differences in cultural frame of reference. *International Journal of Behavioral Development, 16*, 483–506.

Ogbu, J. (2003). *Black American students in an affluent suburb: A study of academic disengagement.* Mahwah, NJ: Lawrence Erlbaum.

Organisation for Economic Co-operation and Development, Center for Education Research and Innovation. (1988). *The social and economic integration of young people.* Paris.

Organisation for Economic Co-operation and Development, Center for Education Research and Innovation. (2005). *The definition and selection of key competencies.* Retrieved January 12, 2012 from http://www.oecd.org/general/searchresults/? q=the%20definition%20and%20 selection%20of%20key%20competencies&cx=012432601748511391518:xzeadub0b0a&cof =FORID:11&ie=UTF-8

Ormrod, J. E. (2011). *Educational psychology: Developing learners* (7th ed.). Boston: Pearson.

Packer, M. J., & Goicoechea, J. (2000). Sociocultural and constructivist theories of learning: Ontology, not just epistemology. *Educational Psychologist, 35*, 227–241.

Packer, M. J., & Tappan, M. B. (2001). *Cultural and critical perspectives on human development.* Albany: State University of New York Press.

Pajares, F. (1992). Teachers' beliefs and educational research: Cleaning up a messy construct. *Review of Educational Research, 62*, 307–332.

Pajares, F. (2002). Gender and perceived self-efficacy in self-regulated learning. *Theory into Practice, 41*, 116–125.

Paris, S. G., Byrnes, J. P., & Paris, A. H. (2001). Constructing theories, identities, and actions of self-regulated learners. In B. J. Zimmerman & D. H. Schunk (Eds.), *Self-regulated learning and academic achievement: Theoretical perspectives* (pp. 253–287). Mahwah, NJ: Lawrence Erlbaum.

Paris, S. G., & Paris, A. H. (2001). Classroom applications of research on self-regulated learning. *Educational Psychologist, 36*, 89–101.

Parker, I., & Shotter, J. (1990). *Deconstructing social psychology.* London: Routledge.

Partnership for 21st Century Skills. (2009). *P21 framework definitions*. Retrieved September 20, 2010, from http://www.p21.org/documents/P21_Framework.pdf

Perels, F., Merget-Kullmann, M., Wende, M., Schmitz, B., & Buchbinder, C. (2009). Improving self-regulated learning of preschool children: Evaluation of training for kindergarten teachers. *British Journal of Educational Psychology, 79*, 311–327.

Perry, N. (2002). Introduction: Using qualitative methods to enrich understandings of self-regulated learning. *Educational Psychologist, 37*, 1–3.

Perry, N., & Drummond, L. (2002). Helping young students become self-regulated researchers and writers. *Reading Teacher, 56*, 298–310.

Perry, N., Nordby, C. J., & VandeKamp, K. O. (2003). Promoting self-regulated reading and writing at home and school. *Elementary School Journal, 103*, 317–338.

Perry, N., VandeKamp, K. O., Mercer, L. K., & Nordby, C. J. (2002). Investigating teacher-student interactions that foster self-regulated learning. *Educational Psychologist, 37*, 5–15.

Peters, M. A. (2001). *Poststructuralism, Marxism, and neoliberalism: Between theory and politics*. Lanham, MD: Rowman & Littlefield.

Piaget, J. (1952). *The origins of intelligence in children* (M. T. Cook, Trans.). New York: W. W. Norton.

Pino-Pasternak, D., Whitebread, D., & Tolmie, A. (2010). A multidimensional analysis of parent–child interactions during academic tasks and their relationships with children's self-regulated learning. *Cognition and Instruction, 28*, 219–272.

Pintrich, P. R. (1995). Understanding self-regulated learning. *New directions for teaching and learning* (63), 3–12.

Pintrich, P. R. (2000). The role of goal orientation in self-regulated learning. In M. Boekaerts, P. R. Pintrich, & M. Zeidner (Eds.), *Handbook of self-regulation* (pp. 451–502). San Diego, CA: Academic.

Porter, R. (2001). *The enlightenment*. New York: Palgrave Macmillan.

Post, Y., Boyer, W., & Brett, L. (2006). A historical examination of self-regulation: Helping children now and in the future. *Early Childhood Education Journal, 34*, 5–14.

Prawat, R. S. (1998). Current self-regulation views of learning and motivation viewed through a Deweyan lens: The problems with dualism. *American Educational Research Journal, 35*, 199–224.

Pressley, M., El-Dinary, P. B., Wharton-McDonald, R., & Brown, R. (1998). Transactional instruction of comprehension strategies in the elementary grades. In D. H. Schunk & B. J. Zimmerman (Eds.), *Self-regulated learning: From teaching to self-reflective practice* (pp. 42–56). New York: Guilford.

Purcell-Gates, V. (1997). *Other people's words: The cycle of low literacy*. Boston: Harvard University Press.

Putnam, R. D. (2001). *Bowling alone: The collapse and revival of American community*. New York: Simon & Schuster.

Puustinen, M., Lyyra, A. L., Metsäpelto, R. L., & Pulkkinen, L. (2008). Children's help seeking: The role of parenting. *Learning and Instruction, 18*, 160–171.

Ratner, C. (2000). Agency and culture. *Journal for the Theory of Social Behaviour, 30*, 413–434.

Ravitch, D. (2010). *The death and life of the great American school system: How testing and choice are undermining education*. New York: Basic Books.

Raymond, A. M. (1997). Inconsistency between a beginning elementary school teacher's mathematics beliefs and teaching practice. *Journal for Research in Mathematics Education, 28,* 550–576.

Read, J. (2009). A genealogy of homo-economicus: Neoliberalism and the production of subjectivity. *Foucault Studies* (6), 25–36.

Richardson, V., Anders, P., Tidwell, D., & Lloyd, C. (1991). The relationship between teachers' beliefs and practices in reading comprehension instruction. *American Educational Research Journal, 28,* 559–586.

Roeser, R. W., & Peck, S. C. (2009). An education in awareness: Self, motivation, and self-regulated learning in contemplative perspective. *Educational Psychologist, 44,* 119–136.

Rose, N. (1998). *Inventing our selves: Psychology, power, and personhood.* Cambridge, UK: Cambridge University Press.

Rose, N. (1999). *Governing the soul: The shaping of the private self.* London: Free Associations.

Ryan, R. M., & Deci, E. L. (2000). Self-determination theory and the facilitation of intrinsic motivation, social development, and well-being. *American psychologist, 55,* 68–79.

Salonen, P., Lepola, J., & Vauras, M. (2007). Scaffolding interaction in parent-child dyads: Multimodal analysis of parental scaffolding with task and non-task oriented children. *European Journal of Psychology of Education, 22,* 77–96.

Santrock, J. W. (2008). *Educational psychology* (3rd ed.). Boston: McGraw-Hill.

Sawyer, R. K. (2002). Unresolved tensions in sociocultural theory: Analogies with contemporary sociological debates. *Culture & Psychology, 8,* 283–303.

Schmeichel, B. J., & Baumeister, R. F. (2004). Self-regulatory strength. In R. F. Baumeister & K. D. Vohs (Eds.), *Handbook of self-regulation: Research, theory, and applications* (pp. 84–98). New York: Guilford.

Schunk, D. H. (2008). Metacognition, self-regulation, and self-regulated learning: Research recommendations. *Educational Psychology Review, 20,* 463–467.

Schunk, D. H., & Zimmerman, B. J. (1997). Social origins of self-regulatory competence. *Educational Psychologist, 32,* 195–208.

Schutz, A. (2000). Teaching freedom? Postmodern perspectives. *Review of Educational Research, 70,* 215–251.

Schutz, A. (2008). Social class and social action: The middle-class bias of democratic theory in education. *Teachers College Record, 110,* 405–442.

Searle, J. R. (2007). *Freedom and neurobiology: Reflections on free will, language, and political power.* New York: Columbia University Press.

Sewell, W. H. (1992). A theory of structure: Duality, agency, and transformation. *American Journal of Sociology, 98,* 1–29.

Shanker, S. (2010). Self-regulation: Calm, alert, and learning. *Education Canada, 50,* 4–7.

Skinner, B. F. (1971). *Beyond freedom & dignity.* Cambridge, MA: Hackett.

Smith, P. K. (2011). Sanctioned global operations: Neoliberalism's domination of place, space, and time. *Educational Studies, 47,* 105–106.

Steinberg, L., Lamborn, S. D., Dornbusch, S. M., & Darling, N. (1992). Impact of parenting practices on adolescent achievement: Authoritative parenting, school involvement, and encouragement to succeed. *Child Development, 63,* 1266–1281.

References

Steinberg, L., Mounts, N. S., Lamborn, S. D., & Dornbusch, S. M. (1991). Authoritative parenting and adolescent adjustment across varied ecological niches. *Journal of Research on Adolescence, 1*, 19–36.

Stoeger, H., & Ziegler, A. (2011). Self-regulatory training through elementary-school students' homework completion. In B. J. Zimmerman & D. H. Schunk (Eds.), *Handbook of self-regulation of learning and performance* (pp. 87–101). New York: Routledge.

Strage, A. A. (1998). Family context variables and the development of self-regulation in college students. *Adolescence, 33*, 17–31.

Streib, J. (2011). Class reproduction by four year olds. *Qualitative Sociology, 34*, 1–16.

Stright, A. D., Neitzel, C., Sears, K. G., & Hoke-Sinex, L. (2001). Instruction begins in the home: Relations between parental instruction and children's self-regulation in the classroom. *Journal of Educational Psychology, 93*, 456–466.

Sugarman, J. (2011). Agency, compatibilism and psychology. In T. Corcoran (Chair), *Critical educational psychology: Enabling conditions in theory and practice*. Presented at the Symposium held during the biennial conference of the International Society for Theory and Psychology, Thessaloniki, Greece.

Sugarman, J., & Sokol, B. (2010). Human agency and development: An introduction and theoretical sketch. *New Ideas in Psychology*, 1–11.

Svinicki, M. D. (2010). Student learning: From teacher-directed to self-regulation. *New Directions for Teaching and Learning, 123*, 73–83.

Swalander, L., & Karin, T. (2007). Influences of family based prerequisites, reading attitude, and self-regulation on reading ability. *Contemporary Educational Psychology, 32*, 206–230.

Teo, T. (2009). Psychology without Caucasians. *Canadian Psychology, 50*, 91.

Tolman, C. W. (2009). Holzkamp's critical psychology as a science from the standpoint of the human subject. *Theory & Psychology, 19*, 149–160.

Trend, D. (1994). Nationalities, pedagogies, and media. In H. A. Giroux & P. McLaren (Eds.), *Between borders: Pedagogy and the politics of cultural studies* (pp. 225–241). New York: Routledge.

Twenge, J. M. (2000). The age of anxiety? The birth cohort change in anxiety and neuroticism, 1952–1993. *Journal of Personality and Social Psychology, 79*, 1007–1021.

Uskul, A. K., Sherman, D. K., & Fitzgibbon, J. (2009). The cultural congruency effect: Culture, regulatory focus, and the effectiveness of gain- vs. loss-framed health messages. *Journal of Experimental Social Psychology, 45*, 535–541.

Vassallo, S. (2010). Teachers' beliefs about self-regulated learning. *Academic Exchange Quarterly, 14*, 45–51.

Vassallo, S. (2011). Implications of institutionalizing self-regulated learning: An analysis from four sociological perspectives. *Educational Studies, 47*, 26–49.

Vassallo, S. (in press). Neoliberalism: Resistance to self-regulated learning pedagogy in an urban classroom. *Journal of Critical Education Policy Studies*.

Vick, R. M., & Packard, B. W. L. (2008). Academic success strategy use among community-active urban Hispanic adolescents. *Hispanic Journal of Behavioral Sciences, 30*, 463–480.

Vidal, F. (1994). *Piaget before Piaget*. Cambridge, MA: Harvard University Press.

Vidal-Abarca, E., Mañá, A., & Gil, L. (2010). Individual differences for self-regulating task-oriented reading activities. *Journal of Educational Psychology, 102*, 817–826.

Volet, S., Vauras, M., & Salonen, P. (2009). Social regulation in learning contexts: An integrative perspective. *Educational Psychologist, 44*, 215–226.

von Glasersfeld, E. (1996). *Radical constructivism: A way of knowing and learning.* New York: Routledge.

Vygotsky, L. (1978). *Mind in society: The development of higher psychological processes.* Cambridge, MA: Harvard University Press.

Walkerdine, V. (2003). Reclassifying upward mobility: Femininity and the neo-liberal subject. *Gender and Education, 15*, 237–248.

Wang, M., Peng, J., Cheng, B., Zhou, H., & Liu, J. (2011). Knowledge visualization for self-regulated learning. *Journal of Educational Technology & Society, 14*, 28–42.

Weber, M. (1997). *The theory of social and economic organization.* New York: Free Press.

Weed, K., Keogh, D., Borkowski, J. G., Whitman, T., & Noria, C. W. (2010). Self-regulation mediates the relationship between learner typology and achievement in at-risk children. *Learning and Individual Differences, 21*, 96–108.

Wegner, D. M. (2002). *The illusion of conscious will.* Cambridge, MA: MIT Press.

Wegner, D. M., & Pennebaker, J. W. (1993). Changing our minds: An introduction to mental control. *Handbook of mental control* (pp. 1–12). Englewood Cliffs, NJ: Prentice-Hall.

Wegner, D. M., & Wheatley, T. (1999). Apparent mental causation: Sources of the experience of will. *American Psychologist, 54*, 480.

Wehmeyer, M. L., Palmer, S. B., Agran, M., Mithaug, D. E., & Martin, J. E. (2000). Promoting causal agency: The self-determined learning model of instruction. *Exceptional Children, 66*, 439–453.

Weininger, E. B., & Lareau, A. (2009). Paradoxical pathways: An ethnographic extension of Kohn's findings on class and childrearing. *Journal of Marriage and Family, 71*, 680–695.

Weis, L. (2004). *Class reunion: The remaking of the American white working-class.* New York: Routledge.

Wertsch, J. V., Tulviste, P., & Hagstrom, F. (1993). A sociocultural approach to agency. In E. Forman, N. Minick, & C. A. Stone (Eds.), *Contexts for learning: Sociocultural dynamics in children's development* (Vol. 23, pp. 326–356). New York: Oxford University Press.

Wiener, N. (1948). *Cybernetics: Control and communication in the animal and the machine.* Cambridge, MA: MIT Press.

Willis, P. E. (1977). *Learning to labor: How working-class kids get working-class jobs.* New York: Columbia University Press.

Winne, P. H. (2005). A perspective on state-of-the-art research on self-regulated learning. *Instructional Science, 33*, 559–565.

Wolters, C. A. (2010). *Self-regulated learning and the 21st century competencies.* The William and Flora Hewlett Foundation. Retrieved April 12, 2012, from http://www.hewlett.org/library/grantee-publication/self-regulated-learning-and-21st-century-competencies

Wolters, C. A. (2011). Regulation of motivation: Contextual and social aspects. *Teachers College Record, 113*, 265–283.

Wolters, C. A., & Taylor, D. J. (2012). A self-regulated learning perspective on student engagement. In S. L. Christenson, A. L. Reschly, & C. Wylie (Eds.), *Handbook of research on student engagement* (pp. 635–651). New York: Springer.

Woolfolk-Hoy, A. (2000). Educational psychology in teacher education. *Educational Psychologist, 35*, 257–270.

Woolfolk-Hoy, A. (2007). *Educational psychology* (9th ed.). Boston: Pearson.

Wright, E. L. (2008). The continuing importance of class analysis. In L. Weis (Ed.), *The way class works: Readings on school, family, and the economy* (pp. 25–43). New York: Routledge.

Xu, J., & Corno, L. (2003). Family help and homework management reported by middle school students. *Elementary School Journal, 103*, 503–518.

Xu, J., & Corno, L. (2006). Gender, family help, and homework management reported by middle school students. *Journal of Research in Rural Education, 21*, 21-22.

Young, I. M. (1990). *Justice and the politics of difference.* Princeton, NJ: Princeton University Press.

Yowell, C. M., & Smylie, M. A. (1999). Self-regulation in democratic communities. *Elementary School Journal, 99*, 469–490.

Yukselturk, E., & Bulut, S. (2009). Gender differences in self-regulated online learning environment. *Educational Technology & Society, 12*, 12–22.

Zeidner, M., Boekaerts, M., & Pintrich, P. R. (2000). Self-regulation: Directions and challenges for future research. In M. Boekaerts, P. R. Pintrich, & M. Zeidner (Eds.), *Handbook of self-regulation* (pp. 750–768). San Diego, CA: Academic.

Zimmerman, B. J. (1998). Developing self-fulfilling cycles of academic regulation: An analysis of exemplary instructional models. In D. H. Schunk & B. J. Zimmerman (Eds.), *Self-regulated learning: From teaching to self-reflective practice* (pp. 1–19). New York: Guilford.

Zimmerman, B. J. (2000). Attaining self-regulation: A social cognitive perspective. In M. E. Boekaerts, P. R. Pintrich, & M. E. Zeidner (Eds.), *Handbook of self-regulation* (pp. 13–39). San Diego, CA: Academic.

Zimmerman, B. J. (2002). Becoming a self-regulated learner: An overview. *Theory into Practice, 41*, 64–70.

Zimmerman, B. J., Bonner, S., & Kovach, R. (1996). *Developing self-regulated learners: Beyond achievement to self-efficacy.* Washington, DC: American Psychological Association.

Zimmerman, B. J., & Martinez-Pons, M. (1986). Development of a structured interview for assessing student use of self-regulated learning strategies. *American Educational Research Journal, 23*, 614–628.

Critical Pedagogical Perspectives

Greg S. Goodman, *General Editor*

Educational Psychology: Critical Pedagogical Perspectives is a series of relevant and dynamic works by scholars and practitioners of critical pedagogy, critical constructivism, and educational psychology. Reflecting a multitude of social, political, and intellectual developments prompted by the mentor Paulo Freire, books in the series enliven the educator's process with theory and practice that promote personal agency, social justice, and academic achievement. Often countering the dominant discourse with provocative and yet practical alternatives, *Educational Psychology: Critical Pedagogical Perspectives* speaks to educators on the forefront of social change and those who champion social justice.

For further information about the series and submitting manuscripts, please contact:

> Dr. Greg S. Goodman
> Department of Education
> Clarion University
> Clarion, Pennsylvania
> ggoodman@clarion.edu

To order other books in this series, please contact our Customer Service Department at:

> (800) 770-LANG (within the U.S.)
> (212) 647-7706 (outside the U.S.)
> (212) 647-7707 FAX

Or browse online by series at:

> www.peterlang.com